RURAL ENGLAND
1066–1348

H. E. Hallam is Professor of Medieval History in the University of Western Australia. His published works include *The Newlands of Elloe* and *Settlement and Society* and he is the editor and a contributor to *The Agrarian History of England and Wales, Volume 2*.

FONTANA HISTORY OF ENGLAND

Edited by G. R. Elton

The aim of the series is to reinterpret familiar and unfamiliar aspects of English history. There will be a pair of volumes on each chronological period which will throw new light on the age in question by discussing it in relation to contrasting themes.

ALREADY AVAILABLE

Malcolm Todd: *Roman Britain 55 BC – AD 400*
Claire Cross: *Church and People 1450 – 1660*
D. M. Loades: *Politics and the Nation 1450 – 1660*
J. R. Jones: *Britain and the World 1649 – 1815*

FORTHCOMING TITLES

Nicholas Brooks: *Warfare, Government and Society 400–1066*
Michael Clanchy: *England and Europe 1066–1272*
Peter Heath: *Church and Realm 1272–1461*
Anthony Tuck: *The Crown and the Nobility 1272–1461*
Maxine Berg: *The Coming of Industry 1660–1850*
Michael Bentley: *Politics without Democracy 1815–1918*
Asa Briggs: *The Growth of Leisure, 1815–1970*

RURAL ENGLAND
1066 - 1348

H. E. HALLAM

Professor of Medieval History,
University of Western Australia

THE HARVESTER PRESS · SUSSEX

HUMANITIES PRESS INC · NEW JERSEY

In association with Fontana Paperbacks

This edition first published in Great Britain in 1981 by
THE HARVESTER PRESS LIMITED
Publisher: John Spiers
16 Ship Street, Brighton, Sussex

and in the USA by
HUMANITIES PRESS INC.
Atlantic Highlands, New Jersey 07716

This edition first published in 1981 by
The Harvester Press Limited and by
Humanities Press Inc.
in association with Fontana Paperbacks

British Library Cataloguing in Publication Data
Hallam, H. E.
    Rural England, 1066-1272.-(Fontana history of
    England)
    1. England—Rural conditions
    2. England—Social conditions
    I. Title
    942.09'2   DA185

ISBN 0-7108-0099-1

Humanities Press Inc.
ISBN 0-391-02303-9

Printed and bound in Great Britain by
Redwood Burn Limited, Trowbridge and Esher

CONTENTS

First, get a house, a woman, and an ox
For ploughing — let the woman be a slave,
Unmarried, who can help you in the fields,
Make ready in your house the things you'll need,
So you won't have to try to borrow tools
And be refused, and do without, and let
The ripe time pass and all your work be lost.
Don't put off work until another day,
Or even till tomorrow; lazy men
Who put things off always have unfilled barns.
Constant attention makes the work go well;
Idlers wrestle with ruin all their days.

Hesiod, *Works and Days*

ACKNOWLEDGEMENTS

Over the years I have incurred intellectual and scholarly debts too numerous to list here. The chapter notes testify their extent. Even so, I would like to mention a few names, several of scholars no longer with us – Professor J. D. Chambers, Professor Sir Michael Postan, Professor H. P. R. Finberg, Professor W. G. Hoskins, Professor G. C. Homans, Professor K. H. Connell and Dr Joan Thirsk. Most of all I wish to thank my wife, S. J. Hallam, senior lecturer in prehistoric archaeology in this university who taught me the ecological approach to history. I would also like to thank the Senate of this university for the opportunity to study for a whole year at Cambridge in 1968 and at Norwich in 1975. Lastly, my warmest thanks are due to Professor G. R. Elton who made me rough hew and shape the ends of these English hedgerows.

Office of the Dean of Arts
The University of Western Australia
Nedlands, Western Australia
20 February 1981

CHAPTER 1

THE MEDIEVAL SOCIAL BACKGROUND[1]

In the 1950s students of pre-Industrial England and the Industrial Revolution tended to stress the importance of an autonomous death-rate as a major factor in population movements. More recently historians have seen that high age at marriage, the effect of social and institutional obstacles and a quite remarkable degree of geographical mobility, laid the groundwork for a competitive and acquisitive society, which kept in a favourable balance resources and population. Individuals used prudential marriage and mobility for self-aggrandizement, and families as a means to make their way to the top. The rich used them to check the blind procreation of the poor.

All over Western Europe, from far back in the Dark Ages, and most particularly among Italian merchants and artisans from the twelfth century onwards, prudential marriage, mobility, and the cult of the individual expressed themselves in the Protestant work ethic, more correctly called the Latin Christian work ethic. The father was a heroic, self-denying labourer, who strove in weariness and danger to maintain himself and his family, and to leave his children richer and happier than himself. 'Consider the lilies of the field, they toil not neither do they spin' was not for him. Idleness was the rust of the soul and all living things, including plants, worked for their sustenance.

The prudential marriage and the Protestant work ethic were not confined to the Italian merchants and artisans of the twelfth century onwards. William Langland was an obscure fourteenth-century cleric, one of that proletariat of unbeneficed clergymen whose continental members produced the *Carmina Burana*. Born at Cleobury Mortimer in Shropshire about 1332, he lived until the end of the century. His father was Eustace de Rokayle, who held land from the Despensers at Shipton-under-

Wychwood in Oxfordshire; he himself may have been a
bastard, and he probably received his education at Great
Malvern Priory in Worcestershire. He knew London well and
lived with his wife Kit and daughter Colette in a cottage on
Cornhill, but he wandered about a good deal, sometimes
dressed as a beggar. He certainly knew poverty.

> I've seen enough of the world to know how they suffer, these
> men who have many children, and no means but their trade
> to clothe and feed them. For many hands are waiting to grasp
> the few pence they earn, and while the Friars feast on roast
> venison, they have bread and thin ale, with perhaps a scrap of
> cold meat or stale fish. And on Fridays and fast-days a
> farthing's worth of cockles or a few mussels would be a feast
> for such folk.

Langland wrote the first version of his great poem *Piers the
Plowman* about 1370. The ploughman was here both the
provider of society and the symbol of the Christian community
– he who tried to set the whole world to work to stave off
hunger, by invoking the principle of 'work or want'. But the
labourers preferred to drink ale and sing songs, so that Piers had
to call up Hunger to chastise them. When at last they produced
enough food to put Hunger to sleep the labourers relapsed into
idleness.

> And then the Waster would not work any more, but set out as
> a tramp. And the beggars refused the bread that had beans in
> it, demanding milk loaves and fine white wheaten bread. And
> they would not drink cheap beer at any price but only the best
> brown ale that is sold in the towns.
> And the day-labourers, who have no land to live on but
> their shovels, would not deign to eat yesterday's vegetables.
> And draught-ale was not good enough for them, nor a hunk
> of bacon, but they must have have fresh meat or fish, fried or
> baked and *chaud* or *plus chaud* at that, lest they catch a chill on
> their stomachs!

To Piers Plowman,

> to DO-BEST is to abstain, by day and night, from wasting
> any words or time . . . . Of all things on earth, God knows
> nothing is more hated by those in Heaven than waste of time,
> and next to it waste of words . . . . Our lord loves all truthful,
> honest men who are willing to work, and gives them the
> grace to earn a living, come what may.

To Langland true marriage was good, 'for married men must
work and earn a living and keep the world going'. True
marriage was 'for love, and not for property', and 'the pleasure
of lechery is a bait from hell'. Langland believed that all traitors,
thieves, liars, wasters, idle wretches, vagabonds, swindlers,
foundlings, imposters and liars – that is, all fringe-dwellers –
were conceived or born out of wedlock or at a time of penitence
or fasting. 'Lacking the grace to earn a living or gain people's
affection, they turn beggars and waste whatever they lay hands
on.' And so Langland connected the true marriage with hard
work (the Protestant work ethic) and fornication with the
degenerate rural proletariat of his own day.

Elsewhere I have pointed out the origins of the twin doctrines
of work and time-saving in the Benedictine Rule and have
briefly traced the track of accountancy through the pontificate
of Gregory the Great, and the estate records of Charlemagne
and the Frankish abbeys to Domesday, the Pipe Rolls of the
English Exchequer and the early accounts of the Bishopric of
Winchester. Systematic estate improvement was already
common in 1066–86, and long before the twelfth century
extensive new settlement was going on all over Western and
Northern Europe. So far had the process gone that the
colonizing movement outside the older lands had already
begun. Towards 870 the Norsemen began to colonize Iceland
and in 986 they started on Greenland. The Red King's coloniza-
tion of Cumbria, Henry I's settlement of Dyfed and Gower,
Strongbow's invasion of Ireland, and the Crusades were all part
of this predatory, expansionist phase of Western European

endeavour, to which there is no real parallel in the history of the rest of the world. Why did it happen?

An environmental factor – the improved weather of the Dark Ages – undoubtedly made expansion easier, just as in the later Middle Ages and early modern times disease made it more difficult, but the weather and disease are not agents. Like Dr Johnson, in spite of what philosophers say, we *know* that man's will is free; however carefully the historian may describe the circumstances of Western European history he still needs to explore its idolum, that is, the West's generally accepted prejudices and assumptions.

Western (Latin) Christianity was a religion strikingly different from Orthodox Christianity. Augustine of Hippo and Jerome, followed closely by Gregory the Great, were the main propagators of these differences which took the form of three related doctrines whose acceptance led to an emphasis upon the Incarnation and Crucifixion of Christ rather than his Resurrection, so that Christmas Day became more important than Easter Sunday. Not for Latins the joyous *Kristos anesti* (Christ is risen) of the Orthodox Eastern service. These doctrines were original sin (understood as something genetically transmitted, not copied from a bad example), grace (understood as something which the sinner had not earned), and predestination. Together with the Benedictine work ethic and discovery of time, they led to the cultivation of the human ego (Augustine was the first autobiographer), the development of machinery, whether administrative or real, and the sanctification of the sins of pride and avarice as the virtues of the successful man. In spite of a revival in the last two medieval centuries, the mystical element of Christianity, so strong at all times in Orthodoxy, slipped away in the West. Latin Christianity became the spirit of capitalism.

The Latin Church's teaching on marriage is one small part of all this. St Gregory Palamas, Archbishop of Thessaloniki (1296–1359), taught that man's body is not an enemy, but partner and collaborator with his soul. God created the whole man in his image, and Christ, by his Incarnation, has 'made the flesh an inexhaustible source of sanctification'. Contrast this with Jerome who in his letter to Eustochium, written in Rome in 384, listed the drawbacks of marriage, for a woman, as pregnancy, the crying of infants, the torture which a rival might cause, the cares of household management, and death, whether of husband or children.

'Be fruitful,' God says, 'and multiply, and replenish the earth.' He who desires to replenish the earth may increase and multiply if he will. But the train to which you belong is not on earth, but in heaven. The command to increase and multiply first finds fulfilment after the expulsion from paradise after the nakedness and fig-leaves, which speak of sexual passion. Let them marry and be given in marriage who eat their bread in the sweat of their brow; whose land brings forth to them thorns and thistles, and whose crops are choked with briars. My seed produces fruit a hundredfold.

What arrogance! Later he says: 'I praise wedlock, I praise marriage, but it is because they give me virgins. I gather the rose from the thorns, the gold from the earth, the pearl from the shell.' Jerome was an ascetic and typical of the highly unpleasant 'saints' which Latin Christianity produced, always domineering over others, but Orthodoxy also had its ascetics. In the West this asceticism bit deep into the consciousness of the Church, since after Gregory the Great the papacy continually took up the cause of clerical celibacy whose shackles the Lateran Council of 1216 firmly and finally fixed upon the necks of the priesthood.

With the coming of the Gregorian mission to England in 597, the way was open for the introduction of Augustinian ideas about marriage. Britain had continued to have contacts with Eastern Europe down to about 550, and British Christianity was full of ideas taken straight from the Cappadocian Fathers. Irish Christianity also had its contacts with the East and Irish interest in Pelagius may explain why we have the manuscripts of twenty-four of Pelagius's writings. The Synod of Whitby (664) and the appointment of Theodore of Tarsus to the Archbishopric of Canterbury (668–90) gave Britain to Rome, and Rome to Britain.

The Penitential of Theodore is a fascinating document. Much of its contents reappeared in the Penitential of St Egbert, Archbishop of York, 732/4–66, and from there, perhaps via his pupil Alcuin, these ideas made their way into the penitentials of the Carolingian Church where they became the basis of the Church's later teaching. They are full of a repulsive prudery. Theodore taught that a husband ought not to see his wife naked, and that anyone who bathed with women should do penance for three days. A man not in orders, and not a monk, who fornicated was to fast twelve months. If he begot a child he should fast three winters; if he killed it, seven winters. The law for women was much more severe. If a mother killed her baby, she was to fast fifteen winters without ceasing, except on Sundays. If she was poor she fasted seven years; if she had fornicated, ten years. If a woman procured an abortion within forty days, before quickening, she fasted (as for murder) three years, twice a week until evening, and three legal fasts. In his second book Archbishop Egbert laid down that if a woman drank a potion to procure an abortion, or used any other means, or killed the baby, she had to fast three years on bread and water, and seven as her confessor prescribed.

Besides these penances for sexual malpractices the two Archbishops placed limitations upon the love-life of laymen. A girl fourteen years old should have power over her own body. Until she was thirteen or fourteen years old she was to be under her parents' control; after that her lord could take her, with her consent. Similarly a boy fifteen years old was to be in his own power and could become a monk. In his second book Egbert laid down the Old Testament practice that after a man has taken his bride home they should remain chaste for the first three days and nights; on the third day they should hear mass and then they might consummate their marriage. All married couples should remain chaste forty days and nights before Easter, the whole of Easter week, and the nights of every Sunday, Wednesday and

Friday. Every woman must be chaste three months before she gave birth, and sixty days and nights afterwards. In book one Egbert required women to be chaste seven months before giving birth and forty days afterwards, and he laid a fast of twenty or forty days on the guilty husband. He also forbade husbands and wives to make love seven days before Whitsuntide and fourteen days before Christmas. These restrictions were so severe that one wonders that anybody could have observed them. They must have greatly lessened the opportunities of the pious for procreation, and greatly inflamed the libidinous tendencies of the impious. Whether observed or not they vividly illustrate the official attitudes of the Latin Church.

The notion that such an immoral institution as matrimony, which, as Shaw said, combines the maximum of temptation with the maximum of opportunity, could be a sacrament, although it occurs in St Paul's epistles and was spelt out in the fifth century by John Cassian who saw it as the symbol of the Incarnation, made the Latin Church slow to accept any reason but procreation for its existence. Augustine of Hippo was well aware that St Paul had said that it was better to marry than to burn with vain desire but he, Jerome, Gregory and others, though they formally acknowledged that 'the relief of concupiscence' was also a function of marriage, turned their back upon it. They left it to St Athanasius and other Greek Fathers to say that physical passion within marriage was good because God made it and God cannot make anything evil. Christ's presence at the wedding in Cana has always seemed, to the Greeks, sufficient reason to believe in the honourable estate of matrimony.

The third purpose of marriage according to the Orthodox Church is companionship. About 1430 Symeon Archbishop of Thessaloniki described the Orthodox wedding service in his *Concerning Chaste and Lawful Marriage*, and the last act was already the blessing and partaking of the common marriage cup, the symbol of the common life of a wedded couple. The Orthodox were already laying stress on Genesis 2.18: 'Then the Lord God said, "It is not good for the man to be alone. I will provide a partner for him!" ' This text was the basis for the Christian companionate marriage.

The new and more favourable emphasis upon marriage which came at the Reformation introduced the companionate marriage into the Elizabethan Book of Common Prayer. The idea was not unknown in the later Middle Ages. Alberti says:

> Let him be minded to marry for two purposes: first to perpetuate himself in his children, and second to have a steady and constant companion all his life. A woman is needed, therefore, who is likely to bear children and who is desirable as a perpetual mate.

Langland was much against marrying for money:

> I think there is nothing more unseemly, than to give a young girl to a doddering old man, or to marry for money some aged widow who will bear no children, except in her arms! For since the Plague hundreds of couples have married, yet the only fruit they have brought forth are foul words, they live in jealousy, without happiness, and lie in bed quarrelling, so that all the children they get are strife and nagging! . . . See that you marry for love, and not for property, when you will gain God's grace and find money enough to live on.

Langland perhaps spoke from experience of a happy marriage, but in the West clerks like himself were the transmitters of the alternate culture of love, not always the licit kind.

Once upon a time the troubadours of Aquitaine were supposed to have been the originators of the love cult, which was (supposedly) always adulterous, a separate, idealistic stream from that of marriage. Closer study of the literature has taught us that it did not exclude marriage, that women wrote or were purported to have written many of the poems and clearly enjoyed their love life, and that in the *pastourela* peasant girls appreciated love just as much as the upper classes. The tradition of *winileodas* or *cantigas de amigo* (songs of a friend) stretches back at least to 789 when Charlemagne forbade abbesses to write them. Two fine examples are *Wulf and Eadwacer*, written in Old English some time in the tenth century, and a Latin *winileod* of great beauty, preserved in the Cambridge Songs' manuscript of the early-eleventh century, the *Levis exsurgit Zephirus*. The alternate culture is a fascinating subject, and it mainly expressed itself in lyric poetry, Latin or vernacular. By the nature of things, only the literate classes have left early evidence, whether that of the knightly troubadours or the disreputable clerks who sang *Potatores exquisiti*, but later folk-song probably descends from a medieval tradition of unwritten lovesongs. K. H. Connell always thought that the poor cabin-dwellers who pastured their cattle on the commons of Ireland in the eighteenth century married for love. The solid peasants, stout burghers and ascetic monks (when they kept the rule) were more interested in money, system, mathematics and capital accumulation than in love. The ideology of the Latin Church aided them, since it was practical, materialistic and tuned to the cult of the individual. No other major society had had this ideological base for its economic superstructure. It is the context of what follows.

CHAPTER 2

THE POSTAN THESIS[1]

Since 1945 agrarian historians have started to turn away from the preoccupation with Marxism which had become fashionable about the time of the Spanish Civil War, so that when, in 1956, Kosminsky's *Studies in the Agrarian History of England in the Thirteenth Century* for the first time became available in English readers found it very old-fashioned. Although it was clearly a work of careful scholarship it seemed to ask and answer all the wrong questions.

Part of the change came from G. C. Homans's *English Villagers of the Thirteenth Century*, the brilliant seminal work of an historian turned sociologist, which first appeared in 1941, at a time when established historians had subjects other than the thirteenth-century villager to think about; it therefore had its main impact upon those undergraduates who surged into the universities of the English-speaking world after the collapse of Nazi Germany.

But perhaps an even bigger part of the change came from the long series of brilliant lectures which Michael Postan delivered to enthusiastic audiences at Cambridge from 1946 onwards. Postan's approach was frankly neo-Malthusian, and although in later years he has changed it a little, the essentials remain. His method required a fruitful wedding of economics and history, and his thesis gained interest in the 1950s, especially after his retirement, because of the world's realization that it had too many people.

The Postan thesis lays down that a great population expansion with a related new settlement made the demand for food outstrip the supply, so that by about 1280 in England and Wales there was great hunger. Between then and the Black Death of 1348-9 population had already started to decline because the food supply was so precarious that any sudden climatic change brought famine and disease. During the course of the thirteenth century, as the population increase pressed more and more severely upon resources, greater and greater areas of marginal land came under the plough. As pasture and meadow grew scarcer so the peasant could keep fewer and fewer animals and, since he depended upon livestock to fertilize his fields, decreasing flocks and herds brought poorer grain yields. Moreover, on the poorer marginal soils the peasant was compelled to grow the 'poorer' grains, barley and rye instead of wheat, maslin and dredge; oats instead of all these. Yield ratios therefore grew smaller as the thirteenth century advanced. Lastly, in many parts of England, as population growth outstripped new settlement, holdings grew impossibly small. The state of the English populace by 1280 was that of a dwarf peasantry devoted to grain monoculture.

The Postan thesis contains a number of hidden assumptions which neither its author nor his numerous pupils have examined or documented in any way. The first assumption is that agrarian trends, particularly in new-settlement and population movements, were generally the same everywhere. Although the supporters of this thesis have conned the lesson of the Leicester school of local historians, have read the works of the numerous historical geographers who have come to life since R. A. Pelham showed the way nearly half a century ago, and are aware of the example of the Cambridge school of prehistorians and the virtues of survey and comparative study, they do not study regions as much as they should. Their mainstay, the archives of the Bishop of Winchester, have no real parallel in England, for Hampshire is not England just as England is not the world.

The second assumption concerns grain yields and links to the third assumption. J. Z. Titow has claimed that yield ratios of wheat, barley and oats declined on the Winchester estates in the thirteenth century and then improved down to 1350. Professor Postan has complained recently that his thesis is not entirely Malthusian, but that Ricardo's theory of rent, which dictates that marginal lands fall out of cultivation when rents rise too high, is even more relevant. The concept is most valuable and has good uses, and those who attended Professor Postan's original lectures can certainly testify to the stress he laid on this idea. Deserted medieval villages have received a good deal of attention in recent years both in England and on the Continent, but although many were on marginal lands, many were not, and many marginal-land villages have existed ever since an English-speaking peasantry named or re-named the villages which now bear English names . When therefore Dr Titow links the declining area of demesne arable with declining yield ratios and deduces that demesne land was falling out of cultivation, with the lord, presumably, letting it to his tenants, the reader asks for evidence but does not find it. Demesne acreages certainly declined on many English manors in 1250–1350, but on some the demesne increased and there are manors where the demesne decreased but the crops grown were larger. Account rolls do not speak of the area of the demesne, but of the area under the plough each year; they show, not a contraction of the arable, but the use of less exhausting crop rotations. As P. G. Brandon has shown too, declining or static yield ratios can be deceptive if the lord increases the thickness of his sowing from two to six or eight bushels to the acre, as was often customary with oats and barley.

The next assumption may be called the good grains and bad grains assumption. Wheat, rye, barley, oats is the order in weight of a bushel of these grains, though the moisture content may upset this order. Cold, wet, high lands in the north of England and in Wales would grow only oats, and the people therefore ate oat-cakes. Bread was a luxury in Cheshire, but it was not a luxury in the lowland zone where people ate a lot of it. The Winchester estates grew a great deal of oats, but there is no evidence that the English peasantry grew more of the 'worse' grains because they were occupying more marginal land, because of population pressure, or the failure of their fields' fertility. Lords and peasants alike grew oats because they had horses, and especially in eastern and south-eastern England and the East Midlands horses were becoming more popular. The horse population of Domesday England was much smaller than that of England in 1300. Many peasants also grew oats because they ate oats pottage.

The fourth assumption is that no technological progress took place in medieval agriculture. The late Professor Finberg used to fulminate against the use of the word 'medieval' because it suggests an age betwixt times which are better – between ancient and modern history – a sort of dark tunnel with light at both ends. Much modern writing would contravert this idea for the Middle Ages was a great innovatory period, the mother of many great and beneficial inventions, and in agriculture saw the beginning of the Agricultural Revolution. In this respect, the writings of Ester Bœrup and Colin Clark both implicitly criticize the Postan thesis. The former does not mention his name and the latter does so only once, and incidentally, but both put forward a strong case for the dynamic nature of agrarian societies whose population is increasing fairly fast. The wars and plagues of the later Middle Ages made innovation unnecessary, but the population pressure before the Black Death brought innovations.

Dr Titow has discussed technological progress and dismissed the possibility. Although the rising yield ratios on the Winchester estates went with a considerable rise in the acreage of legumes, crops were still small; he suggests that their fertilizing power was insignificant. He may very well be right for the Winchester estates, which were notoriously backward, but all over eastern and south-eastern England and the east Midlands, and sometimes elsewhere, legumes, especially peas, were often one of the larger crops, and sometimes produced increased fertility. Even in southern England catch-crops of peas on the fallow (*inhokes*) were a common practice by 1300. Titow also underestimates the effects of crop nutrition. Professor Postan himself has often claimed that lords took all the peasants' dung in East Anglia and that foldsoke has its Malthusian significance. References to foldsoke sometimes put a value upon it, and the peasant could often pay not to avail himself of the lord's fold. The custom was by no means universal on the Ely estates, and sometimes only the cottars, who had no folds of their own, followed it. As in other matters, the lord was providing a service for which the tenants paid. Titow also discounts the effect of marling – one of Coke of Norfolk's 'new discoveries' – which, as the following pages show, was much more common than has been supposed. Future historians will find much more evidence of this practice, as also of sanding, the use of sea-weed, and liming.

Neither have crop rotations had the attention they deserve. The comparative lateness of the three-course rotation, which was not very common before 1300, and the evidence of a changeover from the two-course system to the three-course system, are surely significant. Legume-growing and good crop nutrition made this possible, and particularly in parts of the west Midlands and southern England, where two-course rotations were more general, planting legumes on the fallow converted the fields, at least partly, to an informal three-course crop rotation. East Anglia, and perhaps other advanced areas in the eastern part of England, had almost reached continual tillage. Fallows still existed, but only every six, seven or eight years. In eastern England, where barley was king and sowing heavy, even yield ratios were often much higher than on the Winchester estates; the total amount of grain grown per acre (especially if we include the fallow) was very much greater. The progressive parts of England also had large herds of dairy cattle whose milk the people drank and made into butter and cheese. On the Winchester estates the lord generally made cheese out of ewe's milk, a sign of a primitive economy, for a ewe gives only a quart of milk a day and is difficult to milk, whereas a goat gives a gallon and a cow two gallons. Eastern England and the east Midlands also used stots and affers (small horses) instead of slow oxen for ploughing and could therefore plough twice as much land in a given time. In 1086 one in every three Englishmen lived in eastern England which forms less than 17 per cent of the area of England, and by 1300 eastern England had grown so rapidly that nearly half (46 per cent) of the people of England lived in the five counties between the Humber and the mouth of the Thames. Far from being short of food, eastern England shipped quantities of wheat overseas from the Norfolk port of Lynn and the Suffolk port of Ipswich. If this is not agricultural progress the reader should ask what is.

Several other deficiencies of the Postan thesis deserve attention. The first of these is diet. A recent book by Edward Miller and John Hatcher, and Edward Britton's splendid study of the Huntingdonshire manor of Broughton, underline this point. The first of these is the best account of rural England between Domesday and the Black Death so far written, from the Postan point of view. It deals with realities, not with administrative history masquerading as economic history, and is thus a true product of the Postan revolution. The reader is therefore delighted to find, for almost the first time in a book on the English peasantry, two pages on the peasant's food. Since Ashley wrote *The Bread of our Forefathers* historians have written about all sorts of things much less important than food. Miller and Hatcher point out that the fully grown medieval male peasant ate up to five pounds of bread a day. This fact is grist for the Postan mill since it greatly affects the size of the holding needed for subsistence. When, however, the authors describe this as a 'carbohydrate' diet they show little acquaintance with nutrition. The medieval peasant ate good wholemeal barley or maslin (sometimes wheat or rye) bread and was able to command 5000 calories a day and over 200 grams of protein, mainly second-class, out of the bread. Peasant societies are not usually meat-eating societies but more often subsist on grains and pulses. Even a nodding acquaintance with the peasant cooking traditions of Mexico, Spain, the Near and Middle East or China makes this clear. Meat is not necessary for health – it came late to man's knowledge during the last Ice Age – and in pre-industrial societies is usual only amongst herdsmen and shepherds. Northern England and Wales had plenty of it in the Middle Ages, but the lowland zone had little and did not need it because it had good bread and dairy products, herrings, onions, leeks and garlic. Salads are not necessary for survival, are Mediterranean, and not very acceptable in a cold climate. Edward Britton has criticized the Postan thesis in a similar way, but has added further ideas. His study of alewives and brewers has convinced him of the importance of this employment to the income of poor cottagers and has shown how much ale our ancestors drank. He also comments upon the large number of butcher's as well as baker's shops and thinks that the Huntingdonshire peasant ate a lot of meat. He may well be right, but the Huntingdonshire peasants were well-to-do compared with some other English peasants. Britton also stresses the importance of the medieval garden. Here is a subject for someone to study. Whole societies in Polynesia and Melanesia live largely on garden produce. This is easier in the tropics but could still have been an important source of nutrition in medieval England. The medieval agrarian historian really must learn to cook before he sets pen to paper.

Miller and Hatcher both lay great stress upon the famine period and agrarian crisis of 1315–22. Again I must stress the importance of regionalism. Evidence of famine is hard to find in eastern England. Lords were slow to rebuild their dairy herds because part of their profits always came from fatted calves, for which reason they sold the issue of the herd at a good price rather than keeping all of it. The medieval cow was often quite fertile, so that nearly all cows had an annual calf. Unless over half the dairy herd died of murrain only one year's issue was needed to restore it to its former size.

In recent years historical demographers have divided between those who, like the late Professor J. D. Chambers, believed in an autonomous death-rate as a prime factor in population changes and those who have preferred to emphasize changes in the birth-rate. The over-population of some parts of Asia and the advances in modern epidemiology have made Malthusianism popular. Professor William H. McNeill sees the impact of new diseases as a major factor in world history. No social historian would deny disease its due, and Professor McNeill's theme is attractive as an interpretation, but (as the previous chapter has shown) recent interest in family history, and particularly in the nature of marriage, counsels a corrective. Here I have spelt out a few criticisms of the Postan thesis; in my last chapter I shall try to be more positive.

CHAPTER 3

DOMESDAY ENGLAND[1]

Any book on English agrarian history between the Norman Conquest and the time of Edward I must come to terms with the Domesday Survey as a reasonable basis for a description of new settlement, population movements, and social structure.

Eastern England was a very highly developed region in 1086 with many ploughteams and a high recorded population to each square mile; Norfolk and Suffolk were settled very densely, and Lincolnshire, Cambridgeshire and Essex densely enough. There was much scope for further development in Axholme, the Witham Fens, the Fenland of Lincolnshire and the Isle of Ely, the Suffolk Fenland, the Norfolk Marshland and the Norfolk and Suffok Breckland, and there was some scope for development in the Essex woodlands. The whole region was a land of very large villages with an average of 31.3 households each, except in Lincolnshire and Suffolk where they were smaller. Some 37 per cent of the peasantry were freemen and sokemen and only 5 per cent of the peasantry were slaves. Freedom and great density of recorded population corresponded remarkably well, as did slavery and sparseness of recorded population. Most of the freemen and sokemen, some 29,968 out of 31,169, lived in Lincolnshire, Norfolk and Suffolk, the most densely populated counties, while most of the slaves, some 2335 out of 4223, were found in Cambridgeshire and Essex, the least densely populated. Domesday recorded no slaves in Lincolnshire.

South-eastern England was a fairly highly developed region in 1086. Middlesex and Kent were densely settled and Surrey and Sussex moderately so. Densely populated regions generally had more than five recorded inhabitants to the square mile. There was much scope for further development all over the great extent of the Weald in Surrey, Kent, Sussex and in Romney

Marsh. Numerous densely settled areas with large or very large villages adjoined these great wastelands. As in eastern England the land contained very large villages except for the smaller villages in Sussex and Surrey which were less populated counties. Only 0.2 per cent of the recorded population were free peasants and all of them in Kent, the second most densely populated county, but 8 per cent of the recorded population were slaves: of these only 913 out of 2185 belonged to Surrey and Sussex and over half (1160) to Kent.

The east Midlands was a highly developed region in 1086. Leicestershire, Rutland, Northamptonshire, Huntingdonshire, Buckinghamshire, Bedfordshire and Hertfordshire were all heavily settled, but Nottinghamshire was less advanced. There was much opportunity for further growth on the western uplands, Sherwood Forest, the Wolds, and the alluvium of the northern Trent lowlands in Nottinghamshire; in western Leicestershire and Charnwood Forest in Leicestershire; in the Soke of Peterborough, Rockingham Forest, the southern and central parts of the eastern clay region and Whittlewood Forest in Northamptonshire; in the Huntingdonshire fenland; in the Chilterns and the Burnham plateau in Buckinghamshire; and in the Chilterns, the south Hertfordshire plateau and the Vale of St Albans in Hertfordshire. In Nottinghamshire the sparsely inhabited uplands seem to have undergone an economic regression some time before 1086. The east Midlands was covered with large villages with an average size of 23.1 households, but the whole region was less densely settled than either eastern or south-eastern England. The villages in the various counties were very different in size. Rutland's villages, which were the largest in England and Wales, were almost exactly twice the size of the small villages of Nottinghamshire. Nottinghamshire, Leicestershire and Northamptonshire formed a block of counties in the north of the east Midlands the average size of whose villages, at 20.6 households, was considerably smaller than that of the rest of the east Midlands. The same three counties also had 4488 out of 4813 free peasants in the east Midlands, 23.8 per cent of their recorded population being free.

On the other hand, Leicestershire, Northamptonshire, Buckinghamshire, Bedfordshire and Hertfordshire accounted for 3005 out of the 3054 slaves, about 11.7 per cent of the recorded population in the east Midlands; the last three counties, Buckinghamshire, Bedfordshire and Hertfordshire were especially enslaved. There was therefore no close correlation between density of recorded population and relative freedom, but opportunity for expansion was perhaps greatest in the three northernmost counties.

The west Midlands varied greatly in stages of development from north to south. Only Oxfordshire was highly developed in 1086; Worcestershire, Warwickshire and Gloucestershire were less advanced, and Staffordshire and Derbyshire had far to go. There was much scope for further development on the southern upland, the northern upland and the south Pennine fringe of Staffordshire, the northern moors of Derbyshire, the north-west upland, the Triassic sandstone area, and the north-east plateau of Worcestershire, the Tame-Blythe basin and the east Warwick plateau of Warwickshire, the Forest of Dean in Gloucestershire, and Otmoor and Wychwood Forests in Oxfordshire. There seems to have been an economic regression before 1066 in the northern upland, in the southern upland round Cannock Chase, in Staffordshire, and in the valley of the upper Dove, Longdendale, and in the south and east of Derbyshire, recorded in the Domesday Survey as waste or uninhabited villages. The average size of the west Midland villages was small at 17.2 households, but the average conceals great variation. Staffordshire and Derbyshire were hamlet country; Warwickshire, Gloucestershire and Oxfordshire were covered with large villages. Only 1.4 per cent of the peasants were comparatively free, only Derbyshire and Gloucestershire had a considerable number – 319 out of 433 – of free peasants, and Derbyshire had by far the highest proportion of its population comparatively free. Some 15.7 per cent of the population were slaves, but this included 251 men out of 4922 in Staffordshire and Derbyshire, and 3087 out of 4922 in Gloucestershire and Oxfordshire. Gloucestershire had the highest percentage of slaves in England. The figures show a good contrast between the anciently settled and enslaved south and the newly settled north. The dividing line is between Feldon and Arden in Warwickshire.

Southern England was a densely inhabited region of old-established villages although eastern Berkshire and the forests of Hampshire, which were only moderately densely settled, had ample scope for development. In Somerset there was room for expansion in the marshlands, the Mendips, the Quantocks, the southern hills and Exmoor. In Dorset the heathlands were the only thinly inhabited region. Wiltshire had room for expansion mainly in the Cotswolds, the Grovely-Great Ridge upland, Ebble Downs, the Forest of Braydon and the eastern forest areas of Savernake, Chute, Clarendon and Melchet. The average size of the southern England villages was 24 households and they were therefore large. Somerset had the smallest villages and Berkshire the largest. Hampshire was also near the bottom end of the scale, but Wiltshire was a county of large villages. Only in Berkshire was the percentage of freemen even as high as 0.1, while the average percentage of slaves throughout the region at 16.25 was one of the highest in England. The striking fact about the region is its comparative homogeneity. Hampshire was clearly less well-developed than the rest of the region and there were considerable sparsely inhabited uplands in Somerset; the contrasts common in the west Midlands are not found in southern England.

The condition of Wales in 1086 is poorly known, but Flintshire and Denbighshire were clearly in a primitive pastoral and forested state. On the whole the Marches were rather thinly settled and poorly developed. Cheshire was sparsely inhabited and hamlet country. Both Cheshire and Shropshire showed considerable signs of economic regression before 1066. Herefordshire was richer, lying between Shropshire and Worcestershire in its development. The average size of the settlements was 10.7 households – meaning small villages. The proportion of free peasants in the Marches was 3.6 per cent and of slaves 16.6 per cent. The Marches was therefore an old settled region but with big differences inside it. Out of 395 free peasants, 310 were in Cheshire and Shropshire; out of 1802 slaves, 1661 were in Shropshire and Herefordshire. Cheshire had a high proportion of freemen; Shropshire had a high proportion of both freemen and slaves; Herefordshire had a high proportion of slaves. These figures have their significance for settlement history.

There is considerable difference between the state of development of the two south-western counties of Devon and Cornwall. In 1086 Devon was moderately well-developed and moderately densely settled, but there were two regions of sparse or very sparse settlement – the Exmoor border with the northern part of the Culm Measures belt, and Dartmoor and a smaller adjoining southern portion of the Culm Measures belt. Devon, with 19.2 per cent of its peasants slaves, was one of the least free counties in England. It was moderately densely settled by small villages whose average size was 17.6 households. Cornwall was a poorly developed and sparsely settled county in 1086, in strong contrast to Devon. The granite massifs of Bodmin Moor and the Land's End peninsula were especially sparsely settled. Cornwall was also a land of many slaves; the general percentage of 21.4 was one of the highest in the country. Cornwall was sparsely settled but by small villages of an average size of 16.3 recorded households rather than by hamlets. It therefore contrasts with the counties of northern England.

Of the six counties of northern England Cumberland, Northumberland, most of Westmorland, and Durham were not surveyed in 1086. Lancashire was sketchily and the wildest parts of Yorkshire inadequately surveyed. The whole of northern England was very wild and empty in 1066 and 1086. The north was thinly settled but comparatively free, but only for Yorkshire are figures really available to illustrate this. Here 505 out of 7566 inhabitants, or 6.7 per cent, were free, and the West Riding was much freer than the North and East Ridings. Yorkshire and Lancashire were both hamlet country, and in Yorkshire the average settlement had 4.1 households. The whole of the north had a very long way to go before it would be well-developed but the comparative freedom of Lancashire and Yorkshire suggests that new settlement had already begun.

But the relationship of new settlement and social structure is more complex than it seems at first sight. An analysis of the figures in Domesday (using Professor Darby's tables) which give the percentage of 'free' and unfree peasantry in the various counties does produce a sort of pattern but its significance is not so easy to discover. Most Domesday scholars would agree that freemen and sokemen were similar sorts of peasant, and if they are classed together the free rural population appears to have been remarkably concentrated in a very few counties. The average percentage of freemen and sokemen together in the whole of England was 13.9 but in fact 33,623 out of 37,373 lived in Lincolnshire, Norfolk, Suffolk, Nottinghamshire and Leicestershire. All these five counties were most noteworthy for new settlement before the Norman Conquest, while an additional new-settlement county – Northamptonshire – was just below the average figure for freemen with 12.2 per cent. The anomaly is Kent, which was a fast-settling county before the Norman Conquest but had only 0.4 per cent free. Essex, which was also settled fast, had however, a population which contained 7.4 per cent free peasantry. The correlation between fast growth and freedom is therefore good but not complete.

Rural slavery was much more widespread than rural freedom. On average 10.5 per cent of the rural population were slaves, most of them occurring in the southern and western parts of Domesday England. Gloucestershire and Cornwall each had more than double the average percentage of slaves, and there were high percentages in eastern England in Cambridgeshire and Essex, in the east Midlands in Bedfordshire, Buckinghamshire and Hertfordshire, in south-eastern England in Surrey, in the west Midlands in Oxfordshire, Gloucestershire, Worcestershire and Warwickshire, in the Welsh Marches in Herefordshire and Shropshire, in southern England in Berkshire, Hampshire, Wiltshire, Dorset and Somerset, and in south-western England in Cornwall and Devon. This is an extensive list and difficult to understand. Gloucestershire,

Hampshire and Worcestershire were, like the eastern counties, fast-settling and rich in 1086; they had a very high percentage of slaves. The same applies to a lesser extent to all the other slave counties except Wiltshire, Dorset, Somerset, Devon, Cornwall, Herefordshire and Shropshire, all of which had made less than the average progress in new settlement before 1086. Of these last, Cornwall and Shropshire were still markedly poor in 1086, and were to remain so for a long time, but for the rest, comparative wealth went with a good amount of new settlement and a high percentage of slaves down to and in 1086.

And so it seems that by 1086 rapid growth to a high degree of development had taken place in two areas which had markedly different social systems – one (mainly in the west Midlands and southern England) which had a high percentage of slaves, and one (mainly in eastern England and some of the east Midlands) which had an even higher percentage of freemen and sokemen. Both regions were populous and highly arable – Oxfordshire as much as Suffolk – but on the whole the second group of counties was richer and more populous than the first. Before 1086 the contrast between the relative freedom of these societies was probably greater than in 1086, for there is evidence that the sokemen and freemen of East Anglia were freer before 1066 than in 1086. Maitland's count of the sokemen of Cambridgeshire showed that in 1066 they numbered about 900 whereas in 1086 they had declined to 213. R. Welldon Finn has been less willing than Maitland to reach conclusions about the freemen and sokemen of Norfolk, Suffolk and Essex, but a decline in their number in 1066–86 is distinctly possible. Eastern England was perhaps freer in 1066 than in 1086.

How far back did this contrast between the relatively free and relatively enslaved regions go? In recent years a substantial literature has stressed the continuity of institutions between the late Roman period and the Old English period. One of the most influential works has been Professor Finberg's *Withington*, which adopts an idea from Seebohm's *The English Village Community* – that the Old English manor was the successor of the Roman villa. In the context of recent work on the Dark

Ages and, particularly, on the age of Arthur, the continuity theory bears up well under criticism. Yet it is hard to find the same continuity in eastern England as in the west Midlands. A recent most interesting work throws considerable light upon this problem. The distribution of Roman villas, particularly of those which still flourished in the third and fourth centuries, but even more so of villas which are known to have continued after 367, was remarkably similar to the distribution of slaves in 1086. The richer villas were concentrated, in the third and fourth centuries, in Gloucestershire, Oxfordshire, the west parts of Somerset, Dorset, Hampshire and the west parts of Berkshire. In eastern England they were very thinly scattered, except immediately round Rochester in Kent and in the Nene Valley above Peterborough. The villas which are known to have survived after 367 were even more closely confined to the south-west Midlands, especially to Gloucestershire, but much more evidence is required from the late period before a generalization becomes possible.

More specialized studies of the Roman period in eastern England bear out these statements. Villas were comparatively sparse in Lincolnshire, even if one includes substantial debris among the known villa sites. Fenland Lincolnshire, and also fenland Cambridgeshire, entirely devoid of villas, were the home of a numerous peasantry. The archaeologist cannot say whether or not these were free, but even if they were tenants of the imperial demesne or of villa-owners who lived elsewhere, they probably worked for themselves. The combined territory of the Iceni and Trinovantes (which corresponded roughly with modern Norfolk, Suffolk and Essex) had only 55 out of the 604 villas of all periods so far listed, and only 31 out of 313 third- and fourth-century villas. Kent had only 47 villas out of which 25 belong to the third and fourth centuries. It looks very much, therefore, as if the regions which had a great abundance of free peasants in 1066 and 1086 were the regions which were largely given over to peasant agriculture in Roman times, whereas seigneurial England was the land of villa-owners. Eastern England was also the region of the *ingas* new settlement of the

sixth and seventh centuries, that is, of those place-names which
contain the element *ingas, inga,* or *ingaham.*

Place-name study casts light on English farming before 1086.
Sheep and cattle were almost equally important, followed by
horses, swine and goats. Of the counties with many free
peasants, Lincolnshire was the second county by number;
Norfolk, Sussex, Kent and Somerset were the leading horse-
rearers; Somerset was the first, and Leicestershire the third,
sheep-rearer; and Lincolnshire the second pig-rearer. Thus
Lincolnshire was the second most important pastoral county
(cattle and swine) by number. But Lincolnshire is a very large
county, and the density of animal names is perhaps a fairer
criterion. By density the only pastoral specialist among the free
peasants' counties was Leicestershire, the leading sheep-rearer.

Before 1086 barley may have been more important than
wheat, and rye than oats. Legumes, mainly beans, grew much
more widely than was once supposed. Eastern and south-eastern
England, and the east Midlands, were the principal grain-
growing regions, except for wheat which was equally popular
in southern England. Beans were particularly popular in eastern
and south-eastern England and in the east Midlands. Northern
England grew barley rather than wheat and cared little for
legumes. Of the counties which had many free peasants, the
barley specialists were Norfolk, Northamptonshire and Suffolk;
the rye specialists Norfolk and Suffolk; and the oats and legumes
specialist Suffolk. Thus Norfolk and Somerset were the greatest
mixed farming counties; Norfolk and Suffolk were the greatest
arable counties; and Lincolnshire was the second greatest
pastoral county, after the West Riding of Yorkshire. Mixed
farming, with some agrarian and pastoral specialization, was
characteristic of England before 1086.

Domesday provides information on demesne stock-farming
in Cambridgeshire, especially the Isle of Ely, all Norfolk,
Suffolk and Essex, four manors in Hertfordshire, about half of
Dorset, all Somerset, Devon and Cornwall, and six places in
Herefordshire. All over Domesday England sheep, followed by

swine, goats, cattle and horses were the most important demesne
animals, except that in Essex cattle were more important than
goats and in Devon and Cornwall cattle were second in
importance and swine followed goats in the fourth place.
Domesday England was more pastoral than the England of
Edward I. Long before 1272 goats had virtually disappeared,
while swine became less numerous than cattle. In 1086
everybody still ploughed with oxen; by 1272 the most advanced
parts of England used horses.

Gildas and Bede both mention vineyards, but the Norman
Conquest brought fresh interest in the grape. In Suffolk there
were four vineyards, and in Essex ten. Several of these vineyards
were new and not yet fully in bearing. The vineyard at Rayleigh
produced twenty *muids* (≠60 gallons?) of wine in good years.
There was also a vineyard at Ely. Vineyards were a distinctive
characteristic of south Middlesex which had seven, two of them
newly planted. In Kent there were three vineyards and one in
Berkshire. There are four references to vineyards in Wiltshire.
The entry for Wilcot raises a smile. There was a new church, an
excellent house and a good vineyard. Such enthusiasm suggests
that the royal commissioners had, somehow or other, sampled
the products of the good vineyard. In Dorset there were two
vineyards. Both estates belonged to Aiulf the Chamberlain,
sheriff of Dorset in 1086, and the Tollard Royal vineyard in
Wiltshire was also his. There were seven vineyards in the
lowlands of central Somerset, one in Bedfordshire, one in
Buckinghamshire and three in Hertfordshire, of which one was
newly planted. At Stonehouse, near Stroud in Gloucestershire,
there was a vineyard, probably on the warm south-western
slope of the hill, and in Worcestershire a newly-planted one.
That there were no vineyards in northern England or the Welsh
Marches is not surprising, although they did exist two centuries
after Domesday. That there were none in Devon and Cornwall,
nor more astonishingly in Surrey and Hampshire, the main
centres of modern viticulture, seems hard to believe. The *lacunae*
of Domesday are notorious, but at least the reader can perceive a
new interest in wine-making in England after 1066.

The Domesday Survey tells us what proportion of the rural population were smallholders, since it divides the people into freemen, sokemen, villeins, bordars, cottars, slaves and other minor categories. Bordars held a *bordagium* or small tenement of about five acres, cottars held cottages, often with crofts and gardens, and slaves were either unmarried *famuli* (farm-servants, dairy maids and house-servants), or *cassati* (married housed slaves, living on smallholdings and sometimes liable to work as the lord's ploughmen). These, and the various tradesmen and craftsmen, formed the rural proletariat. Villeins were usually virgaters or half-virgaters, or, in the north, oxgangers, who held a standard share of ten to thirty acres in the open fields and did week-works for the lord. Sokemen could be free or unfree and, when less substantial, held bovates and were exempt from week-works for a *mal* or regular money payment. Villeins, sokemen and freemen were usually able to support their families from the produce of their shares in the village lands, including their rights in the waste. In which parts of England were they in a majority?

In 1086 more than half the men of Lincolnshire were sokemen, and in all south-eastern England, all the east Midlands, except Hertfordshire, in Oxfordshire, Warwickshire, Staffordshire and Derbyshire, and in all Yorkshire, more than half the rural population were villeins. In Norfolk and Suffolk freemen, sokemen and villeins together formed more than half of the rural population. Since sokemen and villeins were of the same economic status, in these counties the typical peasant was a half-virgater or virgater.

More than half the rural population of Essex were bordars, and in Cambridgeshire, Hertfordshire and all southern and south-western England except Devon more than half were bordars, cottars and slaves. In Hampshire, Dorset, Somerset and Cornwall more than one-third of the rural population were bordars, probably the descendants of manumitted slaves, for in all these smallholder counties more than one-tenth, and in Cornwall more than one-fifth, of the rural population were slaves. In all these southern and south-western counties there were also significant numbers of freedmen, so named. Besides this, more than one-tenth of the rural population of Wiltshire were *coscets*, a type of cottar, perhaps also descendants of slaves, and significant numbers of *coscets* existed in all the southern and south-western counties except Berkshire and Cornwall.

To the list of smallholder counties rightfully belong Devon, the Marcher counties, Gloucestershire and Worcestershire. Just under half the rural population of these counties were bordars, cottars and slaves, but there were numerous miscellaneous workers who had little if any land of their own. Except for 28 fishermen in Cambridgeshire, 10 shepherds in Sussex, and 10 oxmen in Lancashire, Domesday pays little attention to these people in eastern and south-eastern England, the east Midlands and northern England, but elsewhere they form a very important part of the survey. Wiltshire and Somerset had numerous swineherds; Dorset had 56 salters and Somerset 10 fishermen. Devon had 370 swineherds and 61 salters, besides freedmen and *coscets*; Cornwall had 40 brewers. More than a quarter of Gloucestershire's rural population were slaves, and there were significant numbers of freedmen and *coscets*. Worcestershire, Herefordshire and Shropshire all had more than one-tenth of their rural population slaves. Worcestershire and all the Welsh Marcher counties had large numbers of oxmen. Herefordshire had 142 and also 11 free oxmen, so that the oxmen, who existed in various twelfth-century surveys were probably, many of them, housed slaves (*cassati*). Herefordshire also had a number of smiths and freedmen, and Cheshire 14 fishermen. And so the smallholder country embraced Essex, Cambridgeshire, Hertfordshire, all southern and south-western England, and the Welsh Marches, Gloucestershire and Worcestershire. Put in other terms, in southern and south-western England and the Welsh Marches 58, 55 and 51 per cent of the rural population had insufficient land to give them a subsistence income. In eastern and south-eastern England, the east and west Midlands, and northern England 38, 41, 35, 45 and 25 per cent of the rural population respectively were in that condition, and the general figure for the whole of England was

42 per cent. Domesday England was predominantly a land of half-virgaters and virgaters.

Reginald Lennard, studying the economic position of the Domesday sokemen and villeins, found that the villeins were neither richer nor poorer than the sokemen, and that the regional distribution of poverty amongst the villeins was much the same as amongst the sokemen. The poorest villeins and sokemen were in Lincolnshire and Norfolk, the poorest sokemen in Suffolk and Essex and the poorest villeins in Kent and Rutland. Of these, only Essex was a smallholder county, but in Norfolk and Suffolk, because of the very large number of freemen, sokemen and villeins made up less than half the population. Into the category of the poorest come the villeins and sokemen of Leicestershire, the sokemen of Derbyshire and the villeins of Suffolk, Cambridgeshire, Nottinghamshire and Northamptonshire. Except in Yorkshire, there were no significant numbers of Domesday sokemen outside eastern England and the east Midlands. The villeins of Surrey, Hampshire, Somerset, Wiltshire, Oxfordshire, Warwickshire, Staffordshire, Derbyshire, Cheshire and Yorkshire were in this class of the second poorest. Cambridgeshire, Hampshire, Somerset, Wiltshire and Cheshire were also smallholder counties in 1086. The second richest sokemen were in Nottinghamshire and Northamptonshire; the second richest villeins in Essex, Bedfordshire, Buckinghamshire, Hertfordshire, Berkshire, Dorset, Worcestershire, Devon and Shropshire. All these counties, except Bedfordshire and Buckinghamshire, were smallholder counties. The richest sokemen were in Bedfordshire and Yorkshire; the richest villeins in Sussex, Gloucestershire and Herefordshire. The last two were predominantly smallholder counties. The poorest villeins and sokemen of all were in Norfolk, where they formed just over a third of the rural population, only a little more than the bordars. The richest sokemen were in Yorkshire, where they formed barely 6 per cent of the rural population. The richest villeins were in Herefordshire, a smallholder county where they formed over a third of the population. Yorkshire and

Herefordshire were much poorer and less populous than Norfolk which contained nearly one-tenth of the Domesday population. Indeed, a great proportion of the poorer sokemen and villeins were in eastern England, for in these five counties lived one-third of the people of Domesday England. Lennard was also able to show that the same regional differences existed in 1066 as in 1086 and that the wealth of the sokemen of Norfolk, Suffolk and Essex declined by over 10 per cent in 1066–86. As these heavily populated counties became yet more populous so the sokemen and villeins became poorer.

Yet in 1086 the poorest people were in Essex, Cambridgeshire, Hertfordshire, southern and south-western England, the Welsh Marches, Gloucestershire and Worcestershire. Much of this was seigneurial England, highly enslaved but becoming freer, and already developing fairly fast. How does Domesday England compare with England in 1348?

The data leave much to be desired, but Fenland Lincolnshire, Cambridgeshire, East Anglia, much of Essex, Kent and Sussex was smallholder country by the fourteenth century. The same is true of Rutland, Nottinghamshire, Leicestershire, and, more certainly, Bedfordshire and Buckinghamshire. Except for Somerset, in the rest of England half-virgaters and virgaters predominated. Only Essex, Cambridgeshire and Somerset were smallholder counties in 1086. The bordars, cottars and slaves who in 1086 had been so prominent in southern and south-western England and the Welsh Marches, and in Gloucestershire and Worcestershire, had given way to a middle and rich peasantry. The freemen, sokemen and villeins who had in 1086 been the mainstay of all eastern and south-eastern England, and the east Midlands, except Cambridgeshire, Essex and Hertfordshire had given place to a massive population of smallholders. The history of new settlement and population growth, of crops and livestock, agricultural techniques, marriage and inheritance customs explains this transformation, and the following chapters will consider the various regions of England and Wales under those heads. The great variety of practices and customs can be demonstrated only by citing individual examples which have been reduced to a minimum; the works listed in the footnotes offer further illustrations. Two matters should be mentioned here. First, in discussing agricultural techniques issue has sometimes had to be taken with H. L. Gray's *English Field Systems* (1915), the fundamental but far from exhaustive study of the subject: this explains the recurrent mention of 'Gray'. And secondly, where place-name evidence tells the story of new settlement it is often important to know the date of a particular survey because these have over the years become more exhaustive and reliable.

CHAPTER 4

EASTERN ENGLAND

1 NEW SETTLEMENT AND POPULATION GROWTH

The creation of new settlements can be deduced from place-names. Here the single most important place-name element is *leah* which means (i) 'a wood, woodland'; (ii) 'a rough uncultivated natural open space in a wood, a glade'; (iii) 'a rough clearing in a wood'; (iv) 'a cultivated or developed glade or woodland clearing, especially one used for pasture or arable'; (v) 'a piece of open land, a meadow'. Since all the localities named in the Domesday Survey either were or had been inhabited places, *leah* there simply signifies 'a clearing in a wood' and its use therefore denotes the formation of a new settlement. Its fault as an index of new settlement is that it shows only assarting from woodland and ignores reclamation of marshland, fen and moor. In Scandinavian parts of England too its use is more limited. For these latter I have used the word *thwaite*, which also means 'a clearing' and is never found earlier than 870.

These two elements by themselves give an interesting picture of the progress of new settlement but there are many other place-name elements denoting new settlement which come from Old English, Old Danish, Old Norse and Old Welsh sources. I cannot discuss all these here but a few observations are useful on the main types used. *Thorp*, 'a secondary settlement, a dependent outlying farmstead or hamlet', is strong in the Danelaw and the north, but the Old English *throp*, 'a hamlet, an outlying farm', does something to redress the balance elsewhere. *Thorp* is not nearly so important as some Danish enthusiasts have implied, and I have carefully desisted from the use of *by*, *byr*, since there is no evidence that its use denoted the creation of a new settlement. *Beretun*, *bertun*, *baertun*, 'a barley enclosure, a barley farm', and more generally 'a corn farm', becomes in

Middle English 'an outlying grange where the lord's crop was stored, a demesne farm, especially one retained for the lord's use and not let to tenants'. Such seigneurial farms often grew into villages, and the name is a useful sign of seigneurial influence upon settlement. The Old English *wic*, 'a dwelling, a building or collection of buildings for special purposes, a farm, a dairy farm', and in the plural, 'a hamlet, a village' is a useful indicator of new settlement, also often seigneurial, and is found nearly everywhere. The Old English *feld*, 'open country', rapidly assumed the meaning 'land for pasture or cultivation' and when applied to a settlement is a sign of new cultivation. Similarly, Old English *wudu*, 'a wood, a grove, woodland, a forest', applied to a settlement, shows that it is new. With these go a few examples from the Danelaw of Old Norse *lundr*, 'a small wood, a grove'; Old English *wald*, *weald*, 'woodland, a large tract of woodland, high forest-land'; and Old English and Old Norse *holt*, 'a wood, a holt, a thicket'. From all over England too we get *wordig*, *weordig*, *wurdig*, *wyrdig*, 'an enclosure', and Old English *wordign*, 'an enclosure', names particularly common in the south-west. Old Norse *topt* and Old Danish and Late Old English *toft*, 'curtilage, the plot of ground in which a dwelling stands', are also useful signs of new settlement. Occasionally there are place-names in *cot*, *cote*, 'a cottage, a hut, a shelter, a den', *denn*, 'a woodland pasture, especially for swine', *croft*, 'a small enclosure of arable or pasture land', *graf*, *grafa*, *grafe*, 'a grove, copse', *saetr*, Old Norse, 'a mountain pasture, a shieling', *sceaga*, *scaga*, 'a small wood, a copse, a strip of undergrowth or wood', *erg*, 'a shieling, a hill-pasture', and *hyrst*, *herst*, 'a hillock, a copse'. Lastly, there are commonly in each county a number of place-names with the element 'new'. Newton is frequent, but I have also included Newbold and its variants, Newhouse, Newsham and Newland. More stringent and lengthy examination of the main English place-names would probably have brought in others – such as, for example, some of the Westons, Eastons, Nortons and Suttons – all villages whose position may have related to that of an older settlement, but the material is sufficiently bulky for conclusions to be firmly based.[1]

The late first occurrence of place-names containing an element which denotes new settlement is not too bad an index of new settlement after 1086, provided that the first occurrence is after 1280, for many years could elapse between the creation of a new settlement and its appearance in any record. In eastern England no new-settlement place-names occurred for the first time after 1350 in Norfolk, Suffolk and Cambridgeshire, and only one each in Lincolnshire and Essex. In 1281–1350 no new-settlement place-names occurred for the first time in Essex, only one each in Suffolk and Cambridgeshire and two each in Lincolnshire and Norfok. There was probably not much new settlement of entire new villages in eastern England after 1086.

Most of Lincolnshire's new settlements came into existence before 1066, and most were on land under 100 feet above sea-level. Axholme and other marshy regions, especially the Lincolnshire Marshland and Fenland, were especially favoured. Very few new settlements were at over 300 feet above sea-level, and these mostly in the upper valley of the Witham, and in the central Wolds. Many new settlements were in woodland in Kesteven, and on the east and south fringes of the Wolds. The Lincolnshire new settlements were therefore for the most part not on marginal land. Where this existed on the Lincoln Edge and Cliff it remained uninhabited until modern times.

Highland Lincolnshire showed signs of new settlement during the twelfth century, particularly in the area rather more than halfway along the Lincoln Edge north of Lincoln. In north Lindsey sea and fen were being reclaimed at Stallingborough, and by about 1233 there was a seadyke.

By about 1189 there was active reclamation in Axholme on the lower reaches of the Trent. A dyke forty feet wide, and a large timber sluice with vertically hinged gates existed in 1310, and there was a weir to drain the common fields into the river Don. Reclamation was still proceeding in 1337.

There was also new settlement of heathland and fen in the north of Lindsey, by about 1150, and several other parts of Lindsey show similar signs. South of the Lincolnshire Wolds round Horncastle and Alford new settlement was taking place about 1180.

In Kesteven, particularly in the fens and on the heaths of the Lincoln Edge round Sleaford, there are ample signs of new settlement from the middle of the twelfth century onwards. Catley Priory, like many Lincolnshire monasteries, was busy developing granges at this time.

Three late assarts bring the practice, in Kesteven, down to the middle of the thirteenth century. These were in the woodland west of Bourne, in 1240, in 1252, and on the line of settlements between Lincoln Edge and the Witham Fens in 1234.

With the exception of the last, all these new settlements were small enclosures of woodland, heath and marsh in a densely inhabited county. In Fenland Lincolnshire the new settlement, instead of being small and piecemeal, was very extensive and led to the creation of new hamlets and monastic granges; instead of being the work of individuals or of groups of peasants, or of monasteries, the creation of the seadykes and fendykes was the work of whole communities, and was not complete on the seaward side until 1286 and on the fenward side until 1241.

Late new settlements grew up in most parts of Norfolk, except the Breckland. In the more heavily wooded area of mid-Norfolk there was quite a batch of them. They also arose in the Marshland, in the good sand region, in north Norfolk, in or near the Broads, and in south Norfolk. Some of the soils of mid-Norfolk are light, but few of these new settlements were on land which was markedly marginal, and many are now quite large villages.

In the good sand region of north Norfolk, east of Hunstanton, the arable increased between the twelfth and thirteenth centuries. Three good assarts (land reclaimed from the waste) are known from the loam region, north of Norwich. Six assarts, mostly mentioned late, are known from mid-Norfolk, and of these one was still proceeding in the 1260s. Two assarting settlements are known from south Norfolk, but assarting in Broadland is not well vouched for.

In the Norfolk Marshland and the Wiggenhalls reclamation was almost as extensive as it was in the Lincolnshire Fenland after 1086. According to Dugdale, there was little in the Wiggenhalls before 1181, and the great event for the whole countryside was the raising of the Old Podike about 1223. In fact, there was already a new purpresture (or enclosure) at the Podike in 1199–1216, and the bank might easily be much older. On the seaward side there were already, by 1186, eight newlands (new enclosures) and by about 1250 there were two more.

Of the twelve late new settlements in Suffolk four were in west Suffolk and eight in east Suffolk. Ten of these settlements are still thriving. Only two of the new settlements were in the Sandlings and both were on or very near the coast. There were no late new settlements in the Suffolk Fenland, or the Breckland, so that the remaining ten settlements were in various parts of High Suffolk, often in the regions most densely inhabited in 1086. The four west Suffolk new settlements were all on relatively high land. The distribution over High Suffolk was fairly even.

After 1066 there was a certain amount of new settlement in Suffolk, much of it in the twelfth century. Most of it is found in High Suffolk, but east Suffolk, especially the Sandlings, had its share. Here there were several late references to assarts made earlier. The surveys of the Sibton Abbey estates, made in 1325, provide ample evidence of assarts in east Suffolk probably made long before.

Most of the late new settlements in Essex are thriving settlements to this day, but five are only hamlets. Only two were in the Essex Marshes, and three were in the Tendring-Colchester loam area. Several new settlements were on the London clay, none of them on high ground, but the London clay was well-wooded. The rest of the new settlements were in remote country in the interior of Essex on the boulder clay plateau.

The Essex place-name survey of 1935 records 108 clearances (names containing *leah*), including those which grew into settlements. Of these seventy-three were first recorded after

1086, forty-six of them after 1280. These do not include place-names which do not appear in the records until the eighteenth and nineteenth centuries.

King Stephen acquitted the two hundreds of Tendring round and east of Colchester from assarts and pleas of the forest in 1141–54, but there may have been much earlier new settlement than this in the Tendring–Colchester loam area. On the London clay, new settlement took place from the earliest to the latest times.

In the Lea Valley, assarting took place in 1181–1222, and was still active in 1222. Near Maldon assarting took place in 1155 and continued for most of the thirteenth century, certainly until 1272, and perhaps until 1290. Near Epping, new settlement had already taken place by 1185–7, and in 1275 corn grew on new assarts from heath and wood.

Further south, along the river Lea, there were river walls in 1255, and on the London clay, towards the marshes of the Thames Valley, there was also a good deal of new settlement. On the boulder clay plateau in 1181–1222 the arable increased and the woodland declined. Assarts both by lord and peasant proceeded steadily in 1140 and 1222.

By 1310 the demesne land at Lawling had almost ceased to exist and compared with the lord's the peasants' interests were great. There was little unspoilt wilderness and the assart holdings were not many. All were new, and may have been in the same general area, perhaps adjoining the open fields. The assarters seem all to have been humble men, and some lived close by their assarts which were in small enclosures or crofts. Thus assarting still continued, in Essex, on a small scale, in 1310. Essex was less typical of eastern England than Lincolnshire, Norfolk or Suffolk.

There were seven, or possibly eight, new settlements in Cambridgeshire first recorded after 1086. They fell into fenland and upland settlements. Two of the three fenland new settlements were in the blacklands of the Isle of Ely – a region not suitable for settlement until modern times – and one was in the siltland of the far north of the Isle of Ely. The new settlements on the chalk uplands of Cambridgeshire were east and west of the Cam and its tributaries. All these new settlements except one are substantial settlements to this day. The Cambridgeshire and Isle of Ely place-names survey of 1943 lists only seventeen names compounded with *leah*, all post-1066, and eight of them post-1280. The list is not exhaustive.

Cambridgeshire divides easily into the heavily settled upland of Cambridgeshire proper, and the lightly settled fenland of the Isle of Ely. Many of the new settlements in the former were recorded well before the Domesday Survey and are good evidence of an early settlement of the county. The new-settlement period in Cambridgeshire's history was between the Viking invasions and the Norman Conquest. In villages like Chippenham, on the edge of the fenland, the lord was ploughing the heath by 1144–6, and the work of clearance had spread to the limit of cultivated land in the sixteenth century. By 1141–6 Gamlingay Heath was under the plough.

The empty fenland in the Isle of Ely tells a different story. Settlement there took place on the islands in the fen and on the siltland in the north long before 1086, but it was not extensive. The Isle of Ely had plenty of room for expansion, many new settlements grew up after 1086, and settlement went on unusually late. Seven new settlements were recorded for the first time in the twelfth century, three in the thirteenth century, and one was not recorded until 1315. Reclamation was still going on in 1251–1307. On the siltlands of the hundred of Wisbech reclamation was comparable in scale to that in the Norfolk Marshland and the Lincolnshire Fenland. There seem to have been two major intakes at about the same time as the latest intakes in the wapentake of Elloe. In Wisbech and Elm these occurred in about 1189–97 and 1225–8. By 1216–36 the men of Leverington had reached the furthest extent of possible reclamation, some seven miles from the centre of the village.

After 1086 there were few woodland clearings anywhere in eastern England. New settlement in eastern England was slight in highland Lincolnshire, Norfolk, Suffolk and south Cambridgeshire, considerably greater in the woods and marshes of Essex, and very great in the Lincolnshire and Cambridgeshire Fenland, and the Norfolk Marshland, where whole communities reclaimed both fen and marsh together. New settlement took place in the Fenland from the tenth century onward, was very active in the first half of the twelfth century, at its height before and after 1200, and continued until nearly 1300. In duration and extent the settlement of the Fenland had few, if any, parallels in England.

The twelfth century was almost certainly a period of population increase in eastern England. Only on the Lincolnshire estates of Peterborough Abbey is there positive evidence of decline in the forty years after the Domesday Survey. The general rate of increase in 1086–1200 seems to have been 40–100 per cent, and most often about 66 per cent. In Cambridgeshire, on the Ramsey Abbey estates, there was a definite slowing down in the period from the reign of Henry II to c. 1250, and on the Ely estates in 1221–51, but there was perhaps an acceleration in 1251–79. Expansion was very great in the Fenland. The siltland population in Lincolnshire grew six- to ten-fold in the two centuries after 1086, and in Cambridgeshire, Norfolk and Suffolk, the Fenland and Broadland manors also expanded very quickly. On the estates of Norwich Cathedral Priory a five-fold growth occurred in the two centuries after 1086, and in both Suffolk and Essex growth was three times as rapid in 1221–51 as in 1086–1221. Woodland areas were particularly noteworthy for fast growth. In Epping Forest the Waltham Abbey manors grew three-fold in the one and a half centuries after 1086. Direct evidence of population decline in 1280–1350 is very hard to find. Four Lincolnshire manors grew by only two-fifths in 1086–1321, but eight Essex manors had doubled or trebled their population in 1086–1350, and two of these expanded very fast indeed. What was happening to the population of eastern England in 1280–1350 is not clear at all from direct comparisons.

Counts of heads of households exist for 228 eastern England manors in 1086–1350, and they split into five equal cohorts which cover 1086–1193, 1086–1229, 1086–1251, 1086–1278 and

1086–1300. The percentage increases over these five periods are 166, 299, 368, 416 and 434. The Domesday population had trebled by 1229 and quadrupled by 1278, and at no time was there any general decline before the Black Death. Population increase was moderately quick in 1086–1193, very quick in 1193–1229, slower but still quick in 1229–51, slowed further in 1251–78, and slowed yet further but still continued in 1278–1300. These movements accord very well with the history of new settlement.[1]

2 CROPS AND LIVESTOCK

On ten Lincolnshire manors in 1245–72 oats was the most important grain, followed by wheat and barley. The three major grains were evenly balanced, and rye and beans were also very significant. On his demesne lands on the fen-edge, in 1266/7–1306/7 the Abbot of Crowland grew mainly wheat, but north of Boston, in 1297, maslin was the biggest crop, followed by oats, legumes, wheat, barley and dredge. Elsewhere in the Parts of Holland, before 1300, oats was by far the greatest crop.

In the Precinct of Crowland grew legumes, barley, oats and rye, but on the other granges of Crowland Abbey oats was practically the only crop. The provisioning of the Lincoln Parliament in 1301 suggests that oats was the most prominent grain in the whole county. It predominated enormously in Holland, but wheat was more notable in the North Riding of Lindsey, and in Kesteven. Thus legumes appear in quantity in the very county of the Parts of Holland in which oats was foremost.

Records of stints of stock cover the whole of Lincolnshire, and the whole period 1130–1280. They show a vast preponderance of sheep, especially on the Lincoln Edge, the Lincoln Cliff, and in the Lincolnshire Wolds. Milch kine were also numerous, and swine, horses and other cattle followed. Sheep, cattle and swine was also the order of precedence in the figures derived from the provisioning of the Lincoln Parliament in 1301. Holland provided most sheep and cattle, and Kesteven most swine. The Fenland was unquestionably a great pastoral region – perhaps above all a cattle-rearing region – but quantification is difficult. In the Precinct of Crowland over the period 1302–22 the average size of the abbey's sheep flock was over 5000, having risen steadily from an average of over 3200 in the period 1258–83. The abbey's flocks reached their maximum in 1340 and thereafter began to diminish. Both Crowland Abbey and Spalding Priory also kept many cattle in the fens from whose milk they made cheeses. North of Boston in 1297 there were more cattle than sheep, but more sheep than horses, so perhaps the ordinary fenland peasant followed the parochial clergy and went in for cows rather than sheep.

In 1274 and 1287 the fenland peasantry grew corn, hay, flax and hemp, kept pigs, cockerels, geese and bees, and made cheese and salt. Here was diversity enough, and nowhere a suggestion that animals were few. There were thousands of sheep, many cattle and probably many horses. Swine were not so worthy of notice. Oats grew where it might naturally best grow, and, as the record of Lincolnshire diet shows, fed horses rather than men. Beans were well-known north of Boston on the glebe-land of the clergy, and in the Abbot of Crowland's granges in the Precinct of Crowland.

Lincolnshire consisted of two principal farming regions in the period down to 1350. Highland Lincolnshire specialized in wheat, barley and sheep; the Fenland in oats, and, after 1300, maslin, sheep, cattle and dairy products. The Fenland also grew some flax and hemp. Inside the two regions there were sub-regions. Sheep were most plentiful in the North and West Ridings of Lindsey; wheat best in the same area; barley grew best in the South Riding of Lindsey, and oats in the same and in Holland. Swine were most numerous in Kesteven and the South Riding; cattle along the fen-edges, on the Marshland, and in the Fenland. Legumes grew freely in the Fenland, especially round Boston, and in the Precinct of Crowland. The two halves of the county illustrate the arable and pastoral types fairly exactly, but in Kesteven and the South Riding of Lindsey there was a tendency towards a woodland economy which went in for barley and pigs.

Like Lincolnshire, Cambridgeshire divides into arable and pastoral parts – upland Cambridgeshire and the fenland of the Isle of Ely, some of it blackland, almost impossible to cultivate and maintain dry at this period, and some of it, round Wisbech, fertile but still marginal siltland.

In Cambridgeshire, crops grown are known on twelve manors in 1312–53. In upland Cambridgeshire wheat and barley were by far the most considerable crops, but rye, maslin and, occasionally, dredge were not to be overlooked, whereas oats was generally one of the least substantial crops. Nearly all these manors grew either peas, sometimes in large crops, or beans. On seven fen-edge manors more oats grew, and over 14 per cent of the land grew peas. There is a hint of an association between barley, legumes and swine. In the siltlands round Wisbech oats predominated.

Less is known about livestock. There seem to have been comparatively few cattle in upland Cambridgeshire, but in 1251 the Isle of Ely was a major breeding and dairying region. Swine were plentiful in upland Cambridgeshire, and in the Cambridgeshire Fenland.

In Norfolk wheat may have been the largest peasant crop on ten manors in 1126–86. Generally speaking, in 1250–1350, barley was overwhelmingly the principal crop, often greater by far than all the other crops combined, but rye, oats and peas could also be prominent. The peasants grew mostly barley, but the lord's fodder-corn rents sometimes compelled them to grow oats, which went to feed his horses. The existence of many horses, not the presence of marginal land, is the reason for large oats crops all over East Anglia. The lord used his oats but sold most of his peas, wheat and barley. Only once do we find peasants growing rye as their largest crop, and only twice were peas outstanding.

For Wymondham the records show some development. Between 1286–1325 and 1327–1344 the total production increased by two-thirds. All crops except maslin and beans increased – wheat greatly and oats slightly. Both barley and peas more than doubled. Compared with 1290–1330 the acreage sown in 1331–44 was about 83 per cent. The decline covers a big drop in the acreage of peas sown, to less than half the acreage of oats, a slight fall in the acreage of wheat and a slight rise in the acreage of barley. With the exception of oats, yields were improving. Wymondham was turning more and more to barley and peas in 1300–50, and was fallowing and grassing the arable in a more and more complex system of crop rotations. The market demand for grains probably stimulated their growth. The lord sold most of his wheat and maslin.

The monks of Norwich Cathedral Priory farmed sixteen Norfolk manors for which we have the accounts for about thirty of the years between 1255 and 1350. The agrarian crisis of 1315–22 is well-represented, but the prosperous period 1325–50 is poorly documented. The manors mainly produced immense crops of barley, most of which the monks consumed as mountains of bread and seas of ale. They sold the rest. Peas were of moderate account and grew more significant over the period.

Yield ratios are available on some manors from 1273 onwards. Compared with 1272–1318 the period 1321–36 shows twenty-three declining yield ratios, thirteen which improved, and three that remained static. Conditions seem to have been deteriorating, but the number of yield ratios is too small for firm conclusions. These figures are less reliable than the sizes of crops and yields per acre. Crops became smaller on ten manors in 1255–1349, and yields per acre deteriorated in ten out of twenty-one examples.

Whether 1315 really was a bad harvest year all over Norfolk is not known. Compared with the period 1293–1315 the demesne harvest of 1315 at Sedgeford was above standard. At Kempstone in 1315 the lord's crops were all below average, but the peasants' crops above the mean. At Calthorpe in 1315 the lord's wheat crop was above normal, but the other crops below it. The peasants' barley crop at Calthorpe was well above the average in 1315. On the other hand, at Hinderclay, in Suffolk, in

1314, there was clearly a major harvest failure on the lord's demesne.

Two rolls of the Master of the Cellar for the years 1263/4 and 1315/16 suggest that the famine was not very serious in Norfolk. In 1263/4 Norwich priory received from its manors 650 quarters of wheat and bought 214 quarters, which, with the remainder in the barns and the granary increment, made a grand total of 964 quarters for making bread. The priory also received from its manors 1438 quarters of malt (always barley malt) which, with the remainder in the barns and the granary increment, made a grand total of 1673 quarters for brewing. In 1315/16 the priory received from its manors 781 quarters of wheat and thirty quarters of barley 'because of a shortage of wheat this year'. The priory also bought 300 quarters of wheat, which with the remainder in the barns made a grand total of 1104 quarters for bread. For brewing the priory bought no barley, but received 1157 quarters from its manors and, with 240 quarters still in the barns, disposed of 1397 quarters of malt. The brewer actually brewed 1410 quarters in 1315/16, compared with 1481 quarters in 1263/4. There was no shortage either of ale or bread in Norwich Cathedral Priory.

Two other ways remain of checking the impact of the supposed pre-plague famine. The monks would perhaps be the last to suffer destitution, but they would be amongst the first to respond to poverty, as were also the people who ran the Great Hospital close by. We have records of grants of food to the poor for many places between 1261/2 and 1345/6. Most years there were such grants on one or two manors, but only in 1294/5, 1295/6, 1297/8, 1305/6, 1312/13, 1322/3, and 1324/5 were they found on from three to six manors and seldom reached as much as ten quarters of peas.

The monks' charity may have been cold, but no lord was averse to receiving heriots, a clear indicator of mortality. In eastern England six manors recorded heriots in 1277/8–1349/50. Usually there were from one to three deaths each year, and over the famine years the number of deaths did not alter. Then the Black Death showed up in the figures. At Hinderclay in 1348/9 there were thirty-two deaths, at Worlingworth six in 1348/9 and sixteen in 1349/50, at Crondon in Orsett four in 1348/9, and at Redgrave sixty-three in 1348/9 and seven in 1349/50. The Redgrave reeve also received forty-four animals of various types as heriots from Palgrave. The Black Death may still have been a major factor in English agrarian history, but in East Anglia and Essex the earlier 'famines' were not.

On the demesne manors of Norwich Cathedral Priory the worst yields of grain per acre were at Gateley in 1294–1318 (0.9 quarters) and the best at Hemsby in 1272–1312 (2.7 quarters). The average yield over the whole period, and on all manors, was 1.4 quarters per acre. A peasant holding of twelve acres, of which, in Norfolk, ten would be under the plough, would produce enough barley bread to feed a man, his wife and two children, but nothing would be left for seed or the stots. The peasants grew mainly barley and generally had good crops of peas.

Sheep continued to be significant, and swine played a major part in the Norfolk economy of the twelfth century. The tendencies in stock-rearing are difficult to discover. At Forncett between 1272–85 and 1289–1305 there was a shift from arable to milk production. The number of plough-beasts went down much more than the number of other cattle, but swine tended to increase in numbers. After 1290 the economy was more pastoral.

Of ten Norfolk manors four as a rule had no sheep in 1328–36, but three kept good-sized flocks. Sheep were only one interest among many to the Norfolk farmer. There were five large cattle-manors but all the manors had dairy herds, usually let out to the cowman. Swine were plentiful on four manors, but less profuse than cattle. Oxen were more abundant than stots on three manors, but fewer on six. The ox was already losing ground very slowly in Norfolk. Sometimes the number of plough-beasts fell at a time when the area of demesne under the plough was slowly shrinking while the productivity of the land rose quite rapidly, and the dairy herd shrank. Sometimes oxen staged a comeback, but stots remained more numerous, and the arable area increased. Cheese-making was a major activity, and some manors also produced a little wool. The fleeces were very small – usually under two pounds in weight.

Norfolk farming already depended almost entirely upon stots and other horses, which suggests that there was enough oats to make the speed of the horse a worthwhile investment. On the estates of Norwich Cathedral Priory there were no oxen at all on three manors, and at various periods there were none at five other manors. Only on three were oxen more plentiful than stots. On seven manors the number of stots also declined over the whole period, in step with the declining arable, except that at Sedgeford (which never had oxen) the number of stots declined but the arable expanded.

Sheep were negligible, except at eight manors at various periods. All these flocks together were less than the immense flocks at Sedgeford 1263–1349, on the chalk heaths of the East Anglian heights. On the whole flocks of sheep declined in size over the whole period, and disappeared altogether at four manors. The peasant flocks at Sedgeford, on the other hand, grew from an average of 1067 in 1272–1305 to a mean of 1661 in 1309–27.

Cattle (other than oxen) increased their numbers over the whole period at eight manors but became fewer at five. Cheese-making, as elsewhere in Norfolk, was significant, and, although occasionally the custom of milking the ewes for drink for the harvesters still obtained, Norfolk cheeses were generally of cow's milk. The herds were large and let out to the cowman at eight manors at various periods.

Nothing suggests that dairy-farming was anything but prosperous and profitable right down to 1350. Thirteen manors have furnished details of the cattle murrain of 1319–20. Two were not affected, five recovered within three years, and six took four to eight years. The prior could easily have halved the recovery time of his herds while he built up again from his own calves, but he preferred to sell many of these at good prices and delay stocking his own herds. Various manors had swine.

In 1086–1350 Norfolk was one of the most highly arable counties in England, but it also practised mixed farming. Barley was outstanding, but wheat and rye were also major crops. There was a flourishing market in wheat and barley, but oats was grown mainly for horses and to make pottage. Peas were moderately worthy of notice and grew in regard in 1300–50. On some manors yields of grain grew, sometimes on a shrinking area of arable, during this period, but on many both productivity and area of arable declined. The effects of the famines of 1314 and 1315 were sporadic. Sheep were numerous, especially in Breckland and on the East Anglian heights, but fewer on the smaller manors, and a good proportion of manors had no sheep at all. Cattle led the way, and most manors made cheese and butter out of cow's milk. Goats disappeared after 1086. Swine sometimes existed in large herds and were generally popular. On some manors oxen still outnumbered stots, but on many manors the latter replaced the former in 1255–1350, and some had already given up oxen by 1255. There are no signs that the cattle murrain of 1319/20 had a permanent effect upon dairying and cattle-rearing. The agricultural interests of the peasantry seem not to have differed materially from those of the lords.

In Suffolk on eight demesne manors of the Abbey of Bury St Edmunds in 1250 wheat was well ahead of oats as the leading crop; barley and rye were much less to the fore, and peas were not as yet popular. The abbot was already sowing his barley twice as thickly as his other crops.

The detailed local survey made for the Lay Subsidy of 1283 in the hundred of Blackbourne gives invaluable evidence of crops grown and stock held in this part of Suffolk. Most of the hundred was in the lowland portion of High Suffolk, but the western and northern fringe were part of the Breckland. In 1086 this Breckland part of the hundred had a heavy sheep population, and no part of the hundred was heavily wooded. The hundred was not a great arable area. The Breckland part of the hundred was one of the less heavily populated parts of Suffolk in 1086, and the High Suffolk part moderately densely populated. The contrast between the two parts of the hundred should be borne in mind.

Barley was overwhelmingly the most important grain and accounted for a greater saleable surplus than all the other grains together. Rye and oats were next in prominence and about equal. Legumes were very nearly as significant as rye, and oats was one-third greater than the wheat crop, which was least in size. The number of sheep – over 17,000 – was enormous, far greater than in 1086, but there were over 5000 cattle, the overwhelming proportion of them beef and dairy cattle, so that this hundred was a considerable milk and meat producer. Stots and affers (small plough horses) were more plentiful than oxen, and the total number of horses – over 1400 – was more than three and a half times the number of oxen. There were also over 2000 swine – not an enormous number, but sufficient to make their presence felt. Since 1086 Suffolk had greatly enhanced the position of beef and dairy cattle, had supplanted most of its plough oxen with stots and affers, had maintained the consequence of swine, and had abolished goats. The great arable improvements were the dominance of barley and the emergence of peas and beans.

There were twelve manors and other tenements which ecclesiastical lords held. Here barley was still a very considerable grain, but oats was even more important. Wheat was almost as notable as rye, but legumes were only half as prominent as either. Oxen were many more than stots, but fewer than the total number of horses. Swine, in relation to cattle, were proportionally nearly twice as plentiful as in the sum total, and there were twice as many sheep proportionally as in the sum total. The church manors preferred sheep and wheat to cattle, barley and legumes, and ploughed with oxen rather than horses.

There were eighteen lay manors and other tenements. Barley retained its place there as the major grain, but oats was still very much more favoured than in the hundred as a whole. Compared with the ecclesiastical manors, and even more compared with the hundred as a whole, rye was insignificant. Legumes were about as substantial relative to the other grains as on the ecclesiastical manors. Oxen outnumbered stots, but were scarcer than horses. Swine were more profuse than cattle on the lay manors, but sparser on the church manors. The greatest difference was in the status of sheep. The twelve church manors had twice as many sheep as the eighteen lay manors. The churches specialized in sheep-farming, and any statements based on church sources will contain a bias towards sheep-farming.

Barley was overwhelmingly the grain of the people of the hundred in 1283, and rye was second and about a quarter of the quantity of barley. Oats was not far behind rye, but wheat lagged a good distance behind oats and was the least-favoured grain, only one-seventh as popular as barley. Legumes, mainly peas, came third in importance after barley and rye. Stots and affers were markedly more common than oxen, and the total number of horses was nearly five times the number of oxen. Cattle were nearly three times as prevalent as swine. The lords, especially the church lords, had proportionally more sheep, but altogether sheep formed by far the most important element on the pastoral side of the economy.

The hundred of Blackbourne splits into three farming regions: seventeen High Suffolk (arable) settlements, fifteen Breckland settlements, and one fenland settlement. None of the High Suffolk settlements were poor, unlike eight out of fifteen Breckland settlements. The Breckland was infertile and stood little chance of gaining fertility from the use of legumes. The only crop it could grow well was rye, and it contained most of the largest sheep-rearing settlements. High Suffolk did everything well, except grow rye and rear sheep, but it was especially good at growing wheat and legumes, and at rearing swine, with a lesser emphasis upon barley, cattle and horses. The fenland settlement was neither rich nor poor, grew wheat, oats and legumes badly, but grew rye and barley, and reared horses and cattle well. Farming in the hundred of Blackbourne in 1283 was therefore fairly mixed, but the lineaments of three regions emerge from the mixture.

Ipswich is on the boundary between the Sandlings and High Suffolk; in 1086 it was close to one of the most highly developed and most densely populated parts of Suffolk. In 1282 the surrounding countryside grew mainly wheat and barley, with rye and oats about half as significant. The great quantity of malt suggests that barley was the major grain. Stots were very few, but the number of horses was more than double the number of oxen. Swine were fewer than cattle (including oxen), but more than twice as numerous as sheep. Cheese and butter were extraordinarily plentiful, and herrings a favourite food. In 1281–2 Edward I levied upon Suffolk fifty quarters of wheat, fifty quarters of malt, 300 quarters of oats, 100 quarters of beans and peas, 200 sides of bacon, 5000 hard-fish and 100 quarters of salt.

A good impression of farming at Freckenham, in Suffolk, comes from the inventories of Walter of Merton's goods, made between December 1277 and January 1278. As usual in Suffolk, stots exceeded oxen and cattle swine, barley was seven times as abundant as wheat, and peas almost as significant as wheat. At Blakenham, which is on boulder clay in High Suffolk, in 1288–9 legumes were not grown very much, and their comparative absence may partly account for the infertility of Blakenham, and the emphasis given to oats. Even so, wheat and rye were almost as plentiful, and barley not far behind.

The Bury St Edmunds manor of Hinderclay furnishes the opportunity to look at a demesne over the whole century 1250–1350. Barley formed in the first period (1250–78) slightly over, and in the second period (1278–91) rather under half the crops grown. In the warm, dry period (1278–91) wheat did particularly well. In the subsequent period (1291–1303), all crops except rye were less productive. In 1291–1350 the total crops improved, but wheat and rye were less productive in 1291–1303 than in 1330–50. This last period (1330–50) was almost as productive as 1278–91. In the period 1278–91 legumes nearly doubled their 1250–78 total, and they maintained and slightly improved upon the new high level to 1350, with some falling off in 1291–1303. Barley and rye both improved substantially, over the century, but wheat and oats declined a little. The decline of both crops was marked in 1291–1318. Legumes were the fifth crop in 1250–78, but the third crop, after barley and wheat, in 1330–50. The area tilled shrank by nearly one-seventh in 1302/3–1317/18 and continued to decline slowly down to 1350. Productivity grew by 40 per cent. Over the whole century the lord sold half his barley and more than half his wheat, a proportion which increased after 1318. After 1310 the lord also sold more than a third of his legumes. Thus the demand for wheat, barley and legumes affected the lord's choice of crops.

Oxen were generally more numerous than stots; the number of plough-beasts declined down to 1322, and then recovered. Hinderclay was conservative in the matter of draught animals. The number of beef and dairy cattle was still smaller in 1334–50 than in 1250–83, even though the herds had been increasing since 1307. Swine usually outnumbered beef and dairy cattle but their numbers fluctuated. There were few or no sheep until 1303–4, when the Abbey of Bury St Edmunds started sheep-farming on a large scale. Cheese and butter were both being made from 1256 onwards at least. In 1271–84 and 1286–95 the average number of cheeses which each cow produced rose from seven to eleven. The herds were doing very well until 1293, when productivity fell off. The lord let out the herd in 1296. Wool production was at its peak in 1307–8, dropped to a lower level in 1314–15, and picked up in the 1330s as the flocks recovered from murrain. The 1290s were not a great wool-growing period.

Worlingworth was in 1250 an oats, wheat and barley manor, but by 1350 peas and beans had supplanted barley as the third crop. Their rise probably explains why, in 1277–1350, the manorial crops increased by a quarter, but the area under the plough by only 7 per cent. As an oats manor Worlingworth was not so interested as other East Anglian manors in the sale of grain. As befitted a prospering manor with increasing crops and (after 1323) growing arable, the number of plough-beasts, mainly oxen, grew by nearly half in 1277–1350. Dairy-farming was not going properly until 1323–4. Swine existed only sporadically, and sheep did not appear until 1333–4.

At Redgrave in 1323–50 the crops were barley, oats, wheat,

with legumes the fourth crop and rye nearly its equal. The average amount of land under the plough seems to have increased by over 21 per cent in 1323–50. Only oats and wheat were significantly commercial crops. Redgrave had every sort of animal. Oxen were more numerous than stots. There was a very strong dairy herd, and the flock of sheep was very large indeed.

Suffolk therefore varied a good deal, and there were differences between the Breckland, Fenland, High Suffolk and the Sandlings. The county was in general highly arable. Barley was the chief grain, and sheep the most plentiful animal, but rye and oats could be significant on the Breckland, and even in the apparently fertile Gipping Valley and round Ipswich wheat was not outstandingly important.

Essex farming in the twelfth century is not well documented but sheep and pigs were prominent. On eleven manors in 1222 sheep were by far the most common animal, swine exceeded cattle, and horses were very few. There seems to have been little scope for animal husbandry, and the estates of St Paul's Cathedral were perhaps largely corn-producers by 1222, when Barling was sending corn to London by boat. The shortage of woodland and the great areas of arable in these manors cut the vast numbers of swine counted in 1086.

The taxations of 1295 and 1301 give accounts of grain and livestock held in Colchester and four neighbouring settlements. In 1295 affers and other horses were nearly twice as prominent as oxen, cattle were two-thirds and swine half as frequent as sheep. Oats was slightly more plentiful than barley, rye half as significant and wheat a quarter. There were very few legumes. Cattle were pretty numerous in the neighbourhood of Colchester, and at least sixteen tanneries flourished in the town. The lesser people greatly preferred affers and other horses to oxen. In 1301 rye and barley were about the same, oats was double either, wheat one-sixth of the barley, and legumes were few. Affers, stots and other horses were five times as common as oxen, sheep three times as many as cattle, and swine two-thirds as frequent as cattle. The lords and gentry had a slight preference for oxen over horses, but the lesser people had very few oxen.

Essex presents a varied figure in its different parts. It was not a great wheat-growing county, even for manorial lords, but favoured oats. There were enormous numbers of sheep, sometimes a good many swine, and more cattle than is sometimes assumed. Stots and affers sometimes tended to replace oxen in the plough, but there is little evidence of substantial crops of legumes, such as fertilized the fields of Suffolk. Essex was not such a progressive county as Norfolk and Suffolk, but it shared most of their characteristics.

Before leaving eastern England, a note about wine and cider. Vineyards were fairly common in Essex. Twelve are named in the Tythe Awards, and there were seven other vineyards by 1310. Cider is less well-known, though besides cider orchards in Essex there were by 1205 at least three in Norfolk.

In Lincolnshire new settlement was still taking place in Axholme in 1337, until the mid-thirteenth century in the woods and fens of Kesteven, and in the siltland villages of Holland until 1241 on the landward side, and until 1286 on the seaward side. Reclamation is not known to have taken place in the Norfolk Marshland after about 1250, and evidence of late new settlement in Suffolk is scanty. Some villages in the Essex woodlands were still actively assarting in 1272–90, and perhaps as late as 1310. Reclamation was still taking place in the Cambridgeshire Fenland in 1250–1307. The two centuries before the Norman Conquest were by far the greatest period of new settlement in all these counties except in Axholme and the Fenland. The twelfth century was the most active period of new settlement after the Norman Conquest and the process was largely complete by 1250. Population increase exactly followed this pattern, except that in eastern England numbers were still growing until 1300. What happened after 1300 is not very clear, but the agrarian crisis of 1315–22 seems not to have afflicted Norfolk, Suffolk and Essex very severely. There may have been very little change or even a decline of population in the Lincolnshire Fenland in 1260–1300, but the population probably grew again in 1300–48.

On the other hand, the Black Death of 1348 cut the population very heavily. Land under the plough cannot have grown very much in area in 1250–1300, yet the population continued to grow. This is not a period of famine, and the food supply seems to have been adequate.

The reader will quickly perceive the mixed and diverse nature of medieval English farming. Seldom is the evidence sufficient to illustrate the emergence of distinctive farming regions, but in eastern England there are quite, clear differences between highland and fenland Lincolnshire and Cambridgeshire, or between the Suffolk Breckland and High Suffolk. But the agrarian economy was not merely a matter of what crops and livestock would grow in what habitats. Both lords and peasants had their own requirements which admitted but used the characteristics of nature and led, or failed to lead, to a more prosperous economy and a more numerous people. Medieval agriculture could be progressive or unprogressive in crops, livestock and techniques. On the whole eastern England was progressive in all three, but there were some divergences.

In the period 1086–1348 progressive farmers grew barley and legumes, made cheese and butter from cow's milk, ploughed with horses, were interested in pig-keeping and (sometimes) made cider and wine from their own apples and grapes, and ale from barley malt; backward farmers grew wheat, oats and rye, or mixtures of these grains, kept sheep for their wool and made cheeses from ewe's milk, ploughed with oxen, kept goats, and made ale from malt other than barley malt. In 1086 all England was still agriculturally backwards; in 1348 some regions were progressive.

Lincolnshire was a mixture of these two categories. Except in the South Riding of Lindsey barley was not predominant, but legumes were a major concern in the Fenland which also grew flax and hemp, two significant industrial crops, and made cow's milk cheese and salt. Cambridgeshire laid great stress on barley and legumes and reared pigs. In Norfolk and Suffolk barley, beans and pigs often went together. On the other hand the Lincoln Edge, Lincoln Cliff, Lincolnshire Wolds and Fenland, the East Anglian Heights behind Lynn and Hunstanton, the Breckland and parts of Essex had great numbers of sheep. Seldom did their owners milk them to make cheeses. All parts of eastern England had good herds of cattle, but Norfolk and Suffolk used horses rather than oxen for ploughing. This development had almost certainly not yet taken place in 1086, but it was there by 1250 and grew over the next century. Seldom can we detect other tendencies. Goats virtually disappeared soon after 1086, since they figure in none of the many twelfth-century charters in which this region is so rich. Barley was increasingly popular in East Anglia, since it grew well and provided both bread and ale. A modern farmer can produce about four-fifths the number of calories per acre of wheat that he can get from barley. Some of the Norfolk and Suffolk manors studied also grew more crops to the acre in 1350 than in 1250. Everywhere beans and peas were becoming much more important and their nitrogen-fixating properties increased the fertility of the soil. On the whole farming in eastern England was improving, in 1250–1350, especially in Norfolk, Suffolk and Cambridgeshire. This improvement, which lords and peasants shared, surely made possible the continued population increase down to 1300 since, for the most part, there were no new settlements of the waste.[2]

3 TECHNIQUES – FIELD SYSTEMS

The open and common fields of England have called for a larger specialist literature than almost any other subject in agrarian history. Earlier writers saw them as fully-fledged right from the start, and valued them, according to their particular racist prejudices, as evidence of the German, Roman or Celtic strains in the English people. Today they seem evidence of particular stages in economic development, as the outcome of new-settlement and inheritance customs, and as a reminder that the village community of shareholders, which so often took action through its lord, was a reality. 'Township' is not a very common

word in early times, but Alfred the Great used it about 890, and
Edgar in 962, to denote a village community.

In his *English Field Systems*, H. L. Gray laid down lines on
the map which defined the province within which there was
an open-field system in the Middle Ages. He excluded from
the open-field region all Cumberland, Westmorland and
Northumberland, all Durham except the east, Pennine
Yorkshire, Lancashire and Cheshire, Pennine Staffordshire and
Derbyshire, all Wales, west Shropshire, the Forest of Dean, west
Somerset, Devon and Cornwall. On the east he drew his line to
exclude the Parts of Holland, Norfolk, Suffolk, Essex, most of
Hertfordshire, the south of Buckinghamshire and Oxfordshire,
east Berkshire, Middlesex, Surrey, Kent and Wealden Sussex.
Since 1915 historians have been modifying his statement and
extending here and there the area of open-field England. Some
of these open fields were less fully-developed than others but
nevertheless in regions which were otherwise regions of closes
rather than of open fields there were open fields, and the closes
were often a later, sometimes post-medieval, development.

Gray excluded much of eastern and south-eastern England
from the classical midland open-field system, and with good
reason, for they operated a more advanced form of open-field
system, as befitted the most extensively settled and most fertile
part of medieval England. He was himself much preoccupied
with the East Anglian *eriung*, *tenementum* or *plena terra* and with
the Kentish *iugum* or *dola*, and made very valuable observations
about the impact of partible inheritance upon the system, but he
was also very worried about Britons, Danes and Saxons and the
pseudo-problem of 'origins'. Yet he was wide awake to the
economic implications both of the East Anglian fold-course and
the Kentish continuous cultivation and remarked about the
former:

It was an arrangement far better for the soil than was that of
the midlands, since by it each parcel of arable was assured of
fertilization during the fallow season. Some of the thriftless
convenience of the midland system may have been sacrificed,

but superior agricultural method and profitable sheep-raising were compensations.

And:

> Arable fallow was naturally better fertilized when sheep were folded regularly upon it than when the township herd and flock wandered aimlessly over it every second or third year, as they did in the midlands.

These superior open-field systems were a response to the pressure of population, not a legacy of the Danes or of the Jutes.

There is a good deal to add to Gray's chapters on eastern England. He was very uncertain about the Fenland, and this I have now described fully elsewhere. Gray insisted that the open field must itself be the unit of rotation (which it frequently was not, even in the Midlands), and by his criteria rightly placed the Parts of Holland outside the open-field system, but many modern historians would not define their open fields so narrowly. The early East Anglian crop rotation was by seasons, not by fields. At Groton, in Suffolk, in about 1191, the Abbey of Bury St Edmunds let out certain land. The survey of the property includes the following statement:

> and the lands in demesne very well sowed with wheat, rye and barley, that is, each culture according to the time and its opportunity, and the lands which ought to be in fallow, very well fallowed and restirred.

In 1325 in six granges of Sibton Abbey the only fold was at North Grange. The arable lay partly in closes and partly in open fields. Enclosure came early in East Anglia, for the field-system lent itself readily to this innovation.

Gray complained bitterly about the lack of open-field evidence for Essex. A statement about Runwell, in 1222, is an early proof of open-field crop rotations: 'There is there no certain pasture unless when the demesne lands lie alternately uncultivated.' There was also fallowing in 1222 at Tillingham: 'Item upland pasture can be between the arable lands 100 (five score) sheep'.

Some points about the field-systems of Norfolk are still obscure, and much work is needed on the medieval period, but the general outline of an open-field system more advanced than that of the Midlands is now clear. Gray supposed a haphazard distribution of strips throughout the open fields. The strips of each tenant were concentrated in one part of the arable, not scattered evenly throughout the open fields, and, since there was no village crop rotation, strips with various crops and fallow intermingled. Hurdles kept the flocks from the corn until 'shack' time, and the sheep grazed in foldcourses, or defined areas of the open fields, heath and pastures, where a particular flock grazed.

The wattle hurdles seemed an unnecessary complication and there is an alternative. The strips of each tenant were concentrated, but 'shifts' or compact areas were set aside for each crop, as in northern and western Norfolk. In this way a three-course rotation overlay the haphazard distribution of strips and ensured a compact block of fallow for the flocks in summer. A similar notion applies to western Suffolk.

In Breckland a basically similar field-system, over some 250 square miles, possessed more conservative and more complicated features. The main arable unit was the furlong, *stadia* or *quarentina* (sometimes called a field) in its precinct. The *quarentina* consisted of *pecie*, which sometimes numbered over 2000 in some villages. There were 'meer baulks' between parcels of land, and, at Thetford, in 1338, a shift system of eight shifts. A three-course rotation was common, but extreme flexibility allowed less debilitating rotations.

Since 1935 historians have known that the infield-outfield system was widespread in western Norfolk, and the natural way to change from extensive to intensive cultivation. In Breckland the infield-outfield system was a three-fold, not a two-fold, system. Elsewhere there was an intensively cropped infield, and periodically tilled outfield 'intakes' from the waste. The

Breckland had an infield-outfield-breck system with duality of cropping within the open fields – Infieldland and Outfieldland – and brecks. Dual cropping allowed intensive and less intensive land-use in the same open field and existed at Fornham in the fifteenth century.

Gray considered that the parcels of one holding were originally concentrated in one area and identified this concentration as the original East Anglian unit of villein tenure – the *eriung, tenementum* or *plena terra*. Gavelkind had partly scattered it, but the Norman manorial system checked the scattering. At Elveden in 1217–18 four holdings were fairly evenly divided between six shifts, so that the tenants had a sufficient portion of each crop. The demesne holdings of the Bishop of Ely at Feltwell in 1277 were distributed between five *felds* (or shifts). Concentration was, in fact, a pre-enclosure phenomenon, and the *eriung* was therefore not materially different from the virgate.

The important features here, which distinguish common fields from mere open fields, are common on the fallow, common rights on the waste, a regulated crop rotation and village by-laws. Dr Thirsk rightly says that common fields developed in England and Wales at different times in different places, but she claims that in many parts the crucial period for their development was in the twelfth and thirteenth centuries. She says comparatively little about communal regulations, but is impressed by Professor W. O. Ault's failure to find by-laws earlier than those of Newington in Oxfordshire in 1270. More recently she has stressed this aspect of the problem in the east Midlands. She is inclined to consider the thirteenth century the period during which the open fields matured. Her earliest reference to a crop rotation is in 1156–7, and the earliest reference to common pasture of stubble and fallow is in 1240.

I have gathered over 200 early references, all from Lincolnshire, as sufficient evidence for the existence of a common village crop rotation. Forty-five highland Lincolnshire villages had two-course communal crop rotations before 1200. In addition, between 1143 and the late-twelfth century, four villages had a three-course crop rotation. Of the whole list four villages are a few years earlier than 1156–7.

Lincolnshire as a whole was a well-settled county whose open (and perhaps common) fields developed very early. The sheer bulk of the evidence shows that this was not an isolated affair, and since Lincolnshire (outside the Fenland) created no new settlements at all after 1086, and few in 870–1086, open and perhaps common arable fields probably had a long history. Recent writers on common fields have tended to assume that there were only immature open fields in highly pastoral regions; I shall now pursue the open (and common) fields into the pastoral Fenlands of Lincolnshire.

Villages like Rippingale, on the fen-edge were, in about 1200, conventional Lincolnshire open and common-field villages with a two-field system. The many *inliks* (open fields) of the siltlands of the Parts of Holland, and the flexibility of the whole system, have made historians claim that the Fenland had no common fields. No doubt some of these *inliks* were outfields, but whatever the flexibility, there were also communal crop rotations. Precisely how these worked is not at all clear, for there is no regular division to take account of a crop rotation anywhere visible. The existence of *ollands* (leylands of a special type) both in the siltland of Lincolnshire and in East Anglia suggests an open-field fallowing system whether common or not, but there was also both a two-course and a three-course communal crop rotation. Two-course rotations existed in four villages in 1260–98. Crop rotations which may have been either two- or three-course rotations existed in three fen-edge villages in 1294–1303. In the siltlands there was a three-course rotation in five villages in 1170–1298. Cambridgeshire was predominantly a three-field county from an early period.

The laws of England recognized the *inhoke* or *inheche*. A trial in 1274–5 called it cultivating the fallow for wheat, oats or barley. Of two Lincolnshire *inhokes* in 1238 and 1262 the second was at Billinghay in the fen-edge country where there was a normal Lincolnshire two-course system. The Prior of Catley and certain other tenants had sown an *inhoke* four times in the previous twenty years, and in 1260–2 brought their dispute over this custom to the king's court.

In eastern England, therefore, complex crop rotations in East Anglia and Essex ensured that by 1250 lords and peasants alike could keep 85–90 per cent of the land under crops. They sowed extensive areas of peas to ensure the continued fertility of the soil. Complicated crop rotations, which need further elucid- ation, also existed in the Isle of Ely. Highland Cambridgeshire had the less advanced, but still comparatively progressive, three- course crop rotation typical of the east Midlands. Lincolnshire modified its very ancient two-course crop rotation by ploughing parts of the fallow in *inhokes*, usually sown with peas. To this combination of advanced crop rotations and the cultivation of legumes we must add effective crop nutri- tion.[3]

4 TECHNIQUES – CROP NUTRITION

A good indication of the technical level and effectiveness of medieval agriculture is its knowledge and use of marling and manuring. Information about these is hard to come by, for the main tradition of English rural studies has hitherto been manorial rather than manurial. I intend therefore, to deal with manuring, marling and other methods of enriching the soil, and to relate what is known to the current problems in medieval English agrarian history.

Manuring is best known in eastern and south-eastern England and the east Midlands. In Norfolk by the middle of the thirteenth century dung was scarce and valuable. The tenants had to carry dung with a cart or waggon, or spread it with a fork, sometimes as much as twenty heaps, without food. The lord's courtyard was a main repository for dung, and after Michaelmas, before 1300, his tenants at Forncett came with forty-three carts to carry it to the fields. After 1300 the lord commuted this work so that henceforth the lord's carts carried the dung and the peasants merely scattered it. The carriage of dung cost eighteen shillings at Michaelmas, but at the seedtime for wheat, which would be in October, the ploughmen in five works spread dung on only ten acres. Marling is well-known in eastern England. In Essex there was marled land on three manors in 1222, and elsewhere in the county the Cathedral Priory of Canterbury marled twenty acres in 1225.[4]

5   THE LIFE OF THE PEOPLE – THE PEASANT'S RESOURCES

All eastern England, apart from some of Essex, was a land of smallholders, many of whom were craftsmen, traders or men who lived on the resources of woodland, fen and saltmarsh. They made salt, fished eels, cured herrings, made charcoal and pottery and wove cloth. Their sons and daughters squatted on the extensive commons and worked as day-labourers for great lords like the bishops and priors of Ely and Norwich. Usually too there were substantial virgaters and yeomanly peasants, sometimes in large numbers.

Lay Subsidies tell a good deal about the possessions of taxpayers, but nothing about those too poor to pay taxes. In 1283, in the double hundred of Blackbourne there were 1363 peasant taxpayers. Each family had, in marketable surpluses of grain, on average less than four bushels of wheat, less than one quarter of rye, more than three quarters of barley , less than six bushels of legumes, and more than two bushels of oats. Every family had four cows or other cattle, and eleven or twelve sheep. Every four families had one stot, more than three other horses, and rather fewer than three pigs. Every five families had an ox. The milk, butter and cheese consumption in Suffolk must have been high, and the surplus grain in store was sufficient to feed one man for a year.

The taxation of Ipswich for the Welsh war in 1282, tells us something about the possessions of 277 taxpayers. Each household had less than four bushels of barley, less than four bushels of wheat, more than four bushels of corn (unspecified), more than two bushels of rye, oats worth over sixpence (about

two bushels), more than four quarters of malt, and legumes
worth more than threepence (about a bushel). Each family had
2s. 4d. worth of wine, nearly six pounds of salt, geese worth 1s.
11d. and geese and ducks worth 1s. 9d., under a halfpennyworth
of herring, nearly three halfpennyworths of fish, and nearly a
halfpennyworth of fish and cheese, cheeses worth nearly three
farthings, butter worth nearly a farthing, ale worth over a
halfpenny, and hemp-seed worth over a farthing. Every two
families had more than one horse, more than one cow or other
cattle, and more than one swine. Every three families had nearly
one sheep, and every four families more than one ox. The
surplus grain was less than half the yearly bread supply of a man,
and although there was a good variety of other products, they
existed in very small quantities in each household. Neither was
there much stock. The inhabitants of Ipswich had few worldly
goods.

The taxations of Colchester and four neighbouring villages in
1296 and 1301 are also informative. Most of the taxpayers were
poor. In 1296 more than half of those who held surplus grain had
less than one quarter. Median holdings of barley, oats and rye
were also less than a quarter, but median holdings of wheat one
or two quarters. There were a few wealthy barley growers, and
many poor oats growers. In 1301 too grain surpluses were less
than a quarter in over half the holdings, and the median holding
of wheat, barley and oats considered separately was also under a
quarter, but the median holding of rye one or two quarters.
Again there were many poor oats growers, but since either the
tax assessors came at a different time of year, or the harvest was
poorer, no taxpayers had over ten quarters of grain for sale. In
1296 the ox-owners had more than two each; in 1301 more than
four each. The wealthier tax-payers owned oxen. In 1296 the
owners of affers and stots had fewer than two each; in 1302 every
two owners had about three affers and stots. Affers and stots
were the draught animals of the poor. In 1296 every owner of
cows and other cattle had rather more than two; in 1301 fewer
than two. There were more small owners of cows and other
cattle than of affers and stots. Other horses were not numerous.

In 1296 their owners had rather more than one each; in 1301 every two owners had more than three of them. In 1296 there were nearly three pigs per owner; in 1301 more than three pigs to every two owners. Most of the pig-owners were poor. In 1296 every owner had more than fourteen sheep; in 1301 every two owners seventeen sheep. Like the pig, the sheep was the animal of the poor. Considerable poverty is apparent in these Colchester assessments. The inhabitants were not so well off as the people of the double hundred of Blackbourne, but had more resources than the men of Ipswich.

Discussion of resources depends upon many other factors. J. R. Maddicott has claimed that the incidence of taxation under Edward I and Edward II was so heavy that the lesser peasantry succumbed to it, but he has had his answer. I have suggested above that in East Anglia, which was most vulnerable because of its huge population, the bad harvests and cattle murrain of 1313–20 were not, except locally, a very serious cause of starvation compared with the Black Death. The political troubles which stemmed from the expensive Scottish and French wars of Edward I, and the civil disturbances which came from the incompetence of Edward II, men forgot in the sunny youth of Edward III. In spite of the horrors of the Black Death England was a much happier country in 1360 than in 1320.

Yet the really basic problems remain. How many people lived in a household? How much did they eat? What was their budget? On the first point, research in England has not advanced since 1958, for lack of source material from before the Black Death. I then showed that on three large Lincolnshire manors of Spalding Priory, in 1267/8, where more than half the population had less than five acres of land, and the median holding was one to three acres, the average household contained 4.7 people. Subsequently I demonstrated that the more land people had the larger the household size. Households living on five to thirty acres could be as large as 5.3 people, and households living on over thirty acres could rise to 6.9 people. A half-virgater's household we can therefore reasonably suppose to have contained five people, whatever its stage of development. With households of this size the Lincolnshire Fenland achieved, by 1260, a population density of over 100 people to the square mile.

Study of the peasant's diet has given a very good idea of his material needs. He relied very heavily upon wholemeal bread, usually barley or maslin bread, less frequently, and on special occasions, wheaten bread, and more rarely rye bread. He ate it at breakfast, for his bait at noon – 'As one who in his journey bates at noon' says the poet Milton – and for supper, and he consumed on average about four pounds of it a day, sometimes as little as three pounds, sometimes five pounds, occasionally more. Like Brueghel's harvesters, eating under the shade of a tree in sixteenth-century Flanders, he ate the pottage to taste which Esau sold his inheritance. Brueghel's harvesters also had sippets in their pottage, but the basis was oats, flavoured with meat juices, or in Herefordshire, as late as 1868, with pieces of bacon in it and frequently peas, beans or vetches. Pottage was normal at breakfast, at the noon-meal, and at supper, and the pot, flavoured with salt, could last many days.

Pease porridge hot, pease porridge cold,
Pease porridge in the pot, nine days old.

The medieval peasant ate little meat, usually mutton – some old, toothless crone past lambing – or, on special occasions, a cullion. More rarely he ate beef, and, at Christmas, chicken, cooked in the lord's oven. Venison, hare, rabbit, pheasant, partridge, geese, swans, pigeons, doves and ducks were the food of the upper classes. In some parts of England he could get freshwater fish. In Elizabethan London, the apprentices went on strike because the masters were giving them fresh salmon for breakfast much too frequently. In coastal areas fresh sea fish, such as cod and ling, were freely available, but, above all, especially round the eastern and southern coasts, salt herring, usually three a day, were part of the staple diet. The Dutch did not start kippering herrings until the fourteenth century, and one of the main purposes of the salt-making industry of eastern England was to salt the produce of the Grimsby and Yarmouth fishing fleets. Board-hard stockfish, which you soak for several days in water before you can use it, still common in Italy, was known to medieval Englishmen.

But the essential accompaniment to bread was cheese. By the time of Edward I, the cheeses of Melton Mowbray were already known in Northamptonshire, and most villages in eastern England and the east Midlands made their own cheeses out of cow's milk. In Hampshire, Devon and many other parts of England farmers milked the ewes and made small cheeses, presumably like the ewe's milk feta of Greece. Nothing is known about goat's milk cheeses, since goats were not very common. The peasantry also ate butter when available in the summer. With cheese, again like Brueghel's peasants, the English peasant ate onions. Garlic (which grows wild in Gloucestershire churchyards), leeks and onions were highly prized, and an essential source of vitamin C. Few other vegetables were available. Aelfric's salter made salt to pickle cabbages round about the year 1000, and the humble 'wort' was well-known in cottage gardens. Root vegetables were little known in the thirteenth century, and in Henry VIII's day Anne of Cleves was astonished to find that London had never heard of lettuces.

Apples, pears, medlars, quinces, plums and cherries were known in lordly gardens and perhaps not unknown to peasants. The latter certainly gathered nuts and hedge-fruits in autumn. The main drinks were ale and water, but in East Anglia, Sussex, Somerset and Devon there was cider. The normal Englishman's daily ration was a gallon, but in harvest-time could be double that amount. Some peasants may have been so poor that, like Borrow's Spanish peasants, they drank only water. In eastern England, especially on the estates of Norwich Cathedral Priory, the lord gave the harvesters milk to drink, and on one Dorset manor, wine. Vineyards existed in many parts of England but there is no evidence that peasants usually drank wine. In the highland zone meat and fish played a much greater part in the peasant's diet, and in Wales, Cheshire and Northern England oat-cakes and girdle-cakes often replaced bread. Wheaten bread was virtually unknown in Cheshire, and the Backstanes on the Wear, near Finchale Priory, took its name from the flat baking stones which were the original griddle-stones. Pancakes must have played a part in popular diet, as they still do all over Europe, but there is no evidence that, as in Brittany and Russia, anyone ever made them out of buckwheat. With cheese or herrings to provide more protein, this gave the working peasant about 5000 calories a day.

The essentials of the diet were bread and ale. For a man's annual supply the ale required a quarter of grain a year, and four other persons in the household might well take two more quarters. Bread came in quartern (4 lb), half-peck (8 lb) and peck (16 lb) loaves and the latter might well be the daily bread consumption of a household. A bushel of barley will make three of these loaves, and at two bushels a week thirteen quarters of barley would be necessary every year for bread – sixteen with the drink corn. Sown at six bushels to the acre, with a yield of four-fold, barley will produce three quarters to the acre, and to produce sixteen quarters five and a third acres are necessary. Since four quarters have to go for seed just over seven acres is necessary to produce basic food and drink for a family. On a two-course rotation the peasant household needs fourteen acres, which is near the half-virgate size which seigneurial opinion considered appropriate for a peasant. On a three-course rotation just over ten acres would be adequate, and with the elaborate rotations of East Anglia, and plenty of legumes, marl and manure, eight acres. With rye or wheat the total yield would not be higher, because the farmer sowed them more thinly. With oats, the yield would be much less again, and any yield much under four-fold would cause difficulties. On the other hand in good years East Anglian barley could produce ten-fold. We are bound, therefore, to place the line at ten acres. Below this a family could not easily be self-sufficent in grain. What saved the peasant most of all was his stock, since it gave him milk, butter, cheese, some meat, including bacon, and wool. He also kept chickens, which greatly supplemented his diet with both meat and eggs. The common was the salvation of the cottar, who was extremely numerous in eastern England. The common was important everywhere, but in seigneurial England even more important was prudential behaviour. This affected especially inheritance rules and marriage.[5]

6   THE LIFE OF THE PEOPLE – INHERITANCE CUSTOMS

The medieval English peasant derived much of his living from his tenements, and, unless he chose to go to town and exercise a trade, a course which many adopted, he had to wait until his father died or retired, or until some vacant holding, hard to find in a time of growing population, came into his hand, before he could marry. The ancient word *cassatus*, which means a slave whom his lord has housed, reflected in the modern Spanish and Portuguese words for 'married', *cassada* and *casada*, aptly connects the two conditions. If a man could obtain a tenement early he could marry early; if not, in a society of few opportunities he had to wait. If a man had many sons, and only one could inherit, the others had to stay single or shift as best they might to get a wife. Where partible inheritance existed the young man's lot might be easier, provided that a reduced inheritance would make him a living, as it would where undivided and profitable wilderness was near. In many parts of England, after a first divison of the original land-shares into bovates or half-virgates, the lords were strong enough to prevent further sub-division. A family could not easily live on less than ten acres of land, and the lord was anxious to maintain his tenantry in such a state that they could pay his dues. In seigneurial England holdings were sufficient, one son inherited, marriage was late, the child-bearing period reduced, and population increase under control; in communal England the exact opposite was true.

In highland Lincolnshire, where most holdings were of bovate or half-bovate size, there is only a very little evidence that holdings were divisible, and where partible inheritance was the practice it affected matters very slightly. In Fenland Lincolnshire, where holdings were tiny, partible inheritance was the usual custom. It existed round the fen-edges in 1282–98, but was above all the custom of the freemen, bond sokemen and molmen of the siltland of the Parts of Holland. The *operarii* (or workmen), who held the larger holdings for which they did week-works, did not hand down their holdings to all their sons. Bovates which sokemen held in Moulton and Weston consisted of minute fragments of many interlocked tenancies. In five very large fenland manors, and two entire villages which contained two of the five manors, 28 per cent were partible, and the percentage varied from under 20 at Weston in 1259/60 to under 55 at Moulton in 1259/60.

Four Norfolk manors of the Abbey of Ramsey, in ten villages, show no signs of partible inheritance in 1160–1250. Surveys of eight Norfolk manors of the Bishop of Ely, all in the Norfolk Marshland, exist for 1221/2 and 1251. The size of the holdings shrank on five of these manors, and in all manors the percentage of holdings held partibly increased. On three manors the fraction of holdings held partibly in 1221/2 was over half, and this was so on five manors in 1251. The percentage varied from under 17 in 1221 to 87 in 1251. So considerable was the increase in partibility that only a great and simultaneous increase in the amount of cultivable land could keep the size of the holdings unaltered. At both periods the holdings were so small that fen profits and wage labour alone could make life possible.

The bishop held six manors in upland Norfolk which he surveyed at both dates. The percentage of holdings held partibly grew on five of these manors, and on three of these the size of the holding also fell. More than half the holdings were partible on one manor in 1221 and on two manors in 1251. The percentage of partible holdings varied from 0 in 1221 to over 71 in 1251. Feltwell and Northwold both had extensive fens, but no apparent urge to proliferate. Dereham and Shipdham were both market towns, and many of the tenants were shopkeepers and tradesmen. Pulham was a settlement without these means of employment.

The fluid condition of the land-market, and the poverty of the tenants of the Prior of Norwich's manor of Hindolveston are reflected in the record of surrenders and admissions in 1309–26. In sixteen complete years there were 748, or 48 a year. More than the average number of surrenders and admissions took place in 1310 and 1312, the famine years 1315–18 and in 1323. Death of the tenant and admission of the next heir accounted for only 74 of these entries. By far the largest number – 443 – resulted from private convenience, including marriage arrangements. The next largest number – 136 – came from transferences the tenant made during his lifetime, so that barely more than a third of the tenants died holding their tenements. Retirement of old men to the chimney corner accounted for 73 transferences of property to sons or brothers, 46 to daughters or sisters, and 17 to others not members of the family. Stress of bad seasons brought about a further 100 surrenders. In March 1316 to April 1317 there were 176 surrenders in thirteen months at five courts, and the roll contains the perpetual refrain: 'Surrender made for great hunger'. Unhappily no details of the 1316 harvest at Hindolveston have survived, but the 1317 demesne harvest was 93 per cent of the average for 1295–1317. The condition of the hordes of tiny land-holders was precarious, and, in spite of evidence quoted to suggest that the famine was, in East Anglia, no universal killer, bad seasons could affect manors like Hindolveston very adversely.

Martham, in Norfolk, was a splendid example of the wildly proliferating East Anglian manor. Early in the thirteenth century 107 tenants had shared about twenty-two and a quarter twelve-acre *eriungs*, which by 1292 were greatly sub-divided. For example, early in the thirteenth century Roger of Hill had held ten acres of *mulelond*; by 1292, eleven tenants, three of them his descendants, held it, and four of the others, the Sco family, were relatives. Subdivision had gone a very long way indeed, and seems to have been the custom for all types of tenure.

Surveys of five other manors of Norwich Cathedral Priory exist. Percentages of holdings held partibly varied from 0 to 37.5 Of these manors Catton affords a remarkable opportunity to study the origin of the land the tenants held. Most tenants had inherited their land, presumably from some male relative, and

29.8 per cent of the holdings were partible. One tenant had inherited one and a half acres from his mother. Six tenants were under age and had probably inherited land from their father, since they were under their mother's guardianship. Pairs of brothers held two of these holdings, pairs of sisters two more, and the tenants of the remaining two holdings were probably cousins. In addition, two other young brothers had inherited one and a half acres from another relative, since their father had custody of the land. Altogether the tenants held 77 pieces of inherited land, but over 50 acres, in 42 pieces in sizes varying from a half rood to 5.25 acres, was bought land. Nearly half the tenants had some bought land, but purchases were small, affecting only 11.5 per cent of the land. There were eleven marriage portions, varying in size from a rood to eleven acres, or 6.5 per cent of the whole. Less than a tenth of the wives brought any land to their husbands. Partible inheritance made the marriage portion less important. A further six acres, in two pieces, was land which the wife had inherited. Lastly, and surprisingly, eight pieces of land, measuring 7.75 acres, came as gifts. And so, even in East Anglia, inheritance (often with a sibling) was the means by which a man most often came to possess land.

Seven manors of Binham Priory were all in North Norfolk. In 1282–3 percentages of holdings held partibly varied from 0 to 36.7. Partible inheritance already existed at Binham itself in 1102–7, but may not have been a decisive factor. Partible socage was really important only on three manors.

Norfolk was unquestionably a land of smallholders in the thirteenth century and this tendency was most marked in the Norfolk Marshland and Broadland, particularly by about 1280, because of the variety of occupations available and the existence of extensive common fens, marshes and heaths. Many were molmen or sokemen – descendants of former slaves, who, at an earlier period, when there was extensive new settlement, had made favourable contracts with their lords, and these generally held in partible socage. This inheritance custom, though widespread, was not everywhere in use, and where in use was not always significant. In the thirteenth century it tended to become more popular, particularly in the Norfolk Marshland and in small market towns. After the end of new settlement, extreme *morcellement* could arise.

Partible inheritance existed on the estates of the Abbey of Bury St Edmunds by 1186–8, when holdings were already small. The smallest holdings were apparently not divided to absurdity but kept united. Brothers, uncles, nephews, parceners or fellows shared them, and often split the duty of attending the hundred court which went with the land. The abbot was not in favour of partible socage. By 1186–8 sub-division among the sokemen had gone a long way, but had not reached the minuteness common in the Fenland. On twelve manors three-quarters of the sokemen and freemen held partibly, and partible inheritance was at work in 1186. It often led to a decrease in the size of holdings, and an increase in the number of tenants.

In Suffolk partible inheritance existed on seven manors of the Bishop of Ely in 1221, and eight in 1251, and on four manors of Eye Priory in 1301–2. On the bishop's manors it increased in 1221–51, but at Barking the new enfeoffment of Needham Market, with its large creation of shops and messuages, greatly reduced the size of the median holding. In the soke of Bedfield, by 1301–2, holdings had become so small that holdings of molland descended to the eldest son, and of villein land to the youngest.

Holdings in Essex were often partible. The custom existed on three of the Bishop of Ely's manors in 1221–51, on nine manors of the Abbey of Waltham Holy Cross about 1230, and on one of Canterbury Cathedral Priory's manors in 1310. The Waltham Abbey manors were in Epping Forest and the wooded parts of West Essex where late assarting made partible inheritance acceptable. At Lawling holdings changed hands very frequently, but at some stage within a generation of 1310, perhaps within ten or a dozen years, certain holdings ceased to be the property of many holders and reverted to single or dual tenure. The agrarian crisis of 1315–22 may have been responsible for this change.

The Cambridgeshire manors of the Bishop of Ely divide into three groups. In 1221–51 holdings increased in number by half on five siltland manors round Wisbech, but the median holding remained the same size, because the amount of land available also increased as fen reclamation continued. At Wisbech by 1221 there were many messuages, and considerable trading and craft interests. In 1221–51 nine of the bishop's manors on the blackland round Ely practised partible inheritance, and on five of these manors it became commoner. The period saw an expansion of these manors with few parallels in England as the bishop made many new enfeoffments and granted his tenants entire fens. Of five manors in upland Cambridgeshire partible inheritance was a significant factor only on one in 1221–51. Holdings were larger than in the Isle of Ely, since these manors had comparatively small resources of woodland, heath, or fen.[6]

In eastern England after 1250 most new settlement had ceased, but population continued to increase until about 1300, and in the Lincolnshire Fenland until 1348. Progressive, mixed farming, with high barley and legume yields and good supplies of dairy products, pork and salt herrings supported twice as many people to the acre as in southern England. Access to newly reclaimed land, the continued existence of great fens and marshes which supplied a multitude of different sorts of fish and fowl, and, in Norfolk and Suffolk, the presence of extensive heaths, made life possible for hordes of poor cottagers. Numerous crafts and industries, sea-fisheries, and many small but thriving market towns gave employment to a teeming rural proletariat – proletariat in the true sense that all they possessed and produced for the state was children. For eastern England, especially in those regions which had many trades and extensive commons, was also a land of partible inheritance, where the young had early access to holdings and common rights and could marry young. Nevertheless the fertility of the rural proletariat did not run amok. Nobody provided them with free food and circuses. By controlling the inheritance customs, so that, when resources were less freely available, inheritance of the eldest or youngest son supplanted the inheritance of all, lords and communities controlled the marriage age, and so controlled the birth-rate. The end of new settlement spelled the end of partible inheritance, and the end of both brought the end of the medieval population boom, but whilst that population boom lasted it forced the devising of new agricultural techniques to feed the growing number of mouths.

CHAPTER 5

SOUTH-EASTERN ENGLAND

1 NEW SETTLEMENT AND POPULATION GROWTH

After 1350 no new-settlement place-names occurred in the records for the first time in Kent, Sussex and Surrey, but Middlesex recorded three. In 1281–1350 Middlesex recorded one, Kent and Sussex two each, and Surrey three. There was more late new settlement in south-eastern than in eastern England because of greater opportunities in the woodlands of Middlesex and Surrey. For Middlesex, the evidence, though slight, suggests that assarting continued late. The north of the county is hilly, up to 400 feet above sea-level, and much of it is cold London clay; in the Thames Valley are rich loams and, in 1086, well-settled ploughland. Assarting started in the Thames Valley before 1189 but, on the whole, the confines of London were wild and undeveloped until a remarkably late period in medieval history.

Surrey was mostly well-settled, and there was much wasteland near a large population. The northern two-fifths is in the London basin, and from here the land rises to the consecutive strips of the North Downs, the lower greensand belt, and the Weald. The Surrey place-name survey of 1934 lists no fewer than ninety-five clearances (*leahs*) of which seventy-six appeared in the records for the first time after 1086. Of these, thirty-nine did not appear in the records until after 1280, and fifteen until after 1350. Surrey was therefore a county of many late clearings. There was a little new settlement in the Thames Valley, and in Surrey woodland was settled fairly extensively, but even by 1300 there were still wide woodlands in the lower greensand belt, and enclosures were small, the work of poor peasants. The greatest exception was Waverley Abbey's assarts in the west of the county.

The extent and lateness of the Abbey of Chertsey's assarts and improvements provide the intimate detail which backs the evidence of the names of clearings; the full story of the Abbey's purchases and improvements is most interesting and enlightening. They started in 1307, continued and accelerated right through the hard years of the century's second decade for over thirty years, until 1339. The abbey's activities must have been very unpopular, for in 1381 the peasants burnt the deeds and court-rolls which recorded the abbot's many purchases, so that their full tale eludes us, but we have a generalized account. The abbey's immense labours confirm that the economy of Surrey was mixed, with a large pastoral element, and that it was expanding in the 1330s.

Kent is a county of great geographical and geological variety, with its heavily wooded uplands on one side, and its marshes on the other. On the North Downs, Boxley Priory had assarts by 1198, and so had St Gregory's Priory, Canterbury in 1213–14 and 1238. There was also some assarting on the lower greensand, in a society of peasant settlers many of whom had pre-Norman names. On the lower greensand, at the westermost point of Kent, there was very late assarting from woodland, in 1300–50, which created large and increasing fields on the estates of Westminster Abbey.

The Weald of Kent was thinly settled at all times in the Middle Ages, but it contained denes, or swine-pastures, attached to particular villages. The earliest were recorded in 785 and 791, but more came later; altogether there were 473 of them. A good many were mere swine-pastures without inhabitants, but others had become small colonies of the parent village. There were also denes which had Domesday names of their own and some of these were fully-grown villages.

The greatest reclamations took place in the Kentish marshes, which divide into the northern, eastern and southern marshes. There was early settlement in the North Kent Marshes in 664–961. After the Norman Conquest reclamation continued with fresh vigour. There was reclamation in Plumstead Marshes in 1230–40. Christchurch Priory enclosed much land in Cliffe

Marshes in 1290–1300. The nunnery of Lilliechurch made embankments against the sea which enabled the convent to move to lower ground in 1288–93. Christchurch Priory was enclosing, wall-building, trenching, ditching and draining islands in the mouth of the Medway in 1279–1422. Round the mouths of the Thames and Medway there were many *wicks* or marsh sheep-farms, which consisted of huts on a central island. Canterbury Cathedral Priory was still encouraging the peasantry to embank the marshes themselves in 1325.

Reclamation took place in three east Kent marsh-villages. In the Isle of Thanet, the Priory of St Gregory reclaimed and cultivated fifty acres in 1219. Canterbury Cathedral Priory carried out skilful and extensive embanking, widened and deepened ditches, and built wooden gutters on its manors there in 1291–2 and 1317–18. Corn, sheep, cheeses and other dairy produce came from this land, most of which was on lease to tenants.

Romney Marsh, the largest of all the Kentish marshes, contains 24,000 acres. Adjoining it is Walland Marsh, of 23,000 acres. The men of Kent drained this marsh in 1162–1500, much of it by 1339, but the western third not until 1477. Dengemarsh they partly drained in 744–74, but made two large innings there in 1178–1200. Canterbury Cathedral Priory had an important manor at Ebony, on an island in the old Rother Valley. The place was truly a grange, for it had no peasants, and hired servants or *famuli* ran it. They produced corn, stock and dairy goods for the markets. About 1300 the priory inned several pieces of land. There was much expenditure upon maintenance in subsequent years, down to 1331, for which the priory received no adequate return. The great wall of Appledore was the main defence of Romney Marsh which had been settled land for at least twelve centuries. The change in the course of the river Rother in 1287 and the fierce storms which destroyed the wall in 1288 had disastrous effects. Appledore had a large body of rent-paying peasants, and in 1293–4 they retaliated upon the sea by making a new inning whose protection led them to unprecedented technical achievements in the making of embankments and groynes in the next generation or so.

Kent was therefore a county of many contrasts. In the northern, eastern and southern marshlands there was extensive new settlement between the seventh and fourteenth centuries, and especially in the twelfth and thirteenth. Much of this was monastic, and some of it purely domanial, but there were several villages of free peasants who took part in the process. In the Weald, the density of population was thin, but by 1348 there were several hundred denes or swine-pastures, often attached to large parent villages some miles away, and by 1086 some of these had already become small villages. Many remained simply clearings in the woods. Elsewhere in Kent there was some new settlement, some of it as late as 1225–50. Most of this was on the lower greensand or in the North Downs.

The great waste of the Weald covered more than half Sussex, but there was a heavy population on the coastal plain and parts of the South Downs. New settlement was extensive, but greater in the Weald and the marshes adjoining the South Kent marshes and Pevensey Level.

Already in 1070–87 Battle Abbey had received freedom of all assarts throughout all their land and indeed they needed such a licence, for the *leuga* or *banlieu*, the circular estate three miles in diameter which the Conqueror had generously given them, was a desolate waste in the Weald of Sussex. By 1086 new settlement had already begun in much the same way as in the Weald of Kent. In the Hastings rape there were many outlying assart members of parent villages, nameless holdings, usually small clearings in the woodland, which untaxed freemen inhabited, each on a virgate of land. Some of these holdings were attached to no village. Abbot Ralph (1107–24) made himself a farmer, ploughed inhabited lands, brought in settlers for uninhabited lands, and multiplied their value twenty-fold. Settlement was so fast that within forty years Battle had 115 households, and the individual virgates could bear full taxation.

Most of the innings in the western marshes of Sussex date from 1478–1661. Pevensey Level already had elaborate drainage works by 1220. Reclamation still continued in 1250–75. By

1250 the men of Sussex had reclaimed the greater part of Mountney Level, but some of it needed constant attention. Inning continued until 1356. There was also considerable activity on the marshes inland from Pevensey down to at least 1290.

West Sussex was rather less densely settled in 1086 than east Sussex (apart from the Sussex Weald). There was a fair amount of twelfth- and thirteenth-century assarting round Chichester, especially on the Boxgrove Priory manors, and this continued until about 1350 in two places in the Vale of Rother. In nine different manors, which together embraced Weald, Down and Marsh, some idea of the extent of late assarts is possible. The Sussex place-name survey of 1929 and 1930 notes 123 *leahs*, 101 of which were first recorded after 1086. Sixty-two of these were first recorded after 1280, sixteen of them after 1350. The emphasis is overwhelmingly on the period 1190–1350.

This picture of a county still expanding its arable in the Weald and elsewhere in Sussex must receive some modification from comparisons between the years 1291 and 1341. Everywhere the upland arable seems to have been untilled, because of the poverty of the parishioners, and tax valuations were down. Even so, Wealden agriculture was mostly stable, but there was a decline along the coast and on the South Downs.

New settlement in south-eastern England was more extensive than in eastern England (except the Fenland), but its frequency varied greatly according to the nature of the terrain and the societies which inhabited it.

South-eastern England contained some of the earliest (seventh-century) new settlement in England, as well as some of the latest. New settlement was still taking place in Middlesex in the fourteenth century and Surrey was extraordinarily active down to the very eve of the Black Death. Similar activity was taking place on the lower greensand in Kent and in the Weald of Kent and Sussex down to about 1350. Battle Abbey assarted its *banlieu* in the forty years after Domesday, and in the Vale of Rother assarting still continued in 1350. In the marshes of east Kent reclamation still advanced in 1317–18. By 1339 much of

Walland Marsh was under the plough. At Ebony the last inning was in 1305, and at Appledore in 1293–4. Wildmarsh in Pevensey Haven was still being reclaimed in 1356. Much clearing from Sussex woodland was after 1280. New opportunities still opened up to the peasantry right down until 1350. At the same time, the numerous denes in the Weald of Kent and Sussex were not always inhabited clearings in the full sense, and the most extensive reclamations took place in the Kentish marshes, including Romney Marsh, and in Pevensey Level in Sussex. In these areas heavy population bordered unsettled wasteland, whether Weald or marshland, so that much of south-eastern England exhibited a paradoxical contrast between old, settled land and typical new-settlement societies on empty wasteland. South-eastern England, and particularly Kent, was a halfway house between eastern England and the east Midlands.

There is no real information about population movements in south-eastern England in 1086–1200. In the two centuries after 1086 settlements in the woods of Surrey grew by 350 per cent, and the population of the estates of the Archbishop of Canterbury on the Sussex Weald multiplied by 433 per cent. Population continued to grow well into the fourteenth century, and on eight manors in Surrey and nine in Sussex was double or treble the Domesday population. So far no real direct evidence of population decline in 1280–1350 has come to light. Counts of heads of household exist for 92 south-eastern England manors in 1086–1350; they split into three equal cohorts which cover 1086–1250, 1086–1292 and 1086–1315. The percentage increases over these three periods are 260, 260 and 382. Population grew modestly in 1086–1250, was stagnant in 1250–92, but expanded very rapidly in 1292–1315 to very nearly four-fold the Domesday population. These movements accord well with the history of settlement.[1]

2 CROPS AND LIVESTOCK

Two Middlesex manors provide information about demesne farming. Isleworth showed marked pastoral characteristics. In 1296, the crops were oats, barley, wheat, rye and peas. There was a very large dairy herd and a productive vineyard. In 1288 Ruislip produced wheat and oats on a massive scale, small quantities of barley and dredge, and one of the largest crops of beans and peas recorded.

The See of Canterbury had estates in Middlesex and Surrey, and in 1292–5 the archbishop sold enormous crops of oats, maslin (wheat and rye), barley and legumes. Comparison with the archbishop's sales in Kent and Sussex shows that increased quantities of legumes sold went with increased quantities also of wheat; on the other hand, the fewer the legumes the larger the quantity of oats. The archbishop's estates in Middlesex and Surrey specialized in oats and sheep. Swine were more important than cattle and oxen than affers.

Five manors and a rectory of Chertsey Abbey in 1234 grew wheat and oats equally, and barley, dredge, rye and peas. About 1350 wheat, barley and oats were of equal significance on seven manors. Swine were more prominent than cattle, but much less numerous than sheep. The monks also ate geese, capons, hens and cheese.

The Bishop of Winchester's manor of Farnham, in 1210–11, grew oats and wheat equally; rye and barley much less. There were many more oxen than affers, and three times as many swine as cattle. The flocks of sheep were large, and the manor made a fair number of cheeses, kept many hens and produced numerous eggs. This manor, with its stress upon oats, wheat, sheep and swine, was typical of Surrey.

None of this information is very conclusive, but it does show a good mixed economy in Middlesex and Surrey, with plenty of emphasis upon wheat, barley and oats, many sheep, and a fair number of swine. Much of the information is seigneurial, and the economy of the peasantry therefore is not well-known.

Westminster Abbey's manor of Westerham in Kent was unusual. Assarting from woodland had caused the division of large and increasing fields. In 1300 about 500 acres were under the plough, and this had increased to 700 acres by 1350. In 1300–50 there was a shifting and declining area of convertible husbandry. There were no 'seasons', the land was apparently in closes, there was a nucleus of permanent arable, and a shifting area sporadically cultivated. In 1297–1350 the largest crop sown was oats, followed closely by wheat, and there were smaller crops of spring corn, legumes, rye and winter corn. The outfields grew less wheat and legumes but more rye, other winter crops and other spring crops. In 1345–50, compared with 1297–1302, the area of wheat and rye had increased; oats, other winter crops and other spring crops had decreased and legumes had increased greatly because the lord had introduced a partial legume rotation. The wheat crop was the largest at harvest, but oats was important on marginal land. The lord may well have known the fertilizing power of legumes.

In 1292–5 on the archbishop's Kentish manors barley, oats and wheat were all equally major crops. Maslin was nearly as favoured as barley, legumes were well-regarded, but dredge and rye were minor crops. Legumes were one-sixth of the crop, and their presence probably does much to explain the superiority of the archbishop's grain production. The fertility of the soil in these areas of Kent may also be another factor. Some of the archbishop's manors were in seven hundreds in the Weald of Kent. Here wheat and barley were still most of the crop sown, but legumes and oats were insignificant. The fertility of these manors was probably less than that of the rest of Kent. The archbishop's manors threshed large quantities of oats, wheat, barley, legumes and rye. Oxen vastly exceeded affers in their ploughteams. There were nearly twice as many swine as milch kine, and ten times as many sheep as all types of cattle. The archbishop sold practically no horses, but over 900 cattle and over 13,000 sheep. He sold considerable quantities of cheese and butter, milk, and ewe's milk. He also produced some wine and cider.

In 1291 Canterbury Cathedral Priory had thirty-one manors in Kent. On eleven chalkland and three Thanet beds and brickearth manors wheat and barley were the major crops, and legumes occupied almost as much land as either. On four clayland and seven lower greensand manors wheat, oats and legumes were the main crops. The best wheat and oats yields went with the most legumes. The lower greensand is poor soil, but by the standards of the day was well farmed. On six marshland manors oats was the principal crop, and legumes were less grown than in other parts of Kent.

Eleven manors of Walter of Merton in North Kent in 1277–8 grew oats, wheat and barley in roughly equal quantities, but fewer legumes. The manors made wine and cider. The most predominant animal was the sheep. Kent therefore varied a good deal between the long-settled lands of the North Kent lowland, the North Downs, Holmesdale and the lower greensand belt, which formed the major part of the county and gave it its essential character, the woodland region of the Weald Clay plain and the High Weald, and the new-settlement region of Romney Marsh and other lesser coastal marshes. Everywhere except in the marshland legumes were a major crop. Everywhere except in the clayland, the lower greensand and the marshland oats was not a major crop. Everywhere wheat was important, and a leading crop in all regions except the marshland. Except in the clayland, the lower greensand and the marshland, barley shared the position of wheat. Wheat and barley may also have been the major crops round Dartford. In North Kent, on the archbishop's manors, wheat, barley and rye were the major grain crops, and legumes were almost as common. Everywhere in Kent therefore, except on Romney Marsh, great quantities of peas and beans grew by 1300, and these were affecting crop yields. Unfortunately we do not know whether the Kentish peasants were also growing them.

Sussex divides into a long-settled region – the coastal plain, the Vale of Rother, and the South Downs – and a woodland region – the Weald. In 1327 the the most prosperous settlements were on the chalk. By 1341 even on the South Downs corn-growing was more prominent than sheep-rearing. The corn grown was wheat in the chalk zone and oats in the Weald. Sheep were most favoured in certain centrally-placed villages, but in such villages there was less corn rather than more wool. In the chalk zone tax-payers were few, but wealthy, and in the lower greensand there were more poor tax-payers. The lower greensand was poor in corn, the Weald poor in everything, and the lowland rich in both corn and wool.

Sussex had a flourishing wool-trade with the continent by the late-thirteenth century, much of which passed through Shoreham. The trade depended largely upon English boats by contrast with the Kentish trade, especially from Sandwich, where Flemish boats carried most of the wool. There were sheep all over Sussex in the early-fourteenth century, and in 1341 there were twenty parishes, mostly east of the Adur, which had flocks of 1000–2000 sheep. Three major sheep-rearing villages stood on the corn-growing coastal plain west of Shoreham. There were few sheep in the Weald, except in the west. The east and west Downs specialized respectively in horned sheep and polled sheep whose ancestry may have been very far back in time. The coastal sheep were mainly ewes reared for their milk, but the sheep round Lewes were mainly wethers, reared for their wool.

In 1332 in the hundreds of Rotherbridge, Holmstrow and Henhurst, there were more oxen than stots and affers, but, as usual, the peasantry favoured stots and affers and the lords oxen. This preference was not nearly so marked as in Suffolk and Essex. Sheep were much more numerous than milch kine, and there were fourteen large flocks of 50–200 sheep. Over 5000 gallons of cider were produced per year. In general, oats was the principal grain, followed by barley and rye. Oxen were preferred to stots and affers as plough animals, and there were very few other horses. Sheep were very numerous, cattle moderately common, and swine not particularly popular.

In 1332 the Vale of Rother practised mixed farming, grew oats and wheat, was an important dairy region, had a fair number of pigs, and large flocks of sheep. Affers and oxen were equally favoured as plough beasts. The coastal plain was very rich, grew wheat and barley, had very large flocks of sheep, and used oxen almost exclusively for ploughing. The Weald had a few sheep, and many cattle, grew mainly oats, and used chiefly stots for ploughing.

On the coastal plain, in 1283–94, the demesne farm of Pevensey Castle grew oats as the principal crop, and the area under beans was considerable. By 1289 four out of every five acres of arable were under crop. Yields were not very high and the Castle leased out this estate in 1294. There were 400–600 sheep, and 25–30 dairy cattle. In 1341 thirteen marshland parishes of Pevensey Level grew large crops of grain, and sheep were not very significant.

In 1341 Lewes Archdeaconry split into seven farming regions: the High Weald, the clay Weald, the Downs scarpfoot, the Downs summits, the Downs river valleys, the coastal plain, and the alluvium. The High Weald and the clay Weald were very poor corn-growing country, and the Downs summits were average for the whole archdeaconry. A good deal of corn grew at the Downs scarpfoot and in the Downs river valleys, but the coastal plain and the alluvium were about three times as fertile in corn as the poorest Wealden part of Sussex. The coastal plain was rich and the Weald and the upper greensand much poorer, with the poorest parishes on the heavy clays. In 1292–5 the Archbishop of Canterbury sold large quantities of grain, mainly wheat, followed by barley and legumes. Legumes were rather more than one-ninth of the crop sold and grew on one acre in twenty – less than in Kent and Suffolk, but still considerable. Oxen were much more popular than affers, swine than milch kine, and sheep were the most numerous of all. These estates on the coastal plain of Sussex were very rich and produced quantities of cheese, butter, and milk. In general there was good, mixed farming, of the sort so common on the Sussex coastal plain.

In 1220 the Bishop of Chichester laid down the number of stock for ten manors. These manors were to be overwhelmingly sheep-farms, with comparatively few cattle, except for draught purposes. There was one herd of goats. The real stock of twelve of the bishop's manors is known about 1330. Oxen were much more numerous than affers, but affers were very much commoner than in 1220. Swine appeared for the first time and were more popular than milch kine. Sheep had almost doubled in number from a century before, and there were no goats. There were many geese, great flocks of poultry and nearly 10,000 eggs. At Bishopstone, in 1306, about one-third of the bishop's demesne was gratten or fallow; wheat and barley were the major crops, and oats and beans minor crops. It was held at one time that the Sussex peasant never drank ale, but only cider, and that beer, which unlike ale contains hops, came into Sussex from Flanders early in the fourteenth century and replaced cider. The Sussex peasant certainly drank ale, but he also drank cider, as did his lord. At four Sussex manors, after 1244, the Bishop of Chichester's tenants had to crush cider apples for the lord. Cider came from two other Sussex orchards in 1321.

In the early-fourteenth century in south-eastern England the clay Weald and the High Weald were difficult for farming, but they were not completely poverty-stricken. They were regions of mixed farming and animal husbandry which grew oats as the chief grain crop, with some wheat on the clay Weald, and reared swine and cattle. The highest taxation assessments in south-eastern England were in the north-eastern lowland, Thanet, and on the northern edge of the Downs. Assessments round Rochester and in the Medway Valley were slightly lower, but north-eastern Kent in general was the richest region south-east of a line drawn fron Great Yarmouth to Southampton. North central and north-eastern Kent were the most populous part of south-eastern England, and barley and wheat the principal crops. Kent was richer than Surrey and Sussex. In Sussex the Weald formed a larger proportion of the county, and the Sussex Weald, especially the clay Weald and the sands east of Horsham, was particularly poor. Assessments were slightly higher on the coastal fringe between Pevensey and Rye, and the chalk east of Worthing was richer still. The wealth of Sussex, like that of Thanet, was along the coastal plain south of Chichester. This was a corn-growing region, especially for wheat.[2]

3 TECHNIQUES – THE OPEN FIELDS

Kent had multiple open fields, but no common fields in the medieval period. In the Vale of Holmesdale, and at Gillingham, by the late-thirteenth century, there were nucleated villages, and also hamlets and isolated farms, as in the Lincolnshire Fenland. The open fields – more accurately, enclosed fields subdivided into unenclosed parcels – were small and numerous, and based on dispersed farms and hamlets as well as on nucleated villages. At Gillingham there were enclosed fields and unenclosed parcels within subdivided fields. This was a multi-field, open-field village with some concentration of each individual holding in one locality. Tenants often held enclosed parcels as well as parcels in the open fields. The open fields may have resulted from co-operative ploughing, and certainly resulted from partible inheritance, but free alienation constantly modified the pattern of holding. Neither in Holmesdale nor at Gillingham, in the valleys of the Darent, Medway and Stour, nor on the lower dip-slopes of the Downs were there any common fields, that is, open fields subject to common grazing by the livestock of an entire village with village regulations for crop rotations and common grazing. There were no fold-courses, as in East Anglia, and individuals folded their stock on their own lands. Some tenants grazed their livestock collectively in the open fields by mutual agreement, but there were no village arrangements for pasturing the fallow.

In Surrey, in the Dorking area in the Vale of Holmesdale, there were multiple open fields with a pattern of hamlets and isolated farms. Some of the more populous arable villages in Surrey developed common fields. In north-west Sussex, conditions were similar. The open fields below the Downs in Harting, about 1400, were permanent fenced or hedged entities divided into strips called *helua* or *helia*. Above the Downs, West Harting Field may have been a common field, since it had furlongs and there may have been a two- or three-shift rotation.[3]

4 TECHNIQUES – CROP NUTRITION

In Kent about 1322 the dung of sheep was worth £91 6s. 8d. a year to the Cathedral Priory of Canterbury, and there was so little of it that the monks used guano from their dovecotes. In Sussex Battle Abbey seems likewise to have been short of manure. The abbot valued the dung-carrying services of the peasants, since both in Kent and Sussex he fed them in the hall when they did this work. The yardlings of Appledram probably manured only about five and a half acres a year. At Petworth in 1347–8 the lord bought thirty-six wagonloads and eighty-three cartloads of dung. At Preston, a manor of the Bishop of Chichester, the lord dunged only a very small amount of land every year after 1244, but the marginal land received equal treatment with the older arable. The beadle and the oxherd could each borrow one of the lord's wains to dung three and four acres of their own land.

The Cathedral Priory of Canterbury was actively marling in Kent throughout the thirteenth century. In 1225–52 the priory bought marl and applied it to five, eight and eleven acres. These were costly operations. Early in the fourteenth century, the prior issued the following regulations: 'Item, in all the manors in which marl may easily be had let marlers be provided in every manor and let as much land as possible be marled in the summer.' The new innings at Ebony were the scene of intensive marling in 1302–3. In 1303–4 the priory put lime on the same five acres, dressed a further eight acres with marl and spread yard manure on four and a half acres of land. In 1304–5 the priory marled over sixteen acres, put lime on over four acres and spread much dung. In 1305–6 the priory marled over twelve acres, and put lime on four acres. In 1306–7 there was a decrease in the area marled and limed.

The aim of all this marling, liming and manuring was to grow more wheat. At Ebony the main crop was oats, but wheat also sold well. The priory sometimes fertilized the land when it was fallow, and sometimes when the wheat was already sown. In

1303–17 the acreage under wheat increased. A good example of the effect of dressing the land with lime occurred in 1305–6 when the priory dressed over five acres and sowed the land with wheat. The resultant yield was 50 per cent greater than that of undressed land. When dressing ceased in 1317 the acreage under wheat fell. In 1331 marling started again when more land came under cultivation, but at Ebony this policy was a failure. Poverty of the soil and floods brought famine. In 1285–1322 the prior spent £111 5s. od. on marl alone for demesne land held in severalty. The Cathedral Priory of Canterbury was an unusually enlightened, wealthy and laborious house, but the policy of marling and liming marginal lands seems not to have paid at all.

Marling also took place in Sussex. At Drayton there was a marlpit in about 1222–53. On the estates of the Bishop of Chichester at Sidlesham in 1257 the villeins had to quarry marl on occasion and each man dug eight feet long, four feet wide and seven feet deep for one period of work. At Greenstead in 1273 the Priory of St Pancras at Lewes made marling within five years a condition of leasehold tenure. Sussex has also provided perhaps the earliest certain reference to marling in England and Wales. About 1100 at Iford, Ralph de Pleiz granted Lewes Priory 'the marl-pit which is at the way out from our vill with the land which is there adjoining the marl-pit'. Two other Sussex manors practised marling in 1321.

Marling took place at Ruislip in Middlesex in 1288–9, and in Surrey in 1342. The best examples from Surrey are from the estates of Chertsey Abbey, and are all connected with the very late assarting and monopolizing from woodland actively carried out there down to the very years of the Black Death.[4]

South-eastern England was almost as progressive as eastern England. Kent and Sussex were richer and more advanced than Middlesex and Surrey. Wheat and barley were the major grain crops; there were large crops of legumes, and yields were better where these existed. In Sussex the peasants ploughed with stots and there were plenty of milch kine. Cheese, butter and milk were plentiful. Sheep were easily the most important animal, proportionally more significant than in East Anglia. In Kent they supplied milk as well as wool. At Aldingbourne in Sussex their numbers doubled in 1220–1330 and they replaced goats. Geese and poultry were numerous and the peasants ate eggs and drank cider as well as ale. South-eastern England had numerous vineyards. This progressive agriculture came about because the whole region had superior crop rotations like those of East Anglia and Essex, and both lords and peasants practised intensive marling and manuring. The Cathedral Priory of Canterbury also limed its demesne lands.

5　THE LIFE OF THE PEOPLE – THE PEASANT'S RESOURCES

Kent needs much more work on holdings before a definite statement about resources is possible, but large holdings are very unlikely. Sussex varied a great deal from time to time and place to place in the size of its peasant holdings. Everywhere there was a distinct class of rich peasants, but in most places there were a great many small peasants. Often the number of holdings under five acres was more than half the total, and these tiny holdings were particularly common in the new-settlement regions, especially in marshland.

The subsidy roll for three Sussex hundreds in 1332 gives a different picture in each hundred. The hundred of Rotherbridge was in the Vale of Rother, a fairly prosperous tract of lower greensand, with large settlements, in between the Downs and the Weald. There were nine settlements and 100 tax-payers in this hundred. Each family had on average one quarter of wheat, two bushels of barley, nearly three quarters of oats, nearly six bushels of rye, nearly four milch kine and over one pig. Every two families had thirty-three sheep, and every four families three affers and three oxen. There was no shortage of milk, butter or cheese, and enough grain in store for sale to support one man for a year.

The hundred of Holmstrow lay on the fertile coastal plain in the alluvial valley of the lower Ouse. There were three settlements and 110 tax-payers. Each family had less than one and a half quarters of wheat, and less than two quarters of barley. Each family had on average seventeen sheep; every three families had one pig; every four families three cattle; every seven families four oxen; and every nine families one horse. Except for sheep, these people were poorer in stock, particularly in cows, than the men of Rotherbridge and had less saleable grain.

Henhurst was a poor Wealden hundred. Every family had, on average, two stots, one ox, six milch kine, three swine, one sheep, six and a half quarters of wheat, eleven and a half quarters of oats and one and a half cart-loads of hay. Dairying was very important, pigs a valuable asset, sheep unimportant, and there was enough surplus grain in each family to feed three men and a child, or four women and a child.

6 THE LIFE OF THE PEOPLE – INHERITANCE CUSTOMS

Kent was a land of hamlets depending upon some central manor, and of small freeholders who held by the peculiar gavelkind tenure, which required the division of tenements between the offspring of the tenant upon his death or retirement. The resulting fragmentation, and the peculiarly free society which accompanied it, are amongst the main themes of work on Kent, but we must be careful not to overemphasize partibility and personal freedom 'by imagining a world dominated by restless smallholders'. Gavelkind and tenure in parage are known from the Domesday Book, but a clear and objective view of the extent of gavelkind is difficult to attain for the period before 1350, and the reader must rely upon general impressions for an idea of the social structure of Kent and the size of peasant holdings.

A survey of the Battle Abbey manor of Wye serves to support the idea that partition never went ridiculously far and that the number of surviving children was seldom so large that the custom became impracticable. Wye contained sixty and a half *juga* or yokelands, each of four virgates, half of them free and half servile. Some thirty-eight people held the thirty and a half free *juga* and of these twenty-seven tenants held seventeen and three-quarters *juga* as heirs. At most, fifty-five tenants held the thirty servile *juga* and one virgate with two *juga*. There was apparently no very startling amount of sub-division compared with Lincolnshire and East Anglia.

Sussex was in many ways quite a contrast to Kent and its peasantry often both more substantial amd more heavily burdened. The Domesday figures would give it a good many poor families but more substantial and servile peasants than Kent or eastern England. The whole countryside round Alciston seems to have had substantial peasants, but partible inheritance was not entirely unknown. Sussex rural society was comparatively free and fluid.

In 1256–7 there were a good many substantial villeins of the Bishop of Chichester who employed labourers and sub-let cottages. At the oats boonwork the villeins held their rods over the bent backs of their farm-servants and sub-tenants. In 1244 only their wives and shepherds were free of the boonworks. Many poor people lived on the bishop's manors.

The Sussex manors of the Archbishop of Canterbury tended in 1285 to be Wealden manors and were frequently peopled by hordes of smallholders. Wadhurst exhibits the spectacle of highly fragmented holdings in a new-settlement manor. In all there were 305 holdings and more than half of these were under five acres. The median holding was three to five acres, even though there were plenty of large holdings. There were 103 cottars alone. Fifty-two tenants held the fifteen and a half virgates of Wadhurst which varied in size from 80 to 160 acres. The median holding was of twenty acres – much larger than the median of all holdings in the county. Sub-division of the virgates had apparently taken place in the past, but seems not to have gone very far. Out of the 1449 acres which virgaters held only 133 were still undeveloped coppice. At first sight most of the new settlement had already taken place. A closer look at the virgates shows that they were all, in fact, named hamlets in the wood. Two were whole virgates which one person held. Like all the tenants of virgates these were neifs (villeins), and the neifs were therefore the aristocracy of the manor. There were eight examples of partible virgates divided among two to seven parceners. There there were various stages of division in these hamlets, and in each a family which had taken its name from the hamlet. Such families were perhaps the original settlers of the hamlet, but besides these groups of relatives there were other people, sometimes in groups bearing the same name. Some of these may have married into the family of the pioneers, others may have won their interest by purchase. The whole represents the working of partible inheritance in a new-settlement society and may be a model of the original settlement of England.[5]

The great variety of farming regions is more apparent in south-eastern than in eastern England. Even so, the resemblance in settlement, population and agricultural history is most striking. Kent and Sussex, like much of eastern England, practised gavelkind or partible inheritance, particularly in the Weald, where assarting was very late and the common woodlands and pastures extensive. The Wealden iron industry had started by 1253 and mines had developed by 1086. Holdings were not so small as in eastern England, and there is less evidence of crafts and trade. The efficient agriculture of south-eastern England provided a sufficient livelihood for a numerous peasantry, whose numbers increased down to 1315, and supported the great churches of Canterbury, Chichester and Battle.

CHAPTER 6

THE EAST MIDLANDS

1 NEW SETTLEMENT AND POPULATION GROWTH

In the east Midlands no new settlements are recorded after 1350 in Leicestershire, Rutland, Northamptonshire, Huntingdonshire, Bedfordshire, Buckinghamshire and Hertfordshire, and only one in Nottinghamshire. In 1281–1350 none occurred for the first time in Leicestershire, Northamptonshire, Huntingdonshire, Bedfordshire and Buckinghamshire, only one in Nottinghamshire, and two each in Rutland and Hertfordshire. The east Midlands was thus, by about 1280, in a similar state of development to eastern England.

In Nottinghamshire most of the new settlement took place in Sherwood Forest, especially in the north, where there was much waste in 1066 and 1086, but there was some new settlement in the western uplands and the Trent lowlands. Marshy areas near the Trent and the Carrs of north Nottinghamshire were especially favoured. The Wolds and the area south of the Trent had little new settlement. Much of this was early and in progress before 1066, but although Nottinghamshire as a whole was well settled the forest was empty and infertile, and here new settlement went on very late.

The Nottinghamshire place-name survey of 1940 contains only forty-three clearing names, less than either Sussex or Essex. Of the twenty-six clearings first recorded after 1086, only ten occurred after 1280, eight of these after 1350. The survey seems to be very short of late *leahs* and *thwaites*. Nottinghamshire has altogether thirty-six examples of the place-name element *thorpe*, of which fourteen were first recorded before 1086. Eleven of the thirty-six names belonged to parishes, and two are of villages. The remaining twenty-three were much smaller settlements. Of the total, fifteen have Scandinavian first elements, one is English, and two are certainly post-Conquest formations (e.g. names which incorporate Norman Christian names like Walter and Richard). All are names of outlying hamlets or dependent settlements.

Most new assarts were in Sherwood, near Nottingham, and were late. The earliest in the forest was late in the twelfth century. Three other manors had assarts from woodland in 1251, 1266, 1288, and 1291. Assarting seems to have been a great activity in 1292–7 in Tuxford, a large village thronged with people. Nevertheless seven cottars' tofts were vacant because no one wished to hold them; presumably rents were too high. In 1329 and 1338 land was falling out of cultivation in two manors in the Sherwood region, for lack of tenants. And yet assarting from the waste continued until the eve of the Black Death. In three Sherwood manors 113.5 acres of new assarts for growing grain came into existence in 1306–47.

Adjoining Sherwood is the western upland and here too there was late new settlement about 1327. There was also some early new settlement at two places in the Trent lowlands in 1150–89. At South Scarle in 1225–31 twenty-five bovate-holders each held an acre of assart. This is quite a good example of a communal assart, but it was a small one. Bovates, not tenants, shared it.

Leicestershire was more densely settled than Nottingham-shire and freer. Only in Charnwood Forest, and in the later-settled and less fertile hilly region of west Leicestershire, was there much new settlement. The Vale of Belvoir and the Soar and Wreak Valleys were particularly well-settled, and here there was little assarting after 1086. There was very little assarting in the Wolds and in High Leicestershire. Rather more occurred in west Leicestershire, especially in the limestone region north of Charnwood Forest along the Derbyshire border. From Breedon-on-the-Hill, early in the thirteenth century, comes a splendid example of the sort of agreement which lay behind many of the arrangements for common of shack on the stubble in the open fields of England. New settlement in the waste of Charnwood was mainly on the fringes, but in central Charnwood in 1129 there were enclosures on high land. Ulverscroft Priory, also in central Charnwood, was concerned with assarts in 1284.

Northamptonshire contained a great deal of well-settled land in the Nene and Welland Valleys in 1086, but the woods and fens of the Soke of Peterborough, and the forests of Rockingham, Whittlewood, Salcey and Yardley Chase were the scenes of extensive reclamations after 1086.

Northamptonshire has forty-two new-settlement place-names in *leah* – considerably fewer proportionally than Nottinghamshire. Of these fifteen were first recorded before 1086; twelve of the remaining twenty-seven were first known after 1280, eight of them after 1350. The thirteenth century was the most active period of forest clearing.

When we turn to the assarts of the Cistercian Abbey of Pipewell in Rockingham Forest their extent seems enormous. Sums paid to the crown suggest assarts of 13,400 acres in the period 1169–1209. The thirteenth-century assarts were much smaller, but included late assarts of twenty-four acres by 1275, and five acres in 1315. The monks were growing corn on assarts in 1306 and 1308. In 1253, the monks of Peterborough had rights of drift and pannage in Rockingham Forest, and the right to enfeoff their assarts there. Osney Abbey received tithes from assarts in the heavily wooded Tove Valley in 1187–9.

In the Nene Valley most of the assarts were late, but some were extensive. By 1253 the monks of Peterborough had 400 acres of assarts at Oundle, and on two other manors assarting from woodland was active in 1220 and 1289–1340. Most of the assarting in the Soke of Peterborough came late. In 1253 the Abbey of Peterborough had 200 acres of assarts, probably improved fenland, in the Soke. Assarting from woodland near the fen took place extensively in 1155–1260.

Luffield Priory had its Northamptonshire estates in Whittlewood Forest. This was ideal assarting country, mostly 400–500 feet above sea-level, and the adjoining parts of Buckinghamshire settled woodland very actively. Assarting was late and still continued in 1331. Elsewhere in Whittlewood substantial assarts for growing grain came into existence in 1190–1290.

The list of clearings in Huntingdonshire contains only fourteen *leahs*, of which six were first recorded before 1086 and one in 1281–1350. Thus the eleventh and thirteenth centuries were the most important for clearances and there was very little new assarting after 1280.

Many Ramsey Abbey manors and sub-manors appeared separately or more completely developed after 1086. Six of them were above the 100-foot contour and in 1086 there were still about thirty square miles of woodland to assart. The Abbot of Ramsey and his rent-paying tenants were assarting soon after 1086, but others beside the abbot were early settlers. The twelfth- and thirteenth-century assarts on the Huntingdonshire estates of the Bishop of Lincoln were very substantial, but on the whole early-twelfth-century woodland assarts were small.

The late-twelfth and early-thirteenth centuries witnessed renewed interest in assarting; the main bulk of it in the woodlands of Huntingdonshire took place in 1160–1250. The net addition of lands between these dates in four manors doubled the holdings of the peasants.

Bushmead Priory, in Bedfordshire, had several Huntingdonshire estates with rather late assarts. The last assarts, in 1265, were the subject of an important agreement reducing common rights on arable. The medieval farmer cut his corn with a sickle a little below the head of the sheaf, and left the straw standing for common of pasture. The partial extinction of common rights was rare in the east Midlands, but the late assarting was typical.

The Huntingdonshire fenland is blackland or peatland, and therefore more difficult to drain than the siltland of the Parts of Holland and the Norfolk Marshland. Reclamation was not so extensive as in the siltland, and mainly confined to the fen-edge and the islands. The greatest was the Prior of Ely's 280 acres of enclosures made in Somersham Fen by 1198–1215.

Bedfordshire divides into the clay vale of the Ouse Valley and the Chilterns, and in this well-developed county there were few new settlements. To all appearances Bedfordshire produced very few clearings. Altogether there were only twenty-four, proportionally about the same as Nottinghamshire. Ten clearings occurred for the first time in or before 1086, and only one in 1281–1350. The most active period was the thirteenth century and there was very little late new settlement.

Most of the twelfth- and thirteenth-century assarts were in the clay vale. Some are vouched for already early in the twelfth century and in 1123–30; soon after, peasants held assarts for money rents and hidage. By 1150–1200 in one village thirty peasants held 350 acres of assarts on these terms. Two manors in the Chilterns had assarts early in the twelfth century, and there were assarts by the Great Ouse in 1274. The Cistercians of Warden Abbey reduced Ravenshoe Wood to arable in 1154–1252.

To these clay vale manors we must add two manors from the Chilterns near the Hertfordshire border, both about 600 feet above sea-level. On both there were extensive oak and beech woods whose area declined considerably in 1181–1222. In 1222 there were old and new assarts, the latter coming into existence in 1193–1205. By 1222 the manors teemed with people.

Many churches with interests in Bedfordshire were making assarts in practically every part of the county during the twelfth and thirteenth centuries. At Leighton Buzzard assarting was quite clearly still important in the 1240s. The Abbey of Old Warden, south of Bedford, was a considerable assarting centre. In about 1190–1200 the abbey was buying up land as well as improving it. Round Warden Abbey itself assarting was already well advanced in 1135. Further south, round Flitwick, there were assarts soon after 1200. Some of these assarts involved the monks of Warden in disputes with other churches, and the earliest disagreement of this nature was with Newnham Priory in 1199.

The Priory of Dunstable also had assarts in the same part of Bedfordshire. Assarting was going strong in about 1200–27.

The division of Flitton Moor between Dunstable Priory, Woburn Abbey, Beaulieu Priory, Philip of Flitton and their free tenants took place in 1227, and they dug dykes to drain the moor. Agreements between lords and communities were not very common in the east Midlands, for which reason such evidence is the more valuable. There must have been very many more in earlier periods which were never committed to writing. The last Dunstable Priory record of this type, from 1200–30, said that the prior had dyked the fen in Flitwick by the assent and agreement of the neighbourhood of Flitt. By this time the concept of the *visnetum* or neighbourhood as a body whose consent the prior needed was well-established, and here it seems to have meant the whole hundred of Flitt.

The land immediately south of Dunstable is the Bedfordshire portion of the Chilterns, and is 400–600 feet above sea-level. In Studham (500–600 feet above sea-level) assarting was in full progress in 1170–1230. Close to Dunstable one of the prior's manors showed clear traces of assarting about 1300. The area was still well-wooded, but the layout of the fields showed that assarting was still going on. There was apparently no 'normal' open-field system, and here and there were odd crofts. The field on the Down still had unbroken or newly-broken land in it. This was the very image of a late, high, marginal village.

Thus in spite of appearances there was a good deal of new settlement – mostly from wood and fen – in twelfth- and thirteenth-century Bedfordshire. All parts of the county, from the northern boulder clay to the central greensands and the southern chalklands of the Chiltern Hills, took part in this process which was still unfinished about 1240. Communities and communal agreements played a great part in this process, and a thriving land-market accompanied it.

Buckinghamshire has forty-seven clearing names in the county place-name survey of 1925. Fourteen of these clearings already existed by 1086, and of the remainder eight were not recorded until after 1280, five of them after 1350. The thirteenth century was the greatest period of new settlement. The county did not contain more extensive reclamations than did

Huntingdonshire and most of them were from the northern claylands or the southern river-valleys. Eighteen assarts are known from the former in 1189–1306. By 1100 little of Sherington still needed clearing. Thame Abbey had possessions in the woodland eight miles south of Buckingham. From 1195 comes a clear description of a forest reclamation.

The monks of Newington also had assarts in the northern claylands, and in 1311 they, with their men of Newington, agreed, with Sir John de Grey and his men of Bletchley, to cultivate the fallow. There were two intercommoning villages, both with new-settlement names. Newington (or Newton) Longville first appeared in the records in 1086, but Bletchley ('Blecca's *leah*') was not recorded before 1106–9. Both had probably risen from the scrub not many years before, and intercommoning had arisen after partition, settlement and cultivation of the waste. Neither village was in an upland region, and by 1311 *inhokes* were necessary to produce greater quantities of food and, perhaps, to generate greater fertility. The men of Newington were, in fact, cultivating the West Mead of Bletchley as an open field, with a fallow course and *inhokes* on the fallow.

The Abbey of Missenden had most of its estates in the central Chilterns, more than 400 feet above sea-level. Assarting was well underway by the mid-twelfth century. Later, in 1263–92, the assarters paid due attention to the fertility of the new lands by spreading marl. Nearby, in Missenden itself, there was assarting by 1161, and marling on assart lands. There were several tenants of assarts in Missenden in 1234–52. Assarting had proceeded far in another manor by 1300. In the far west of the county, there was assarting in 1152–3, 650 feet above sea-level. About 1220 in the Thames marshes there was an enclosure from marsh to create new meadow. Other Buckinghamshire assarts, mainly in the Chilterns, were recorded in 1199, 1205 (412 acres of assarts), 1213 and 1229.

Three more reclamations belong to the southern river-valleys. On the north bank of the Thames, in 1110, there was an extensive one, divided by many landholders. A much later assart, from about 1260, lay in the Colne Valley. At High Wycombe, in the Wye Valley, well into the Chilterns, there were open fields, and other smaller fields spread along the sides of the valley. There were many assarts among the fields of High Wycombe, and others in the same area ascended the valley sides to a considerable height. These assarts were in severalty, and at the disposal of those who cleared them. The first definite mention of Newland Meadow occurs in 1227; the people probably created it to make up for the conversion of older meadows into the High Street in 1154–89.

Wooburn is also in the valley of the Buckinghamshire Wye just before it enters the Thames. Here, in 1240, assarting was still going on, and the Bishop of Lincoln made an agreement with Sir Oliver de Aencurt which seemed to imply that common rights should continue on assarted land.

The *Hundred Rolls* of 1280, which cover only four Buckinghamshire hundreds, tell much, as far as they go, about late assarting in the county. All the assarts recorded lay in two of the four hundreds, nor did all villages participate in this activity. Out of 10,112 acres of land in the active villages 493 acres were assarts. The lords held in demesne 4111 acres, and of this 144 acres were assarts. The tenants held 6002 acres, but of this 349 acres were assarts. The peasantry was therefore rather more interested in assarting than the lords.

A good deal of clearance was going on in Herefordshire even though new settlements were few in number. The Hertfordshire place-name survey of 1938 had 107 such clearings, and the density was much greater than that found in Essex and Sussex. Only eighteen clearings existed before 1086, and sixty were not recorded until after 1280, forty-six of them after 1350. Hertfordshire, therefore, though well-developed in 1086, showed little sign of new settlement until after 1280. Early assarts were known in east Hertfordshire, in the Vale of Baldock, in 1102, and elsewhere in 1199–1213.

On the whole the east Midlands was not an area of extensive assarting. In the forests of Sherwood in Nottinghamshire, and Charnwood in Leicestershire, on the uplands of west

Leicestershire, in Rockingham, Whittlewood and Salcey Forests, and in Yardley Chase in Northamptonshire, assarting continued until about 1250. The woodlands of Huntingdonshire also attracted clearances until about this time, but reclamation in the Northamptonshire and Huntingdonshire fenland was not on the heroic scale of the siltland intakes. Buckinghamshire saw extensive assarting recently completed by 1279, and Hertfordshire was also active in about 1200–25. There was a fair amount of assarting from wood and fen in twelfth- and thirteenth-century Bedfordshire. All parts of the county, from the northern boulder clay to the central greensands and the southern chalklands of the Chiltern Hills, took part in this process, and it was still unfinished about 1240. Communities and communal agreements played a great part, and a thriving land-market existed.

Information about population movements in the east Midlands does exist. The speed of expansion in the generation after 1086 in Northamptonshire was very great, and there is no positive evidence of stagnation in the times of Henry I and Stephen. In most parts of England in the two centuries after 1086 the population increase was 250 per cent but the Nottinghamshire manors of the Bishop of Lincoln increased more slowly. This may have been because of slowing down, stagnation, or decline in the thirteenth century. On the Ramsey Abbey estates there was a definite slowing down in the period from c. 1150 to c.1250. The fen-edge manors of Huntingdonshire expanded 350 per cent in 135 years, but slowed down in 1221–51. Expansion in the Chilterns in 1086–1300 was 450 per cent in Bedfordshire; in the Buckinghamshire woodland in the same period it was 325 per cent. As elsewhere, population growth in fenland and woodland was very rapid.

On the whole direct evidence of a fourteenth-century decline before the Black Death is hard to come by. It exists for one manor in Nottinghamshire, one in Rutland and eight in Northamptonshire in 1125–1321, but this is not evidence of decline in 1280–1350. I know of no such direct evidence for that period in any part of the east Midlands. The same differences in speed of expansion exist in the fourteenth century as in the thirteenth century. Particularly slow growth took place on three Leicestershire manors, which grew by half in 1086–1321, one Rutland manor, which grew by a third in 1086–1314, and nine Northamptonshire manors, which grew by a half in 1086–1319. A few east Midlands manors grew rapidly. Counties where the fourteenth-century population was double or treble the 1086 population were: Northamptonshire (one manor) and Buckinghamshire (two manors). Six manors in Hertfordshire expanded very fast indeed. On the whole the east Midlands was perhaps not a very rapidly expanding region, since its resources of unimproved woodland and fenland were not very great.

Counts of heads of household exist for 201 east Midland manors in 1086–1350; they split into five equal cohorts which cover 1086–1142, 1086–1244, 1086–1279, 1086–1280, and 1086–1312. The percentage increases over these five periods were 161, 273, 262, 212 and 255. Population grew fast in 1086–1244, but declined considerably in 1244–80. Population increased again in 1280–1312, but failed to reach the level of 1279. These movements accord well with the history of new settlement, and mark out the east Midlands as different from eastern England.[1]

2 CROPS AND LIVESTOCK

Upon four Nottinghamshire manors in 1296–8 there were generally more oats than other grains; on one of them the importance of peas was very striking and, as in other counties, went with a high proportion of barley. Two of these manors were marginal lands developed late. In 1246–1328 ten Nottinghamshire manor-houses had dovecotes, which argue a large grain crop. Variety in food came from fish, and (for the lords) from rabbits. In 1255–1329 ten manors had fisheries, of which two were in the Trent and one in the Soar. In 1274 one fishery produced eels. There were rabbit-warrens in 1295 and 1340. More relevant to actual cultivation and live-stock rearing was pannage for swine, not perhaps so extensive as the existence of Sherwood Forest might lead one to suppose. In 1251–95 it existed in at least five localities. On the other hand, in 1251, Langdon Wood was oakwood and could sustain hundreds of cattle, swine and goats. Nottinghamshire must have had more resources of this sort than other east Midland counties. Lastly, there is a statement of the possessions of the Hospital of St John of Nottingham made in 1305. The grain was mostly rye, but the stock included cider. It is news to read that Nottinghamshire sometimes drank cider in the early-fourteenth century.

One snippet of very early information for Leicestershire comes from 1114–15 and 1126. A western Leicestershire manor had demesne at both dates, and in 1114–15 the stock consisted of oxen, horses and a large flock of sheep. On one Leicestershire manor in 1277–8, oats was nearly as prominent as wheat, barley much less favoured and beans neglected. Oxen exceeded stots in number, and cattle swine. Sheep were few. Leicester Abbey had cows in 1260.

The status of oats in the east Midlands is also clear from excellent Northamptonshire figures. On one manor in 1288–9, dredge led the way, followed by oats, wheat, rye, maslin and beans and peas. Dredge was the drink corn. On another Northamptonshire manor in 1277–8 rye and oats predominated, but one-third of the grain in stock was wheat and dredge. Legumes were also very acceptable. Oxen exceeded affers, but there were no swine or milch kine. There was a good flock of sheep.

The amount of grain sown as seed is known for the Crowland Abbey manor of Wellingborough over three periods – 1258–85, 1289–99 and 1302–14. After a period of decline in 1289–99 the sowings of wheat maintained a steady level. Oats was by far the largest crop sown, but it steadily declined over the whole period as the lord sowed more and more dredge, which latter did not appear until 1296, and not every year until 1305. Sowings were so heavy in 1302–14 that oats and dredge together increasingly predominated. After oats, barley was the largest crop, and its sowing increased perceptibly in 1302–14. Rye was the fourth crop in popularity, and much less preferred than wheat, but it grew by more than half between 1258–85 and 1302–14. The lord grossly neglected beans and peas. In 1267–89 and 1289–1305 we find no record of legumes. To all appearances Wellingborough had a poor marginal economy in 1258–1314, an economy which was becoming markedly more impoverished as the years went by. The lord was sowing more 'poorer' grains proportionally; he also ignored beans and peas and seems not to have known their fertilizing power.

The total grains harvested paint a somewhat different picture. We have evidence for the years 1258–85, 1289–1302, and 1304–22. In 1289–1302, compared with 1258–85, the size of the harvest decreased, but it increased by half in 1304–22, even though that last period covered the famine years. The size of the wheat crops fell considerably, but, especially in 1304–22, that of dredge crops rose very greatly. In 1289–1302 the rye crop was treble the crops of 1258–85, and in 1304–22 quadruple. Barley fell then more than recovered; oats fell and nearly recovered. Legumes were a small crop in 1258–85, almost non-existent in 1288–1302, multiplied twelve-fold in 1304–22, but were still only half as significant as rye and the smallest crop except bolmong (oats and peas mixed). The emphasis upon 'poorer' grains was certainly there, but so was the dethronement of oats, its replacement by barley, and the rise of dredge and legumes. This evidence goes counter to the claim that Wellingborough was a poor marginal manor.

Wellingborough is a particularly interesting manor, because for the period 1292/3–1304/5 we know the quantities and types of tithe corn. Barley was the largest peasant crop, followed by dredge, rye, oats, wheat and bolmong. No legumes were recorded, but the figures certainly do not depict a marginal economy. Peasants often grew less wheat than lords, but a little over half their crops were barley and dredge.

Neither do figures for demesne stock remaining at the end of the year suggest a poor pastoral economy. In 1258–85 oxen were much preferred to stots, but stots and other horses together were rather more numerous than oxen. Cattle were very popular, so popular that they outnumbered sheep in 1258–9 and 1271–2. Indeed, there were few sheep at all until 1276–7, and until 1280/1 they remained below the average number. Swine outnumbered milch kine over the whole period, but were fewer in 1258/9 and 1271/2. They were below the average number for the period for only three years. In 1289/90–1302/3 there were again many more oxen than stots. Draught animals were half as many again in this period. The herd of milch kine fell by over half, and sheep grew steadily in numbers until the flocks were one-third greater than in 1258/9–1285/6. The herd of swine was very slightly smaller. In 1304/5–1322/3 the herd of stots fell to less than one-half its size in 1292/3–1304/5, other horses grew in numbers by one-quarter, and the herd of oxen fell by a little. The decline in the number of draught animals was only 3 per cent. At the latest date the herd of cattle was very slightly greater than in 1289/90–1302/3, but the flock of sheep fell by one-quarter almost back to the figures for 1285/9–1258/6. Swine increased by about one-tenth and were almost twice as many as milch kine. The latter maintained and slightly increased, and swine consistently increased their herds over the whole period, but sheep, after a brisk rise in 1276/7 and subsequent years, reached their maximum in 1285/6, declined thereafter, and disappeared after 1312/13. The period of maximum sheep-farming was also the period of oats and rye, but there was never a period of poor marginal pastoral farming.

The manor of Wellingborough was also a considerable dairy farm. We know sales of cheese for 1258/9–1271/2, of butter for 1258/9–1291/2 and thereafter the total production of both. By far the major portion of the milk not drunk went into cheese rather than butter. The herd of milch kine was slowly diminishing throughout the period as the herd of cattle other than draught cattle diminished. At the same time the output of each cow was slowly declining. Since sheep were also suffering a severe decline in numbers, one may suspect a greater emphasis on rearing beef cattle. After a sharp rise in 1289/90–1302/3 the herd of oxen also began to fall off. Much of the cheese and butter the lord made for the market. The sales of the former went down quite rapidly over the period, and actual production declined to a little over half of what it had been in 1267/8–1289/90. Butter was a perishable commodity and the manor kept no stock. Its production was half for the market, and remained so. Over the sixty-five-year period the decline in yield of both cheese and butter was steady and regular.

A limited amount of comparable material is available from other parts of Northamptonshire. At Kettering in 1294 rye was easily the biggest crop, followed by oats, barley and small crops of dredge, legumes and wheat. The wheat and legumes were quite insignificant, but one-quarter of the beans went in planting the corn-land (viz. the fallow, as an *inhoke*). Horses were here considerably more numerous than oxen, and there were large herds of cattle and swine. In contrast to Wellingborough cattle exceeded swine. The production of hides reminds us that in modern times Kettering has been a centre of the boot and shoe industry. Sheep were also a major interest, and at the start of the year there were goats, geese, fowls, ducks and pigeons. The manor also made cheeses, some of which went to the household and servants. The cows produced butter, some of which the household and servants ate, and the rest went to market. Most of the cow's milk went to the lambs, and the rest to market. The ewes must have been short of milk this year for the lambs to have enjoyed such luxury.

The relationship between the arable products and the flocks and herds is particularly interesting at Kettering. One-tenth of the barley went to feed the pigs, fowls and pigeons. Over one-fifth of the oats went to provender for horses drawing manure and marl. One-ninth of the beans and peas went to fatten pigs, and to feed some of them after they came in from the wood. Over one-third of the rye went to feed the pigs and young pigs, and under half in sheaf to feed the ewes.

Kettering had a windmill, a watermill, a fulling-mill and a bakehouse. A reminder of the town's early cloth industry was the place where William the Walker (i.e. fuller) had a dye-house. In 1294 the lord planted olive-trees – as unpractical a piece of optimism as is imaginable.

Kettering was a manor which practised mixed farming; it had a fair number of cattle, sheep and swine, a bias towards rye and oats and few legumes. Cheese, butter and milk existed, but were not very important. The cattle may have been mainly beef cattle, or grown for hides, for the manor preferred horses to draught oxen. The peasantry had some swine.

In 1298 the Earl of Lancaster's manor at Higham Ferrers had a garden, dovehouse, fishpond and a vineyard (which did not pay). The town had three watermills, a fishery and three bakehouses. In 1313 dredge was more than twice as important (and productive) as wheat, and peas were insignificant. The stock was not very great – affers, another horse, oxen and swine. Some of the peas went to the doves, but most of the rest of the grain which the servants did not eat went to the market. Barley and maslin were the leading peasant crops. There were five stalls in the shambles and eight shops let to linen merchants. Every year at the mills, the inhabitants caught on average 175 eels. The lord's household bought from the manor, in 1313, a quantity of must, but the plants and fruit of the large garden, the grass and nettles of the pinfold and the grass of the vineyard were worth nothing.

Rushden and the Park had, in 1298, a grange with an oxhouse, a sheepfold, two dovehouses and two watermills which were thrown down. In 1313 the demesne farm produced dredge, wheat, and oats and at the end of the year there were affers, oxen, a good herd of cattle and a skep of bees. Like Higham Ferrers, Rushden had no sheep.

Northamptonshire therefore was a county of mixed farming in about 1250–1325. Oats, dredge and rye, rather than wheat and barley, were the major crops, and sheep were significant here and there in the hills. Most villages seem to have had a fair number of cattle, either beef or dairy, and swine were reasonably popular, sometimes more so than cattle.

Huntingdonshire was not unlike Buckinghamshire and Middlesex. An estate of the Earl of Cornwall in 1296 was typical, and, like most Huntingdonshire manors, differed from Buckinghamshire and Middlesex in the emphasis it laid upon legumes. The first crop was wheat, followed by barley and peas (equal), oats and bulmong.

The Ramsey Abbey estates resembled Norfolk and Cambridgeshire in that wheat and barley were the main crops, and legumes were prominent. Most crops declined in yield over the period 1250–1350, especially oats, and the economy was not exactly thriving in 1325–50. Many parts of Huntingdonshire, especially near the fen-edge, were highly pastoral. The cattle produced milk, which the people turned into cheese, rather than use the milk of sheep and goats. Most cows 'ran in the marsh with their calves'. The abundant marsh grasses were at some considerable distance from the manor for convenient pasture for milch kine, and winter hay does not seem to have been of an abundance to ensure a very great surplus after the feeding of horses and oxen. The fens were to develop largely as sheep pasture in the Ramsey economy. Two manors specialized in swine, and one had easily the largest flock of sheep. Oxen greatly outnumbered stots. Statistics available are not enough to show whether pastoralism was increasing in the fourteenth century, as harvests shrank, but between the twelfth and thirteenth centuries the demesne livestock on four Ramsey Abbey manors greatly increased. The abbey was exploiting the waste so much more vigorously that the herds of cows sextupled, and the flocks of sheep and herds of pigs trebled. In 1095–1200 the number of cartloads of hay from the fens of nine manors more than doubled, as did the area of the demesne meadows of six manors in 1086–1390.

The Bedfordshire Lay Subsidy of 1297 offers a splendid opportunity to survey the agriculture and stock-rearing of a portion of the county – the hundreds of Barford, Biggleswade and Flitt and the towns of Bedford, Dunstable, Leighton Buzzard and Luton. Altogether there were thirty-seven villages – ten in Barford, sixteen in Biggleswade and eleven in Flitt – plus the four towns, of which Leighton Buzzard included five neighbouring villages. Most of Bedfordshire is dull boulder clay but parts of Flitt hundred are lower greensand and rise to 400 feet above sea-level.

The general grain and stock totals lead to observations about Bedfordshire as a whole in 1297. Dredge was the principal crop, with the largest quantities growing on Biggleswade hundred and round Dunstable and Luton, but wheat was not very far behind. The country round Luton and the hundreds of Barford and Biggleswade were the chief wheat-growers. The third most popular grain was oats which grew mainly in the hundred of Barford, round Luton and in the hundred of Flitt. These were the major grain-growing regions. Barley and rye were not much grown in Bedfordshire, the former only round Dunstable and the latter in the hundred of Biggleswade. Legumes were more popular than either but much less favoured than oats; they achieved real importance only in the hundreds of Flitt and Biggleswade. Stots and affers were more numerous than oxen. Dairying was by no means a neglected side of the agrarian activities of Bedfordshire. Barford, Flitt and Biggleswade hundreds had most stots, affers, other horses and cattle. Swine were not outstandingly plentiful. The hundreds of Barford and Biggleswade and the country round Luton had most of them – about two-thirds of those recorded – but swine were only rather more than one-third as common as cattle. Sheep were the most prominent animal. Biggleswade, Flitt and the country round Luton had about two-thirds of the sheep, densest in the country towards the Chilterns.

One cannot compare the assessment for the lay subsidy of 1297 in Bedfordshire with similar assessments at slightly different dates in other counties because each lay subsidy affected a different class of people and each assessment took place at a different time of year. Nor can assessments for lay subsidies be used as an absolute standard to guide us to a knowledge of the resources of these people because of the prevalence of bribery and corruption amongst medieval tax-gatherers. The chief use of these assessment rolls is therefore to discover internal patterns (which may or may not be valid) and to say a little about agrarian tendencies. Thus twelve out of thirty-seven villages were good at growing rye and only three out of these twelve good at growing legumes. There was, at first sight, an association between neglect of legume-growing and specializ-ation in growing a marginal land cereal, but then we see that eleven out of thirty-seven villages were good at growing barley but only three out of these eleven were good at growing legumes. Barley is no marginal land crop, so that no correlation appears between lack of legumes and lack of good grains. The figures do, however slightly, suggest a possible correlation between plentiful crops of legumes and good corn crops, but they may simply indicate that the larger and richer villages were good at everything just because they were larger and richer. Similarly there may have been a slight tendency for barley-growing to occur simultaneously with swine-keeping, as in Suffolk. Of the eleven good barley villages five were also good swine villages. The parts of Bedfordshire surveyed were not really strong at rearing sheep. Out of thirty-seven villages fourteen were considerable sheep-rearers and, to press home the point that sheep-farming does not necessarily go with poor arable husbandry, five out of the fourteen were good at growing legumes. One correlation that does seem unquestionable is that villages strong on sheep were usually good at other pastoral activities. Out of the fourteen sheep villages ten were good either at raising cattle or horses or at both.

Dredge was by far the greatest crop in the four Bedfordshire towns; wheat and oats followed. Rye and maslin were negligible, and malt was not a major item for the tax-gatherer. Affers and other horses were much more significant than oxen. Other cattle were more than four times as many as oxen and nearly twice as numerous as swine. Nearly half of the sheep assessed for the subsidy in 1297 in Bedfordshire were in these four towns and of these over half were in Luton. The predominance of the Chiltern sheep-country is very clear.

The Bedford and Dunstable assessments also contain details of a number of miscellaneous items. Bedford had straw, iron, salt, coal, oil, lime, larder goods and tannery. Dunstable had wood, tiles, lime, skins, tanning stock, timber, felt, meat, skinners' stock, fish, grease and tallow, fruit, wood and charcoal, spices, iron, bakers' stock, leather, cloth and poulterers' stock. The most significant items to note here are the various tanners' and skinners' stocks and equipment (such as lime), the meat and the (salt) fish. The fruit is a curiosity not elsewhere encountered. These items stress the mixed nature of Bedfordshire farming and the possible sources of protein in Bedfordshire diet. The evidence of manorial accounts reasonably well supports these tax assessments, especially if one allows for the fact that the latter recorded only the marketable surplus of grain, as well as the wild fluctuations in stock and grain on a medieval farm from one end of the year to another.

Bedfordshire was therefore a county which was predominantly arable in 1086–1348 but which also had a fair amount of animal husbandry. In the sandy areas rye was a favourite crop but on the whole dredge, wheat and oats were most noteworthy – in that order. Barley was not generally a major crop but legumes had some prestige. Sheep were very plentiful, especially in the south towards the Chilterns and there were a good many cattle but few swine.

In Buckinghamshire conditions varied a good deal. Wheat was generally the first crop, but oats was sometimes almost equally to the fore; barley was often towards the top of the list and there was a good deal of dairying and rearing of livestock. Few legumes grew in Buckinghamshire. On one manor in 1296 the largest crop was wheat followed by oats, barley, rye, dredge, peas and vetches. Thus wheat went with oats, but there was a variety of other grains and legumes were not neglected. The manor was a major dairying centre and had a very large herd of cattle, which produced a large number of cheeses and a good deal of butter.

A second manor was very different. In 1296 the biggest yield was of oats, followed closely by rye, wheat and dredge. There were no peas and vetches that year and the manor had in stock only a horse, a few cattle and two geese. In 1288–9 a third manor produced wheat, oats, barley and maslin.

Two very early surveys come from the royal manors of Aylesbury and Brill in about 1155. At Aylesbury there were many oxen, a few affers, cattle, a good number of pigs, a large flock of sheep, two beehives, a piggery, a poultry pen with twenty-five fowls, one lead vat with a tripod, one lead vat with dairy utensils and three wains. There was a barn full of wheat and a barn full of oats. There should also have been a stack containing oats, a stack of wheat and a heap of threshed oats, but the constable found only the latter. There were four cattlesheds and there should have been grain for seed. There was no barley, more oxen than affers and more swine than cattle; in general Aylesbury was a wheat, oats and sheep manor.

At Brill in 1155 there were many oxen and an affer, pigs and sheep. The barn should have contained a stack of maslin, and its other aisle oats and barley. The little barn contained wheat and rye. There was a cattleshed, two wains and grain for seed. Barley and rye were minor crops; wheat and oats major crops. Oxen were ahead of affers and swine more common than cattle. Again this was a wheat, oats and sheep manor.

On a manor of the Bishop of Winchester in 1210–11 oats came before wheat but there had been an excess of wheat the previous year. Mancorn and barley were very much smaller crops and peas were negligible, but that year the bishop bought beans and sowed them. There were geese and the manor made cheeses and sold most of them. Oxen were three times as numerous as affers and as usual on woodland manors there were two or three times as many swine as cattle. There was a large flock of sheep.

At Great Berkhamsted in Hertfordshire, in 1296, the principal crop was oats, followed by wheat and with maslin and barley a long way behind. In stock there were horses, a large herd of cattle and many sheep. The dairy produced cheeses and plenty of butter. Great Berkhamsted was, at this date, very much an oats, wool and dairy-products manor. A Crowland Abbey manor in Hertfordshire in 1296 and 1304 was a butter and cheese farm. In 1296 the stock consisted of oxen, a good herd of other cattle and horses; in 1304 of oxen, other cattle but no horses. The lord made butter and cheese from cow's milk. In 1296 and 1304 the manor made cheeses and butter and sold half of both. The diet of the permanent dairy staff and hired labourers in autumn was

mainly cheese and butter. The percentage of the produce sold
was lower on this manor than elsewhere, which suggests that the
monks fed their staff better than other lords.

In the east Midlands new settlement was largely complete by
1250, but in parts of Nottinghamshire it continued to the eve of
the Black Death, and in Charnwood Forest in Leicestershire
until 1284. In 1086–1244 the number of heads of households
multiplied by 275 per cent, but there was a great decline in
1244–80, followed by another rise in 1280–1312, which failed to
bring the population back to the level of 1279. The decline
corresponded roughly in date to the stagnation in the
Lincolnshire Fenland in 1260–1300 and in south-eastern
England in 1250–92. None of these periods of stagnation and
decline correspond with the agrarian crisis of 1315–22. Why did
they happen? Population declined in the east Midlands because
assarting virtually stopped by 1250 and farming was in-
sufficiently progressive to cope with so many people. Late
marriage then reduced the number of peasants.

The east Midlands is a region where farming was both
conservative and progressive. This is clearest in Bedfordshire,
but clear enough over the whole region. Nottinghamshire,
Leicestershire and Hertfordshire grew oats; Northamptonshire
dredge, rye and oats; Huntingdonshire wheat and barley;
Bedfordshire dredge and wheat; and Buckinghamshire wheat
and oats. Legumes were important only in Nottinghamshire
and Huntingdonshire. Only at Wellingborough in 1258–1322
and on the Ramsey Abbey estates can we see what the
tendencies were and document change. In 1258 at
Wellingborough oats was the largest crop and there were few
beans and peas. By 1322 barley had dethroned oats and dredge
had become very important. Legumes had greatly multiplied
but were still not very popular. In 1292–1304 barley was also the
principal peasant crop, as was maslin at Higham Ferrers in 1313.
On the Ramsey Abbey estates all crops, especially oats, declined
in 1250–1350. Nottinghamshire drank cider, and Higham
Ferrers had a vineyard in 1313. Leicestershire, Northamptonshire, Huntingdonshire and Buckinghamshire ploughed with

oxen; only Bedfordshire used stots and affers. Sheep were numerous in Northamptonshire, Bedfordshire (especially towards the Chilterns), Buckinghamshire and Hertfordshire, and seem not to have been dairy animals. On the other hand milch kine, and the production of butter and cheese, were also important in Huntingdonshire, Northamptonshire, Buckinghamshire and Hertfordshire, and there were many cattle in the woods of Nottinghamshire. Swine were not very popular, even in Bedfordshire. Nottinghamshire had a great many, especially in the woods, but otherwise only at Wellingborough did their numbers rise and surpass the declining dairy herd. Goats existed only in Nottinghamshire. Farming seems to have improved in 1250–1350. Sheep- and cattle-rearing declined at Wellingborough, but cattle-rearing probably increased on the Ramsey Abbey estates in Huntingdonshire.[2]

3 TECHNIQUES – THE OPEN FIELDS

Open fields, in the sense of arable and meadow divided into strips scattered about the fields, certainly existed before 1086. In the east Midlands, in Buckinghamshire, there were eleven early, two-field crop rotations and one from after 1300 unkown to Gray. Buckinghamshire was still vigorously assarting in the two centuries after Domesday, but it had common-field crop rotations by the twelfth century at the latest and probably earlier. That, like Lincolnshire, it was at this early date largely a two-field county with a two-course crop rotation is most probable, though later it became predominantly a three-field county.

Buckinghamshire also provided an example of common pasture on the stubble, communally organized, earlier than 1240, and clearer than the Lincolnshire Fenland examples. At Stowe, an agreement of 1226 listed the Abbey of Osney, Ralph of Lamport, John son of Maurice and the men of Chackmore who had common in Stowe and Lamport, 'in the common field of Westleigh . . . when that field lies at fallow or uncultivated from fifteen days after the feast of Saint Michael to the Lord's Nativity'. Ralph granted the others common in Chackmore and Radclive on similar terms 'and in stubbles and in meadow after the corn and hay has been carried away.' Buckinghamshire may very well have practised communally controlled pasture on the fallow very early since it was one of the counties which had well-developed open fields in the tenth century.

There were many more open-field villages in the east Midlands than those known to Gray. Little early material can be added for Nottinghamshire and it seems unlikely that it ever had an early three-field system. For Rutland we can add one early-thirteenth-century three-field village. Northamptonshire was clearly a two-field county before 1300: to Gray's examples we must add two other two-field villages. Since Gray wrote, Bedfordshire has made seven additions to the list of early two-field villages, and one three-field addition in about 1235. Early Bedfordshire was therefore a county with two-field crop rotations. Hertfordshire was scarcely an orthodox open-field county at all, except round Hitchin, but it furnished an early two-field system in about 1200–10.

Villages which converted themselves from a two-field to a three-field crop rotation are well-known. In the east Midlands one was in Bedfordshire, two in Buckinghamshire, one in Leicestershire, eight in Northamptonshire. Often the change came very late. The three-course crop rotation was not very common before 1300 and rare before 1250. Some villages developed more flexible crop rotations which allowed a larger proportion of the arable to come under the plough each year. These were the *inhechinges* or *inhokes*, found in Huntingdonshire in 1290, where they had been the custom for twenty years past, and in Buckinghamshire in 1305 and 1311. Since there is no certain pre-Conquest evidence, therefore, the open fields in Killingholme in 1143–7 remain the earliest known example of a three-field crop rotation in England.

Of the altogether 669 known open-field villages in 1350 433 were two-field and 236 were three-field. The former therefore outnumbered the latter by almost two to one; before 1300 the ratio was higher than three to one. New three-field villages arose mainly in 1300–50 either by growth from two-field villages or as a result of new settlement. In all parts of England the newly appearing three-field villages predominated in this period over the two-field villages, but this predominance was greatest in the new-settlement areas. The counties where three fields were commonest in 1300 were Cambridgeshire, Nottinghamshire, Hampshire, the Isle of Wight, Derbyshire, Staffordshire and Yorkshire. In 1350 we may add Herefordshire. Huntingdonshire in 1350 had as many three-field as two-field villages. All these counties had a population growing very fast down to 1300 or 1350, and the people pressed hard upon the resources of the land. The northern counties in particular had much marginal land, but there was a lot of it also in Sherwood Forest in Nottinghamshire, the New Forest and other forests in Hampshire and round the edges of the fens in Cambridgeshire. The change to a three-field system was a symptom of population pressure and the need for more grain. There was less need for a three-field system in the comparatively stagnant counties of Dorset, Somerset and Wiltshire, but why did it not develop in the rapidly growing and densely settled counties of the west Midlands and southern England? The answer is that in these counties the two-field system developed more flexible crop rotations which allowed a larger proportion of the arable to come under the plough each year.[3]

4 TECHNIQUES – CROP NUTRITION

Some villages in Nottinghamshire seem to have been very short of manure. In Sherwood, in 1327, the tenants of a king's manor there might collect the leaves fallen from the trees in Clipston Park for manuring their lands. On the Abbot of Peterborough's manor of Kettering in Northamptonshire in 1294–5 there was a livery of oats for horses drawing manure and marl, and work went in carrying manure out of the sheepfold and yard, cleaning out the dovecote, and in spreading manure in the fields. The lord was not alone in possessing and using dung to fertilize his fields.

In the east Midlands there is good evidence of marling. There were marlpits in Nottingham itself in 1279, and at Cossall in Nottinghamshire in 1294 at least one peasant habitually marled his land. Northamptonshire had a marlpit in 1289–1340. On an estate of the Priory of Dunstable in Bedfordshire there was a marlpit in 1205–50, and on another manor, about 1240, the canons had newly-marled land above the heath. In Buckinghamshire marlpits occurred in 1228 and 1250. In 1210–11 the Bishop of Winchester marled 28.5 acres of land. In Hertfordshire in 1222 on an estate of St Paul's Cathedral there was marled land and William the Treasurer had marled 50 acres of land.[4]

5   THE LIFE OF THE PEOPLE –
THE PEASANT'S RESOURCES

Some Nottinghamshire peasants in the north were on the poverty line, but on balance the county had rather more half-bovaters (i.e. peasants with ten to twenty acres) than cottars, thus differing from Sussex. It may well have resembled some parts of neighbouring Lincolnshire. The evidence for an abundant small peasantry in Leicestershire, Rutland and Northamptonshire is neither very extensive nor entirely convincing; it must rely largely upon what emerges from the charters in the period before 1250. Even the charters are not so well-known, so abundant, or so early as those of Lincolnshire, Norfolk and Suffolk, but the combined evidence leaves little doubt that in these counties, and especially in the eastern parts of Northamptonshire, there was by the end of the thirteenth century a high percentage of smallholders. Bedfordshire had a peasant society in which the cottagers (under five acres) were an even larger class than the half-virgater (five to ten acres). In Bedfordshire he would possess not more than 7.5 acres of land, and in many Bedfordshire and Cambridgeshire villages there

were markedly more smallholdings among the freemen than
villeins. The fens of Cambridgeshire supported very many more
smallholders than the clays and sands of Bedfordshire. In the east
Midlands Huntingdonshire seems to have been unusual, for the
median holding was a half-virgate and there were many villein
virgaters. In Buckinghamshire smallholdings were more
numerous than half-virgates, and the median holding was a
quarter-virgate.

In Bedfordshire the Lay Subsidy Roll of 1297 covers three
hundreds and the four towns of Bedford, Luton, Dunstable and
Leighton Buzzard. In Barford hundred each family had in stock
as surplus grain for sale under ten bushels of wheat, over one
bushel of barley, under ten bushels of oats, under one bushel of
rye, under four bushels of dredge and under one bushel of
legumes. This would barely suffice for one woman's diet for a
year. Every family had fewer than two sheep; every two families
one stot, three cattle, and less than one pig; every three families
one other horse; and every eleven families rather more than four
oxen. The hundred was not great stock-rearing country.

In Biggleswade hundred every family had more than ten
bushels of wheat, one-fifth of a bushel of barley, under four
bushels of oats, less than three and a half bushels of rye, under
fourteen bushels of dredge and over two bushels of legumes.
This surplus was almost enough to keep one man in bread for a
year. Every two families had one affer, one other horse, and
eleven sheep; every three families one ox; every four families
five cows; and every five families two swine. These people were
also very poor in stock, but had more sheep to the family than
the men of Barford.

In the hundred of Flitt each family had more than a quarter of
wheat, nearly a bushel of barley, under four bushels of oats,
nearly a bushel of rye, about six and a half bushels of dredge and
three bushels of legumes. This would feed a boy for a year. On
average every family had more than five sheep; every two
families one stot and three cattle; every four families one pig;
and every seven families a little more than two oxen. These
people were especially poor in pigs.

There were 1051 peasants assessed to the subsidy in these three hundreds, of whom 820 had goods and chattels worth less than one pound. The lords owned most of the oxen and the peasants most of the stots. Fourteen settlements, half of them riverside settlements in Barford hundred, had no peasant oxen. Most peasant oxen were the property of peasants assessed at one to three pounds, and few belonged to peasants worth less than one pound. Peasant oxen were unevenly distributed, and a high proportion were in three villages. Half-virgaters did not generally possess more than one plough-beast and therefore had to co-operate with neighbours to form a ploughteam. About 22.2 per cent of the peasants had no cows, and of those who were luckier, seven out of eight had only one beast, and only two had three beasts. The peasant's milk supply was not excessive. According to the Wellingborough figures, most households would have ninety-one pounds of butter and cheese a year, or under six ounces a head each week. This is not very much by modern standards. Sheep were not a major interest of the peasantry, since only 32.6 per cent had any at all. Sheep-farming in medieval Bedfordshire was primarily an interest of ecclesiastical lords.

Peasant wealth in the four towns was not very different. Every family had on average about one and a half quarters of wheat, two quarters of dredge, nearly two bushels of barley, nearly one quarter of oats, over a bushel of legumes and small quantities of rye and maslin. This was enough surplus grain to feed one man with bread for a year. Since this was no better than in several country areas, it suggests that there were no more corn-factors in these towns than in the countryside. Every family had on average five sheep; every five families three affers and two pigs; every six families an ox; and every fifteen families one other horse.

Very occasionally the sources allow a picture of the peasant's goods and chattels. An inventory of 1293 valued a dead man's chattels at 33s. 8d.; it said that he owned a bolster, a rug, two sheets, a brass dish and a trivet. At Chalgrove, in Bedfordshire, in 1279, when customary tenants died the lord took the best cloth as a heriot when they had no animals. Tenants of eight acres could lack animals entirely. A vagrant who died at Tebworth, in Bedfordshire, in 1279, lawfully made his will and left the vicar his surcoat and his sister a cow.

6 THE LIFE OF THE PEOPLE –
INHERITANCE CUSTOMS

Partible inheritance was not very common in the east Midlands. On the whole Nottinghamshire was a county of small peasants, many of them sokemen, and had become increasingly so since the Domesday Survey. In 1250–1300 the tendency towards smallholdings was very marked, and the result of partible inheritance. Two examples of divisible tenements date from 1296 and affect eight tenants.

About 1295 the Dean and Chapter of York Minster made extents of the prebends of the church. At West Burton, near Gainsborough, out of forty holdings the commonest holding, eleven of which cottars held, was under one acre, and the median holding was three to five acres. Of the forty tenants twenty were joint holders and of these six held very small holdings. Quite apart from these there were several relatives amongst the joint holders. At Bole in 1280–1301 the social structure was similar. The median holding was again of three to five acres. The smallness of the holdings partly resulted from the existence of joint holdings. Out of twenty-seven tenants thirteen held partibly, but none of the joint holdings was exceedingly small. Some Nottinghamshire villages had a good many smallholdings, and half of the tenants were tenants of joint holdings.

Three Hertfordshire manors of St Paul's Cathedral were in a new-settlement region in 1222. At Caddington one of twenty-eight free tenants held jointly, but joint tenancies were commoner amongst the cottars. These cottars seem in reality to have been virgaters holding jointly. At Kensworth seventeen out of fifty-nine tenants held partibly, and out of thirty-eight

Dunstable tenants who held land in Kensworth eleven did likewise.

The east Midlands was partly conservative, and partly progressive in its agriculture and was becoming more progressive in the century before the Black Death. This is especially true if we look at the changes from two-field to three-field crop rotations and the generally late occurrence of three-course rotations. This, and the frequent use of manure, with the practice of marling the land, especially new assarts, shows that more intensive methods of agriculture came into vogue in the fourteenth century. Except in parts of Nottinghamshire and in Buckinghamshire the typical peasant had a half virgate – sufficient, with the common, to supply all his wants – and the peasants of Huntingdonshire were even richer. These factors are sufficient to account for the new rise in population in 1280–1312. After 1312 what happened is less clear.[5]

CHAPTER 7
SOUTHERN ENGLAND

1 NEW SETTLEMENT AND POPULATION GROWTH

In southern England no new-settlement place-names occurred in the records for the first time after 1350 in Berkshire, Hampshire, Wiltshire and Dorset, and only one each in Somerset and the Isle of Wight. In 1281–1350 two occurred for the first time in Dorset, four each in Berkshire and Wiltshire, six in the Isle of Wight, seven in Hampshire and nine in Somerset. In 1086, southern England was less fully developed than eastern and south-eastern England and the east Midlands, so that new settlement continued there much longer. This was particularly true of Somerset, which is a highland zone county, but true also of Hampshire and the Isle of Wight.

Most of the Berkshire assarts were in the Kennet-Loddon Vales and the Thames Valley, and there was a little assarting early and late in the thirteenth century. A few early-twelfth-century assarts occurred in the central downland and in Bagley and Cumnor Woods. In the thirteenth century assarts existed in the Vale of the White Horse, in the central downland, and in the far south-west corner of Berkshire under Inkpen Beacon.

In the considerable forests of Hampshire there was a great deal of activity. Monastic clearances were very extensive and went on late. In 1171–82 Waverley Abbey cleared 17,640 acres of forest. Monastic assarts continued on a smaller scale into the thirteenth and fourteenth centuries in Aliceholt, Wolmer Forest and the New Forest.

Late assarts came into existence in Wiltshire in 1281–1350. The Wiltshire place-name survey of 1939 has 101 clearings. This is not a very great density of clearings – less than half of that for Hertfordshire. Twenty-one clearings already existed by 1086 and forty-two were not recorded until after 1280, twenty-two of them after 1350. Clearances before 1190 were few in number, and progress began late.

Wiltshire shows a few signs of extensive assarting round Chippenham, in the forest, but only a little took place elsewhere. Three Wiltshire assarts date from the eleventh and twelfth centuries. In 1066–87 the Thames Valley, near Cricklade had two assarts. In 1179 the nuns of Amesbury were assarting in the Avon Valley, north of Salisbury. An assart and an *inhok* existed near Devizes in 1196. Much greater assarts than these seem to have grown on the estates of Stanley Abbey, near Chippenham, in the thirteenth century. By 1203–4 the monks had assarted 13,340 acres and they were still at it in 1227 and 1304.

Most of the assarts of Malmesbury Abbey were where the Cotswolds fall to the clay vale, in the north-west of Wiltshire, and they date mainly from 1262–97. Both the abbey and the burgesses of the guild merchant of Malmesbury were assarting three miles from the town on Burntheath. At Brokenborough, near Malmesbury, the abbey made an agreement with neighbouring villages which were making *inhocs*. The abbey had been assarting the land on the Down a generation before, but the inadequacy of the Wiltshire two-course crop rotation had led to the introduction of the *inhoc*.

Long Newnton already existed as a new settlement in 681. Three miles away is Ashley, 'the ash clearing', first recorded in 1086. The two villages and their lords agreed that the abbot would not cultivate the land of Newnton between Newnton and Ashley unless he had done so anciently. The agreement defined the commons and laid down that the tenants could only make an *inhoc* with the consent of both villages. This again was a very tightly controlled economy. Other assarts existed in the Cotswolds.

Small assarts, perhaps an illicit encroachment, existed on a Glastonbury Abbey manor near Chippenham, in 1189. Others held legal assart, at a low rent, probably in small individual holdings. Another Wiltshire manor of the Abbey of Glastonbury was assarting the heath in 1297. Late assarts certainly existed in Wiltshire, but they are not well documented. There was assarting in Selwood Forest, in 1283. In 1348 Queen Philippa held assart in the Forest of Chippenham. Wiltshire may have been assarting from the waste just before the Black Death.

Little is known about assarting in Dorset. Before 1178 Alfred of Lincoln marled and cultivated a marsh. This is typical treatment of marginal land and an early example of marling. Waverley Abbey had assart in the Forest of Ashley in 1246.

The name 'Somerset' means 'summer settlers' in the heart of the country, the wild levels in which Alfred took refuge from the Danes in 878. Permanent settlements with summer islands in the fen later became the earliest settlements. By 1086 the coastal belt of clay and silt was better developed than the inner moors which Domesday says rendered nothing. Four great churches held the bulk of the Somerset levels – Glastonbury, Wells, Athelney and Muchelney. By 1126 Glastonbury land by the river Axe was bearing crops. Between the hills near Axbridge the people enclosed eight acres of moor in 1135–54. In six other villages meadows existed in the moors by 1189, usually in five-acre lots. By 1238–60 there had been a considerable advance. In three villages at least fifty-two holdings, of which thirty-four contained 156 acres, existed in the moor. In another village, in 1260, tenants held 108 acres of meadow, and in 1272 there were at least forty-five acres of assarts.

The three island villages of Weston Zoyland, Middlezoy and Othery merit a little more attention. These linked villages were the richest of the Abbot of Glastonbury's holdings in the levels proper, and north and south of the islands on which they stood were many enclosures. In 1238–60 the three villages had in the moors 733 acres of meadow in 177 holdings. In 1238 the abbot had created an extra eighty holdings of meadow from 253.5 acres of moor. At High Ham, near the edge of the levels, assarting continued in 1235–52 and in 1252–61 the west field of one village consisted partly of assarts.

Several late assarting agreements have come down to us. In one village, in 1260, the lord agreed to enclose and dyke his land in the 'wolf's clearing'. Elsewhere, in 1273, the new-settlement nature of the holdings mentioned is fairly clear, whether from down, fen or wood, and the existence of a meadow in the west field, and a wood in the east field typifies the diversity and piecemeal creation of the open fields in many parts of England and Wales.

In and around Glastonbury itself extensive assarts continued until the end of the thirteenth century. A new assart and new meadow existed in 1276. An agreement between the abbey and a tenant in 1294 recites the names of at least ten of the abbey's improvements in Glastonbury and looks forward to the tenant enclosing at least another twenty acres and to the abbey enclosing more land from the moor.

Various types of assarting took place in substantial areas and several parts of Somerset. In 1233–4 the Dean and Chapter of Wells enclosed Stathe Wood, meadowland towards the wood, and part of Saltmoor. Elsewhere, in south Somerset, in 1235–7 the Bishop of Bath and Wells allowed a neighbour to cultivate 103 acres of land, in return for permission to cultivate the adjoining Bishop's Den, outside Bishop's Wood. This is a typical agreement over common rights of the type so often behind the creation of open fields. New settlement continued in the Mendip Hills and in the Axe Valley in 1248–9 and 1253–4. The Dean and Chapter of Wells were assarting in 1227, and in 1263 they began to enclose twenty-two named meadows in 800 acres of moor east of Taunton. Muchelney Abbey also enclosed 100 acres of moor, and in 1327–8 the Dean and Chapter of Wells arranged with the Abbot of Glastonbury to enclose the northern moors not far from Wells.

The contrast between new settlement in the levels, and in the other parts of this varied county, is therefore pretty plain, but we know little about such activities in the Mendips or on Exmoor. Even in the Somerset levels there seems to have been little new settlement before the thirteenth century. Somerset was not scantily settled in 1086, but neither did it have a superabundant population adjacent to extensive fens and marshes, of the sort found in highland Lincolnshire and Norfolk, or in the coastal regions of Kent and Sussex.

The Shaftesbury Abbey surveys show stagnation and decline in recorded population between 1106 and 1144 on some of the abbey's estates in Dorset and Wiltshire, but the evidence is not very good, and the surveys are very difficult to handle. Expansion in recorded population slowed down in Wiltshire in 1189–1252 and 1260–80. Somerset's population grew fairly rapidly in 1086–1189, but stagnation and decline characterized one-third of the Glastonbury Abbey manors in 1189–1252. On the other hand, in the Hampshire forests in the two centuries after 1086, various groups of manors grew 350, 433, 366 and 1900 per cent. In the early-fourteenth century the bulk of the Wiltshire evidence dominates southern English demography, and here quite definitely there was stagnation on two, and decline on ten of the twenty manors for which there is comparative material. One Dorset manor also declined between 1235 and 1326. In most parts of southern England expansion was still the rule right down to 1350, and the same differences in speed of expansion exist in the fourteenth as in the thirteenth century. Particularly slow growth took place on eleven Berkshire manors which grew by three-quarters in 1086–1308, one Wiltshire manor which grew by 6 per cent in 1086–1326, one which grew by 25 per cent in 1086–1315, and one Dorset manor which grew by 33 per cent in 1086–1315. On the other hand the fourteenth-century population was double or treble the 1086 population in Berkshire (six manors), Hampshire (six manors) and Wiltshire (112 manors). Five manors in Somerset grew very fast indeed.

Counts of heads of households in 1086 exist for 319 manors. By equal cohorts, and after scaling to adjust the weight of each county to its Domesday proportion, in the five periods 1086–1148, 1086–1237, 1086–1287, 1086–1311 and 1086–1328 the percentage increases in population were 169, 218, 379, 255 and 306. The Domesday population had more than doubled by 1237 and remained more than treble in 1328. After a fast increase in 1086–1148 there followed a moderate increase in 1148–1237, and a very fast increase in 1237–87, which almost brought the population to quadruple the Domesday figure. In 1287–1311 there was a fast decline, but a rapid increase in 1311-28 made up rather under half of the losses. By comparison, the period of decline in the east Midlands (1244-80) came a generation earlier; the period of stagnation in south-eastern England (1260-92) was also earlier.

Berkshire witnessed the fewest developments after 1086; Hampshire and the Isle of Wight were the quickest growing counties in 1086-1350. Berkshire and Hampshire were also expanding their population very rapidly, and there is no real evidence that holdings became very small. In between came Wiltshire, Dorset and Somerset. Population grew quite rapidly in Wiltshire in 1086-1350, and in some parts of Somerset very rapidly. Holdings were small in Somerset, but sufficient in Wiltshire. In all parts of the region the forest lands and the fens were the types of countryside in which there was the fastest growth over the longest period, but compared with other parts of England development was slow and steady rather than dramatic. Southern England achieved neither the rapid development from a very poor base which was characteristic of the North, of Wales and the Marches, nor the early development, from a good start to an advanced economic stage which was characteristic of eastern England, and much of south-eastern England and the east Midlands. On the whole the South was rather backward and sometimes rather poor.[1]

2 CROPS AND LIVESTOCK

Eight Berkshire manors have supplied information about crops and livestock. In 1189 and 1235-52 sheep were by far the most important livestock on a manor of Glastonbury Abbey. In 1210-11 on two out of three manors of the bishopric of Winchester, wheat was by far the largest crop, and oats the second crop. On the third manor maslin was the first crop, followed by oats. Legumes were non-existent or insignificant. On all three oxen were much more numerous than affers and on two manors swine exceeded cattle. These two manors also had moderate flocks of sheep. The third manor had no cattle or swine and few sheep. Two manors made cheese, one cider, and one manor had geese. On two St Paul's Cathedral manors in 1222 sheep, cattle, swine, oxen and horses was the order of precedence of the stock. Two other manors were, in 1288–9, wheat and barley manors and one of these had a good crop of beans.

In 1288–9 three Hampshire manors were predominantly barley-growing with wheat and oats as major secondary crops, little or no rye, and some legumes. Conditions elsewhere in Hampshire were very different. The manors of the Bishop of Winchester furnish ample early evidence of the state of agriculture in Hampshire in 1210–11. The first point to note about the grain is the great dearth of legumes compared with any other region at later periods so far studied. Insufficient legumes were grown to have any effect upon the fertility of those estates. Oats was the leading crop on fourteen of the bishop's manors in Hampshire. These oats-growing woodland manors also possessed many sheep and, on the whole, few milch kine. Everywhere there were enormous numbers of oxen – far more than usually considered necessary on the greatest monastic estates – and very few affers. Cattle on the whole were used for draught purposes. Milch kine were significant only on six manors, twelve other manors having only casual milch kine or none at all. None the less nearly every manor made cheese in large quantities, and the bishop sold most of this in what was clearly a very good market. Since many manors had no dairy cattle, and since there are several positive statements to prove it, the cheeses were quite clearly ewe's milk cheeses – the sign of a poor economy – whereas elsewhere in England at a later date manors made a great deal of cheese and butter from cow's milk. Even in Hampshire, however, the four greatest cheese manors also had important herds of milch kine.

From cheeses there is a natural progression to sheep. The flocks were generally very large and sometimes immense, 1000–1500 sheep on each of five manors. There were no sheep at one manor and fewer than 100 at another. Sheep were without doubt the greatest factor, together with oats, in Hampshire farming. Swine were significant: though absent from six manors, they were in general popular. The woodlands of Hampshire doubtless played a part in this popularity but swine (like other animals) also benefited from the great crops of oats. Horses were uncommon. Only one manor had any considerable number of affers, but there were wild horses, sometimes bought from Wales, at Bishopstoke, Marden and Twyford.

Altogether, therefore, this was a poor pastoral economy. Oats and sheep with a few cattle and swine were its chief products. The early date is partly responsible for this difference, but so is the poor woodland region – still settling fast – which was so different from the east Midlands. This difference means that it would be dangerous to generalize from the Winchester estates to the whole of England.

Further information for the year 1338 comes from the compotus roll of the Winchester Cathedral manor of Wootton or Manydown, in Hampshire. Oats, barley (including bere) and wheat were the major crops and there was little to choose between them. Legumes at less than a sixth of any one of these major crops were negligible in quantity. The peasantry grew twice as much barley as wheat and oats. Oxen were more popular than affers, swine much more so than milch kine, and sheep very numerous. There were peacocks, fowls and geese, and, in 1210, 400 little doves. The dairying interests of the demesne farm also deserve notice. Winter milk, probably in the form of cheese, brought in twenty pence. The manor made summer cheese at the rate of a cheese a day. The manor used or delivered to the receiver over half of these and sold the rest. The cheeses seemingly varied in weight but were never less than four pounds. The manor also made and sold butter, the milk for which apparently came mainly from a flock of ewes. In addition there were eggs from the Easter render of the peasants.

It is difficult to form a general impression of Dorset farming, but wheat and sheep seem to have been usual, with some preference for cattle (probably to make cheeses) over swine, in the later period, but in 1086 swine came before cattle.

In Wiltshire wheat-growing and dairying accompanied enormous flocks of sheep. One manor specialized in dairying and poultry-raising. Barley was the first crop, followed by wheat, rye and oats. There were in stock horses, a very large herd of cattle and over 600 sheep. The dairy produced large amounts of cheese and butter. The poultry in stock were peafowl, swans, geese, chickens and doves, and there were 5000 eggs. Another manor had on average, in 1272–87, over 2500 sheep not lying in the countess's fold over the winter. On a third manor in 1296 the order of size of yields was wheat, barley, dredge, vetches and *drenia* (perhaps also dredge). In stock there were horses, oxen and over 1700 sheep. The dairy produced cheeses and butter, and since no cows were recorded ewe's milk must have been the basic product.

The normal stock which leaseholders received on eight manors in the twelfth century was nearly 1800 sheep, 167 oxen, twenty swine, five affers and one cow. There was also cider. The demesne economy had room for little else but sheep amongst its stock, apart from sufficient oxen to maintain the arable. On another manor in 1235–52 the miller had 100 sheep. Sheep were therefore important in Wiltshire for the prosperous. On a very large number of lay manors in 1243–50 oxen greatly exceeded affers in numbers, and cattle, though comparatively few, outnumbered swine. Sheep were very many: there was pasture for flocks of 1000 in 1274 and for 1200 in 1300 and altogether pasture for nearly 27,000 in the county.

Some inquisitions describe the farm-buildings. On one manor in 1258:

there is there a certain longhouse in the place of a hall, and one room in one head, and another room in another head, and one outer room and one cowhouse, of the court and two small barns, and one sheepfold upon the hills, and all the said houses are old and in a bad state.

On another in 1257

in the court of the said manor there is one hall, two rooms at one head of the hall near the land, and one room on the upper floor, and a cellar underneath in another head, two barns, one cowhouse, one kitchen, and a stable, and they are sufficient and in good condition.

At yet another in 1257

in the court of the said manor there is one hall and one room with a wardrobe in one head near the land, and in another head there are two sollars with a wardrobe and two cellars; also one kitchen for brewing and baking, also one dairy, also one house for a stable in one head, and in another head is the granary; also one house for pressing [i.e. cider or cheese]; also two barns, one cowhouse, one sheepfold, and one henhouse: all the said houses are fit and sufficient.

There was a garden with fruit, a curtilage with a vine, and a watermill with several fisheries.

The few other descriptions of manor-houses and their outhouses are later. In 1328 a lady's assignment of dower consisted of one-third of the manor house, that is

the middle chamber over the granary and larder, the grange and larder, that chamber called Cokayne, and the grange called Ouerberne, as it is bounded, with the house called the 'Carthous', and another called 'la Couhous'.

Besides this there were two pigsties, an ox-shed, one-third of a croft where the sheepfold was, a third of the garden and a third of the dovecote. Elsewhere the same lady had a chamber next to the chapel of St Andrew on the west, with chimney and wardrobe, covered with tiles, and with a loom; the solar set above it abutting south on the highway; the little grange next to it west of the chapel; the granary on the south opposite its door; the south grange in the barton, the garden, pighouse, one-third of the sheepfold and the cony-warren. Another manor in 1350 consisted of a hall, chamber, chapel roofed with stone, kitchen, bakehouse, brewhouse in a ruinous state, oxhouse, stable, and all other houses, except the grange, ruinous.

Adam of Stratton's manor of Sevenhampton with Stratton provides striking confirmation of the interests of Wiltshire demesne farming during the second half of the thirteenth century. In the two periods 1269–79 and 1280–7 the lord sowed more land with wheat than with barley and oats together. He planted slightly smaller areas with wheat in the period 1280–7, and slightly larger areas of barley, but only three-quarters of the area with oats. In all there was a slight contraction in the area of the arable. The actual crops obtained showed a sizeable decrease in the corn yield by about one-fifth between 1269–79 and 1280–7. A rise in the flocks of sheep, and a constant herd of cattle, accompanied the great decline in grain.

Both horses and oxen became slightly less numerous as the arable contracted, and swine existed in large numbers only in 1269–70 and 1279–82. The most interesting stock development was the sudden start of large-scale dairy-farming. The lord made the conversion at one stroke in 1274–5 by purchasing forty-two cattle. In both periods the manor sold most of its cheese and all of its butter. Some of the cheeses were rowen cheeses, that is, cheeses made from milk derived from cows that pastured upon the stubble after Michaelmas. The manor sold them all. The production of butter by each cow was stable over the whole period, and came in each half to slightly less than one gallon a year. The production of cheese per cow rose over the same period from over seven a head to under nine a head, supposing that the sizes of the cheese remained constant. Dairying was clearly an increasingly profitable activity. There were also a few other profitable sidelines, such as the production in 1269–70 of ninety-one gallons of cider (all sold), or the fattening in 1269–83 of pigs for the market in the winter.

Wiltshire therefore appears as a great sheep and wheat county, with some interest in dairying but little in breeding horses, raising swine or growing legumes. On the whole it was a backward area which grew a great deal of oats, used mainly oxen and produced low yields. None the less there is no evidence of deteriorating conditions caused by over-population and grain monoculture with insufficient manure.

After 1086 the earliest material for the study of Somerset farming on the estates of Glastonbury Abbey is for the year 1189. The account of stock normally found on sixteen manors leased out really gives details of stock actually in the hands of the lessees at the time of the survey. The information is pretty meagre, but coupled with statements about what should be there or was there at a previous time gives a curious picture. Oxen and other cattle were the only beasts which existed in numbers in the hands of the lessees. There were a few swine but very few sheep. On fourteen manors there are also details of what 'could be' or formerly was there, from which we can deduce the missing stock. Cattle and sheep seem to be missing, so that swine, originally barely more important than cattle and sheep, though not so numerous as elsewhere in Somerset, made their presence felt. Five of the manors were well farmed but on others water was a difficulty, and one manor could not keep sheep since they died, probably of liver fluke.

On four manors we know the stock of grain in the barns and the land sown with grain. Wheat and oats were the largest grain crops, but on two manors beans was by far the largest crop in stock; perhaps the Abbot of Glastonbury gathered the beans from all his estates into these barns. For Glastonbury we have the crop evidence derived from an account of the grain received on 27 September 1287 for making the convent ale. The grain available dictated, to a large extent, what went into the ale and more than half of it was oats. Monks did not drink bad ale if they could avoid it, and much of this would go for the servants' use. Oats was therefore the principal grain on seventeen Somerset manors of Glastonbury Abbey in 1287.

We also know the stints of stock in eleven villages. Sheep were a major interest, and cattle and swine were almost equally well-favoured. Swine, in particular, were notably more common than in Wiltshire. In 1210–11 on the Bishop of Winchester's great composite manor of Taunton, away from the marshland and typical of a tract of low-lying country mostly under 400 feet above sea-level, with mainly light, freeworking, stoneless loams, oats was by far the largest crop and there was a great surplus of it in the barn. Wheat followed, and barley and peas were negligible. The peasantry grew wheat and rye. The record of acres sown splits the crops between the constituent members of the manor of Taunton, eleven in number. Three grew no wheat, only two grew barley and only one peas. The area of wheat exceeded that of barley at two places only, and equalled it in one. At one place the areas under wheat and oats were nearly equal and exceeded those elsewhere. Oxen were much more numerous than horses, and swine and cattle were of similar status. The number of sheep was very small, and the cheeses may therefore have been made from cow's milk, since they were a major item in the account. There were thirty-one sticks of eels (775) from the fishpond and the millpond.

Altogether Somerset was a most varied county with a strong emphasis on sheep, a fair number of cattle, comparatively few horses, plenty of oats, and, in places, a fair amount of wheat. Swine were much more favoured than in Wiltshire but otherwise the characteristics of the two counties are not very different. The economy was everywhere very mixed but in both areas sheep and oats as a rule predominated.[2]

In southern England the population nearly quadrupled in 1086–1287, by which latter date new settlement had virtually ceased. Development was later than in other parts of England, and the decline in population – 1287–1311 – also came later. As in the east Midlands the growth in population started again in 1311 and continued till about 1328, but the recovery did not make up for the losses of 1287–1311. This recovery took place right over the agrarian crisis of 1315–22. Why did it occur?

Berkshire, Dorset and Wiltshire grew mainly wheat; Hampshire and Somerset mainly oats; the peasants of the great composite manor of Taunton in Somerset wheat and rye. None of these counties grew many legumes, even at Manydown in Hampshire in 1338, except that in 1189 certain of the Abbot of Glastonbury's Somerset manors had immense quantities of beans in store. Beans were certainly well-known in southern England, since the Domesday manors of Binstead, in the Isle of Wight, Binstead in Hampshire and Bicknoll in Wiltshire take their names from this crop, as do Bincombe in Dorset and Binegar in Somerset, first recorded in 987 and 1065 respectively. They were apparently seldom grown after 1189. Berkshire, Wiltshire and Somerset also made cider, and Wiltshire and Somerset wine. Somerset also grew flax, hemp, garlic, leeks and pears. Berkshire, Hampshire, Wiltshire and Somerset all used oxen and had few horses. Hampshire and Wiltshire had a few cattle, and occasional manors made butter and cheese from cow's milk. This was especially true of Sevenhampton in Wiltshire after 1274. Generally a large number of cheeses came from ewe's milk, particularly on the Winchester estates. Throughout southern England there were immense flocks of sheep. In some parts of Berkshire and Dorset and on the Winchester estates in Hampshire, swine were numerous.

Tendencies are fairly clear. Dr Titow has demonstrated a fall in yield ratios on many of the Winchester estates over the entire thirteenth century, and an equally convincing rise in yield ratios over the first half of the fourteenth century. He has not connected this rise to the steady unspectacular rise in the crops of beans and peas over the whole period, but perhaps this should be done. Both on the Winchester estates and at Sevenhampton in 1269–87 the arable contracted, the lord introduced dairy-farming with cows and increased the size of his sheep flocks. The Crowland and Peterborough Abbey estates in Lincolnshire and Northamptonshire had the same experience. Farming was backward in southern England, but may have improved enough to encourage earlier marriages and an increase in population.

3 TECHNIQUES – THE OPEN FIELDS

Gores, gore-acres, furrows, furlongs and headlands appeared in a number of places in Berkshire in 903–83. In 982 five *cassati* (housed, and therefore married, slaves) were on common land 'everywhere very little divided by boundaries since the yokes lie together joined each to the other'. Land in 956 and 958, lay 'acre under acre'. In 961, nine hides lay intermixed with the land of others in the common fields and meadows. The four manses in the common land in 983 seem to have been standard tenements, akin to the virgates and bovates of 1086. Descriptions of open fields in Hampshire, Dorset and Wiltshire take them back to 870.

Wiltshire, Dorset and Somerset furnish open-field material on a very large scale. In Wiltshire there were fourteen early two-field villages. There are no new early three-field villages to record, but there were twenty-six late two-field systems. In 1329 two manors had more than three fields. Three villages seem to have changed from two-course to three-course crop rotations in 1249–1349. There are three new examples of two-field villages from Dorset, but no early three-field systems. Somerset, which offers much less information for the period 1300–50, was overwhelmingly a two-field county, with eighteen early two-field villages and only four late-recorded three-field villages. In these examples two-thirds or more of the land was sown, and the evidence is therefore about a crop rotation, not about the number of fields. Two villages changed crop rotations. The same is true of Berkshire. There are two new examples of early open fields, but one manor in 1327 and 1331 had five fields.

The practice of taking *inhokes* was most common in southern England and the west Midlands, particularly, but by no means entirely, where there was a two-course crop rotation. We have a Hampshire example from 1265–6, a Berkshire example from 1235–52, three Somerset examples from 1259–60 and two Wiltshire examples from the thirteenth century.[3]

4 TECHNIQUES – CROP NUTRITION

In 1222, at High Wycombe, in Berkshire, the Abbess of Godstow's men tried to build up dung-hills before their front doors and Basset's men came and carted the dung away and spread it on his demesne lands. In Berkshire in 1235–52 on an estate of Glastonbury Abbey, the reeve had one acre of wheat of the lord's corn, except manure and folding.

In 1189–99 the Prior of the Abbey of Abingdon was an improving landlord and 'All the land, which was very bad and unfruitful, both this side of the water and beyond, he made very good and fruitful, by manuring it with the earth which is commonly called "marl".' On an estate of the church of Winchester, in Berkshire, in 1210–11, the lord marled twenty-six acres; in the Isle of Wight, the canons of Christchurch, in 1272, marled all their lands. Two Hampshire manors of the Bishop of Winchester practised marling in 1210–11.

In Somerset in 1334 Taunton Priory had common in the marlpit. Elsewhere in Somerset there are several good references to marling on the estates of the larger monasteries. The Glastonbury villeins, in 1235–52, sometimes had to marl and cart five heaps a day to be quit. In 1225–50 St Mary of Ilminster and the Abbey of Muchelney received land from a donor who reserved the right to marl from the marlpit on the land. About 1220, another donor gave the Hospitallers as much marl throughout all his land as he ever had, wherever they could find it. On the Bishop of Winchester's great manor of Taunton in 1210–11 there were twenty-two marlers.

One of the labour services in Wiltshire, in about 1230, was that the peasant should marl if there was any to do. Such a labour service was unusual and the conditional clause is noteworthy. Two Wiltshire marlpits are known from 1230–40 and 1242. In 1210–11 the Bishop of Winchester marled fifteen acres on two Wiltshire manors and paid the wages of four marlers for a year, and of four marlers for half a year. Marling was expensive and the area marled not very great.

There are several mentions of lime in England in the thirteenth century but only one explicitly states that it was spread on the land. In Berkshire, in 1235, a donor granted the Templars all his assart that he made in his wood for liming.[4]

5 THE LIFE OF THE PEOPLE –
THE PEASANT'S RESOURCES

The evidence is slight and conflicting in Berkshire, and scanty in Hampshire. What there is in Hampshire argues against the existence of many smallholders. In Wiltshire, in the earlier period, the virgate-holder was the most numerous class of tenant on most manors, and on some manors the median holding was the virgate. Yet throughout the county at all times from 1189 to the 1330s the median holding was most generally a half-virgate and manors with multitudes of smallholders were not numerous. At all times too there were some rich peasants with over sixty acres of land, and these were most prominent in 1189 on the Glastonbury estates. Later on, and elsewhere, they were less common, the general movement being towards mediocrity in the size of holdings. There is not enough Dorset material for elaborate comparisons, and there was a certain amount of divergence between manors, but the indications are that the county was like Wiltshire. All over Somerset in 1189–1287 the quarter-virgate was the commonest and median holding. Following the same tendency towards mediocrity as in contemporary Wiltshire, Somerset went in for smaller holdings. None the less, even the Levels were far from the state of *morcellement* found in eastern and south-eastern England.

A Somerset example in 1237–8 casts a little light upon the actual possessions of the peasantry. At South Brent there were two *wikarii*, or tenants of outlying wicks or farms, probably in the moor, named Thomas of Wick and Philip of Wick, one of whom held five acres and the other a ferling or quarter of a yardland, which here contained forty acres. Each had fifty breeding ewes and twelve cows. At Berrow, Agnes Baron likewise held a ferling and fifty breeding ewes and twelve cows for the wick and there were two other *wikarii*. At Lympsham there were three wicks, one of which the whole manor held. The parson had with the lord's cattle six oxen, one affer, twelve cattle, thirteen swine and five fowls.

6 THE LIFE OF THE PEOPLE –
INHERITANCE CUSTOMS

There is very little satisfactory evidence of partible inheritance in southern England. In 1265–6, on the manor of Linkenholt, in Hampshire, five pairs of tenants, not apparently related, held five virgates.

Southern England was rather an unprogressive region, but agriculture was slowly improving. Generally speaking, two-course crop rotations were in vogue, and villages modified them by making *inhokes*. Slowly an interest in legumes was developing, and there was some marling and manuring. There was virtually no partible inheritance and marriage may therefore have been very late. Holdings were generally half-virgates, sometimes virgates and only in Somerset quarter-virgates. Somerset had great reserves of fen, moor and heath, and greater opportunities for hunting, fowling, fishing and pastoralism. Even Somerset could not exhibit great hordes of cottagers. In 1086 the whole region had been smallholder country, full of slaves and *cassati*. Though not poorly developed in 1086 southern England had derived great benefits from the coming of greater freedom. A similar change had taken place earlier in eastern England, with the result that eastern England enjoyed a precocious maturity. The pressure upon land was never so great in southern England that innovation in agriculture became essential. When it came innovation was slow and unspectacular. Ironically, this is the region of the Postan thesis.

CHAPTER 8

THE WEST MIDLANDS

1 NEW SETTLEMENT AND POPULATION GROWTH

In the west Midlands, no new-settlement place-names occurred in the records for the first time after 1350 in Warwickshire and Derbyshire, only one each in Worcestershire, Gloucestershire and Oxfordshire, and two in Staffordshire. In 1281–1350 one each occurred in Warwickshire and Oxfordshire, two each in Worcestershire and Gloucestershire, three in Derbyshire and five in Staffordshire. The west Midlands was not nearly so backward in new settlement as southern England, and most of the late new settlements were in or near the southern Pennines.

Staffordshire's development was very extensive both before and after 1086. Already in 1143–8 the Empress Matilda could grant St Mary of Radmore a forest-clearing on Cannock Chase, and by 1169–70 the Cistercian Abbey of Combermere in Cheshire had assarted 1340 acres of the waste.

Four villages on the flanks of Cannock Chase, not far from Lichfield, were assarting in 1208–9. Twenty men of Osney Abbey held assarts by 1254–67 and in about 1270 the canons of Osney were assarting and building cowsheds, sheepfolds and other buildings. Much of the land grew oak woods, but there were several marshes. Assarters with Old English names had already been at work in 1150–2. In 1175 Stratton Heath came under cultivation. In 1114–50 there was an assart on the Needwood Forest side of Burton-on-Trent.

Late assarting took place all over Staffordshire, but is found to the greatest extent in the Black Country and the Forests of Morfe and Kinver, in the far south, bordering Worcestershire, in and around Cannock Chase, and in Needwood Forest. The Forest of Morfe no longer survives, but three farms in the far south of the county bear the name. In 1296 various wastes were let out. The forest was once very extensive. More is known about the contiguous royal forest of Kinver, south of the Forest of Morfe. In 1296 only three acres of waste were let out, but in 1342 the king granted 100 acres to be asserted. The median assart was three acres, and all of the land cheap, most of it very cheap. A good many of the late asserts were in and around Cannock Chase and the Black Country, with examples occurring as late as the 1340s.

Further south, the tenants of Dudley Castle seem to have had about 660 acres of assart. In 1293 the Dean of the Free Chapel of Wolverhampton had allowed Robert Champion to assart thirty acres, and had let over thirty acres of newly asserted waste. The asserters were numerous and the asserts small. In 1296 there was an assart and eighty-five acres of new wasteland which lay *frisca* (fallow). The manor still had forty acres of woodland. On the royal demesne at Wednesbury in 1307 the tenants complained that the lessee had asserted sixty acres of waste and coppice, and let them in tenements, mostly very small. The Crown stopped the improvement of 450 acres of Calf Heath in Cannock Forest in 1311.

One asserting village was in the Pennines and over 900 feet above sea-level. This was Alstonefield, in the northern end of Dovedale. In 1308 there were eighteen messuages and 488 acres of assart in the forest, divided into forty-seven holdings. The median holding was just over eight acres. The size and nature of the assart is astonishing. At least five of the holdings belonged to substantial tenants, but there was a fairly long list of smallholders. On the whole, therefore, as in other asserting regions, this was a country of cottagers.

Asserting continued until early in the fourteenth century on Needwood Forest. Several villages attested these activities. At Abbot's Bromley, in 1283, the Abbot of Burton's approvements in the outer wood produced cartloads of fencing. Various grants in 1280–1305 mention asserts in Abbot's Bromley Wood and on the heath. King's Bromley is on the Trent, south of Needwood: here in 1300 free sokemen and cottars, most of them virgaters or half-virgaters, had taken over the waste, and 'foreign' tenants held land newly taken from the waste. The other Bromley with late assarts was Bagots Bromley where Croxden Abbey had newlands in 1290, while in 1316–17 John Bagot was leasing portions of Bagots Bromley High Wood to a thatcher and a clerk with leave to assart and cultivate. An assart first mentioned in 1338 may have been the result. These examples suffice to show that assarting continued in central Needwood until 1325–50 at the same time as the Bagots were becoming more interested in rents than in farming.

However, the bulk of Staffordshire assarts were made in 1190–1280. The nuns of Brewood had assarts in 1211–16. In the southern uplands, two assarts existed in 1190–1206, three more in 1194–1206, and two more about 1240. Nearby were two thirteenth-century assarts. The Abbot of Burton's assarts in the Trent Valley near Burton, or on Needwood existed already by 1188–97. The Priory of St Thomas the Martyr at Stafford had at least four assarts in Blithfield before 1253. William de Ferrers was assarting in Needwood near Ridware in 1252–3. In and around the Potteries the uplands provided many opportunities for assarting, and Trentham Priory made several interesting agreements with its neighbours. In 1246, Hulton Abbey was ploughing the heath and marling it. There were assarts of little men – one of them a tailor – in 1277. Hulton Abbey and Trentham Priory were both assarting in 1242. There were other assarts about 1250, and in 1261, in wild country which wolves frequented. Trentham Priory was still assarting in 1280. Dieulacres Abbey had assarts in a number of places on the edge of the Pennines, with extensive pastoral interests in the moors above Leek (1252). Many smaller assarts existed all over Staffordshire. They appeared practically everywhere in 1100–1350, were most frequent in the thirteenth century, and most often found in the southern forests, on Cannock Chase and Needwood, and on the flanks of the Pennines. Needwood Forest is the best-documented region, but assarting spilled over into the valleys of the Trent and the Tame. Great and small alike took part in it. There are many examples of assarting agreements, but on the whole not much evidence of communal activity.

New settlement in Derbyshire was extensive, but limited by the nature of the terrain. The county divided into three regions – the Pennine area, eastern Derbyshire, and the southern lowlands. The first was a region of low population density and few freemen in 1086. Only two early settlements were attested there. In addition fourteen villages whose names imply new settlement are in the Domesday Survey. There were twenty-six new settlements established after 1086, and at least three of these were established after 1280.

Eastern Derbyshire had a low–medium population density and medium percentage of free peasants in 1086. No fewer than sixteen villages were attested as pre-Conquest settlements, and many of these gave evidence of extensive clearing. Besides these well-attested pre-Conquest villages there were twenty-nine villages with new-settlement names in the Domesday Survey of 1086. New settlement in eastern Derbyshire was therefore earlier, and more extensive, than in the Pennines, and there were many early settlements. There were great clearings in eastern Derbyshire just before the Norman Conquest. Clearings after 1086 were sixteen in number, and the latest recorded was 1285. There were, therefore, fewer new villages founded in eastern Derbyshire after 1086 than in the Pennines.

The southern lowlands were the most densely settled part of Derbyshire, and here again there were few free peasants. Altogether there were nineteen attested pre-Conquest settlements in the southern lowland and thirty-five villages with new-settlement names mentioned for the first time in 1086. There were quite a few late new-settlement place-names, and some of these were very late. Nearly all these late settlements were on the rising ground immediately south of the highland area of the Pennines. Five new settlements were on the rising ground south of the Trent in the far south of the county.

Derbyshire was the very type of the late-developing north, and inside the county comparison between the three geographical regions shows few early settlements, a good start to new settlement before 1086, and heavy and late new-settlement in the twelfth and thirteenth centuries in the Pennines. East Derbyshire, which is hilly magnesian limestone, has a fair number of early settlements which led to heavy clearings of woods just before 1086, accompanied by wholesale freedom for the peasants, but a smaller drive to new settlement after 1086 and a less late continuation of it. The southern lowlands had the largest number of early settlements, mostly in or near the fertile Trent Valley south of Derby, and a large number of new settlements both immediately before and a long time after 1086, most of which were on the hilly southern fringe of the Pennines.

As for clearings, I have counted 446 *leahs* and *thwaites* or one clearing every two square miles, one of the highest densities recorded in England. None were recorded before 1190, and the overwhelming majority (208) first appeared in the records after 1500. A great many were not known until the tithe awards of the 1840s. There is no telling when the clearances first came into existence, but that Derbyshire was a county of late and numerous assarts seems assured. None of the really interesting Derbyshire assarts were very early, and fewer than in Staffordshire were very late. The amount of assarting in Derbyshire was astonishingly great, and particularly strong in the upland regions north of the Trent and east of the Derwent. The High Peak has left comparatively little evidence of activity – though activity there was – and although there is plentiful evidence of assarting in the Trent, Dove and Derwent lowlands, it did not reach the level of intensity common in the uplands. Derbyshire's great assarting regions were generally 400–800 feet above sea-level.

In 1086 Warwickshire divided into two contrasting portions – the north-west, which contained the Tame-Blythe basin and the East Warwick plateau, and the rest of the county, which contained the Avon Valley and the Feldon. The former was an area of low prosperity, thinly populated and densely wooded; the latter was intensively cultivated, densely populated and had little woodland. Most of Warwickshire's slaves were in the

Feldon and Avon Valley. Wooded Arden was the home of freedom and intensive new settlement; the rest of Warwickshire was long-settled and servile.

Warwickshire had rather fewer clearings than Worcestershire, spread over a larger area. Altogether the place-name survey of 1936 contains eighty-nine *leahs*, and the density was thicker than in most English counties. Twenty-six clearing names appeared by 1086, and of the remaining sixty-three, twenty-one were first recorded after 1280, eight of them after 1350. Most periods were active, and clearing continued later than in Worcestershire, but less intensively at all times.

One example will suffice. Stoneleigh Abbey stood in a bend of the Avon, east of Kenilworth, on the traditional boundary between the two parts of Warwickshire, where the woods sweep down to the river. The abbey began in 1155 when Henry II gave the monks of Radmore, on Cannock Chase, its site at Stoneleigh together with various assarts. In 1204 King John added Waverley Wood and other assarts. Assarting round the abbey had already gone far by 1215, and no fewer than ten fields and two cultures existed at Stoneleigh Grange. In Echills Wood the home grange of the abbey had brought under cultivation nine fields and four meadows. In Waverley Wood the monks had made closes, and had enclosed a field and made three cultures and four fields adjoining the wood. Four other woods and coverts all belonged to Stoneleigh, and various abbots had enclosed and assarted them and farmed them out to tenants after the peasants had cut down the trees. Assarting had begun in 1100-35 and still proceeded in 1231-58. The abbot granted others waste and woodland in 1250-1 and in 1266 there were peasant assarts. Assarting continued vigorously in 1275, 1277, 1284, 1285 and 1294. The abbot made himself very unpopular in 1277-93, for at great cost, labour and danger, and against the will of almost all the more important people of the whole neighbourhood, he reduced the waste of the manor of Stoneleigh into cultivation. Assarting still continued in 1303, 1307, 1319 and 1325.

There was, therefore, in the soke of Stoneleigh, on the

southern edge of Arden, not far from Kenilworth, extensive assarting from the waste in 1100–1393, both by the Abbots of Stoneleigh and their sokemen, and most of this took place after 1190. Assarting was particularly active in the early years of the thirteenth century, 1275–1300 and 1300–25, so that in the great woods round Stoneleigh, especially Waverley Wood on the south-east, and Westwood on the north-west, an elaborate system of dyked and hedged closes, in which the common right of estovers (taking firewood) was extinct by agreement, had developed by 1350–75. In the thirteenth century the abbey held many granges and by 1215 had fully assarted much of Echills Wood round the home grange. Eight granges came into existence but there was always extensive peasant assarting too. By 1350 wealthy peasants, blossoming into the yeomanry, had some of the granges on lease and the abbot was leasing out the waste, but leases which started with a rose rent and finished with a substantial money rent show that assarting proceeded perhaps more slowly in 1350–1400, though there were no signs of a retreat of cultivation. The profit had largely gone out of demesne farming but this particular frontier society mainly escaped the depression.

The contrast between Arden and Feldon, represented by the villages of the hundreds of Stoneleigh and Kineton, was best seen in 1279. The much greater population densities of the forest villages went with a smaller percentage of arable, so that a given amount of arable in the north often supported four times the population as the same amount of arable in the south. There remained plenty of meadow and pasture to keep up the fertility of the arable in the forest and the heavy population density in an area which still had much wasteland in 1279 prolonged the expansion of the arable right down to the end of the fourteenth century.

We know a great deal about new settlement in Gloucestershire, and in limited areas, especially in the Cotswolds and the Forest of Dean, it was quite considerable. Altogether, there are 465 *leahs* in the Gloucestershire place-name survey, which makes a very high density. They were especially common near the escarpment of the west and north-west Cotswolds, and in the Forest of Dean; less common in the south-east and east Cotswolds. Of the 465 clearance names discovered 250 occurred in the records for the first time after 1500, sixty-five in or before 1086, forty in the fourteenth century, ninety-seven in the thirteenth century, and twenty-three in the twelfth century. Thus the thirteenth century was the greatest assarting period, but assarting probably continued very late in Gloucestershire.

A great deal of assarting took place in the Cotswolds during the twelfth and thirteenth centuries. Robert the second Lord Berkeley (1189–99) gave a tenant all the assart east of Michaelwood and there was also another assart on Michaelwood. John Smyth described Michaelwood or Muclewood (the Great Wood) as a wood of about 1000 acres in his own day but it was formerly much greater.

In 1228 Henry III disafforested the region called Horwood or Kingswood. Henceforward assarting could proceed without payment to the crown. Thomas Lord Berkeley (1220–43)

> reduced greate quantities of ground into enclosures and severalty, by procureinge many releases of Comon from free holders, wherein he bestowed much labor, and the like in Exchange of grounds with them, some in greater, some in lesser quantities, some less than a quarter of an acre . . . also hee much pared the skirts of his chace of Michaell wood by granting in fee many acres thereof to divers men, at three pence, fower pence, and six pence the acre rent.

His successor, Maurice (1243–81), decided to impark Whitcliffwood, near Berkeley, adjoining the lands of tenants and freeholders, many of whom had common of pasture in the wood, 'for no woods or grounds, in effect till the Eve of this age, were inclosed or held in severalty.' When negotiations failed, 'hee on a sodaine resolutely incloseth soe much of each mans land unto his sayd wood as he desired, maketh it a parke, placeth keepers, and storeth it with Deere.' Most of the commoners accepted compensation for the loss of common rights, but some were still unsuccessfully sueing his son.

On the flanks of the Cotswolds above Bristol assarting was much more extensive. When Henry I gave Oakley Wood on the edge of the Wolds near Cirencester to the monks of Cirencester in 1100–35, he forebade assarts, but despite this about 3000 acres existed by 1170–1. In 1342 the men of Cirencester alleged that in 1202–3 the Abbot had assarted a hundred acres in Oakley Wood. Certainly, in 1213, the keeper of the house of Cirencester had agreed with Rainer of the Wood that he should have pasture in Oakley Wood, provided that he kept his animals out of the assart from April to June.

In the Vale of Gloucester there was a certain amount of early new settlement. In 1107, Henry I gave the monks of Tewkesbury hedged woodland to assart. In 1100–35 Henry I ordered his foresters not to interfere with Corse Hill Wood, which belonged to the Abbey of St Peter of Gloucester. By 1150 there was enough cleared land in the Golden Valley for a gift to the monks of Llanthony. In 1154–79 Henry II confirmed to the Abbot of Gloucester all the abbey's assarts, old and new. Near Gloucester, the monks of Gloucester also had assarts in 1154–89. There were also later assarts on the estates of Gloucester Abbey, in 1228–43, and in 1273. At Bishop's Cleeve, the Bishop of Worcester had in 1182 a moderate area of assarts, largely made in 1163–79. Girold held 176 acres of assart and woodland which remained to be assarted. His total holding was divided into halves, one in each open field, and by grant of the bishop he paid a substantial rent. Girold was the very type of the hard-headed, enterprising peasant who flourished as well in the days of Henry II as of Henry V. He or his predecessors had added to an original twelve-acre holding four other holdings, all assarts, and two holdings not called assart. To these Girold had added one very large assart of his own creation, part of which was still woodland. The manorial structure and the open fields of Bishop's Cleeve had absorbed all these assarts by 1182.

On the eastern shore of the Severn there was a certain amount of reclamation from salt-marshes, mainly in the fourteenth century around Berkeley. In 1189 the process had already started. The Berkeleys drained and enclosed a considerable area in 1327–77. The lord of Elburton attempted to improve the drainage of his own land by uniting Old Splott Rhine to Littleton Rhine, which belonged to the Abbot of Malmesbury.

The thinly inhabited Forest of Dean saw more reclamation than the rest of Gloucestershire. In 1151–5, the Earl of Hereford had given the monks of Flaxley 100 acres of assarts and in 1158 Henry II added a grange with 200 acres of assart at Northwood, near Flaxley. The monks of Flaxley began to assart in the forest themselves shortly after their abbey's foundation in 1151, and in 1154–89 they enclosed about 300 acres of new land. Near Monmouth, an extensive assart began, and followed the course of a stream into the Wye. In 1220 the assart had a newly-built church called, in 1221, the church of Newland. In 1305 Edward I endowed it with the tithes of all the extra-parochial assarts in the Forest. Even in the twentieth century twenty distinct pieces of land paid tithes to Newland. Assarting continued late in the Forest of Dean, appearing in 1317, 1319 and 1347. New settlement began in Gloucestershire as far back as history can reach, and the arable reached its peak by 1350.

Oxfordshire was a well-settled, servile county in 1086, which showed some enterprise in new settlement during the subsequent period. Assarts were quite plentiful, and mainly late-twelfth or early-thirteenth-century. Oxfordshire has 100 *leahs* recorded in the place-name survey of 1953–4, so that the density was very high, but not so high as in Worcestershire. Of these clearings twenty-eight existed by 1086, and forty-four were first recorded after 1280, twenty-eight of them after 1350. The importance of the thirteenth century for new settlement was quite marked, and there can be little doubt that in Oxfordshire clearings continued late.

Oxfordshire has two uplands and one lowland. In the north are the Cotswolds and the North Oxfordshire upland; in the south the Chilterns; in the middle are the central claylands. The greatest clearances took place in the large woods along the Buckinghamshire border. In 1245 Osney Abbey received back from the king assarts confiscated in Buckinghamshire and adjoining in Oxfordshire. Assarting in this forest had already proceeded for many years in 1245. There were seven examples of breaches on the Oxford clays in 1154–68, after 1185, about 1190, in 1200–19, about 1230 and 1240, and in 1267–84. Three may have been outfields and one seems to have contained several hedged fields. Three assarts existed in the Cotswolds about 1180 and in 1220–8. The Abbot of Gloucester assarted 115 acres of Wychwood Forest in 1304–7.

Only Worcestershire provided information about the growth of population over the whole century after 1086. Here the speed of expansion was very fast in 1086–1106, but slower in 1106–91. A fair amount of evidence seems to point to stagnation and decline in 1106–44, and 1114/15–26, on the estates of Burton and Evesham Abbeys in Derbyshire, Staffordshire and Gloucestershire, but this evidence is not very good, for the Evesham surveys are very difficult to handle. In most parts of England population increased by about 250 per cent in the two centuries after 1086, but Feldon Warwickshire, most of Worcestershire and Oxfordshire and some of Gloucestershire increased more slowly. This may have been because of slowing down, stagnation, or decline in the thirteenth century. In Gloucestershire c. 1260–80 expansion was half as fast as in 1086–1265. In the Forest of Arden in Warwickshire, in the two centuries after 1086, expansion was much faster, to 375 per cent of the 1086 population. The greatest population growth of all was in the highland zone of the west Midlands, but from a very small base to quite large villages. In Staffordshire the growth was 933 per cent.

On the whole evidence of a fourteenth-century decline is hard to come by. In the west Midlands two Worcestershire manors may have shrunk since 1086, but there is no real direct evidence of decline in the period 1280–1350. On the whole the west Midlands was a region of fast population growth. By the fourteenth century population was double or treble the 1086 population in Warwickshire (eighteen manors), Gloucestershire (twenty-five manors) and Oxfordshire (ten manors).

Counts of heads of household exist for 275 west Midland manors in 1086–1350. By equal cohorts with the various county figures adjusted to the Domesday proportion of the whole, in the periods 1086–1114, 1086–1211, 1086–1273, 1086–1293 and 1086–1315 the percentage increases were 209, 212, 253, 234 and 318. This suggests (unless Domesday is deficient) a very, very rapid increase in 1086–1114, followed by stagnation in 1111–1211, a moderate increase in 1211–73, a slowish decline in 1273–93 and a very rapid increase in 1293–1315. Population was more than double the Domesday population by 1114 and more than treble by 1315, but made little progress in 1114–1293. This is the first region to produce evidence of stagnation in 1114–1211. The late-thirteenth-century decline was earlier in the east Midlands and later in southern England, and was not marked.[1]

2   CROPS AND LIVESTOCK

The Burton Abbey surveys of about 1126 and 1114–15 are the earliest material which exists for the county of Staffordshire. The second survey gives details of demesne stock on seven Staffordshire manors. The abbot had leased his manors to tenants, which explains the smallness of the abbot's demesne stock, or its non-existence on some manors.

There is a little information about livestock from the lands of the priory of St Thomas the Martyr near Stafford. In 1257 the priory received pasture for 400 sheep, affers, swine and horses. In about 1240 the lord of Tixall gave the priory common of pasture for sheep, affers and swine. In the thirteenth century Dieulacres Abbey had pasture for oxen, cows and affers. In 1252 Hulton Abbey gave Dieulacres common pasture for 200 cattle beyond the water of Churnet. The economy of these monastic houses in Pennine Staffordshire was highly pastoral.

The preoccupations of the Audley family are clear from the inquests held of their estates. In 1299 there were six watermills, two vaccaries, iron mines and millstone quarries. In 1308 there were four watermills, two meres with a fishery, four iron-mines, a quarry of millstones, a coal-mine and three fishponds. There were iron-mines and coal-mines on the manor of Sedgeley in 1291 and the Earl of Lancaster had an underground coal-mine in Stoke in 1296.

Many parts of Staffordshire were like Little Sardon. Here in 1291 there was common pasture without stint, pannage for swine and oak for firewood. At King's Bromley in 1259 there was a fishery, a mill, pannage of the villeins and pannage of strangers. The existence of strangers' pannage shows that there was plenty, and since the probable rate of pannage was a halfpenny or a penny a pig there must have been at least 180 and perhaps 360 swine belonging to villeins and strangers in King's Bromley, which was in the heart of Needwood.

On the royal estates, probably in 1249, the pannage of the whole manor of Wigginton supposes 208 or 416 swine. In 1273 eight south Staffordshire manors could support at least 684 or 1368 swine. Penniak Wood could support 240 swine, but there were rarely so many. At Cradley the pannage was for 16 or 32. There was also pasture for 100 sheep on the common pasture.

The Honour of Tutbury was similarly pastoral in 1296. Here the customary tenants gave oats (which we must suppose their typical produce) to collect dry wood in the forest. There were three free fisheries in the River Dove. The significance of forest products is clear in Needwood Forest. The forest itself belonged to the Earl of Lancaster in 1296 and was divided into five wards. The main profits were from the agistment of cattle, customary payments of hens for bark, the sale of lime-tree bark, pannage, herbage, mast, old wood and fishery.

Staffordshire was poor and pastoral and at all times, especially in the Pennine uplands, and in such forests as Needwood, Cannock and Kinver, tended to rear horses, cattle and swine, rather than sheep, and to grow oats before all other grains. There were also a great many fisheries, and forest products such as timber, lime-bark, nuts and hedge fruits like sloes and hawthorn berries. The number of cattle is not precisely known but if pannage for each was a penny then agistment cattle alone numbered 928. Simi'arly pannage for swine in Needwood presupposes herds totalling about 1400 pigs and perhaps double that number.

Derbyshire was very like Staffordshire in most respects. Pasture stints of six villages in 1200–22 mention 1640 sheep, which was a much larger proportion of sheep than in Staffordshire, but much of the territory covered is dry limestone country rather than wet millstone grit country – the Low Peak rather than the High Peak. Further north conditions were different.

In 1113 William Peverel gave Lenton Priory, in Nottinghamshire, two-thirds of all tithes in ten parishes, and two-thirds of the tithes of all High Peak pastures. He added all the tithes of all the horses wherever he had a stable. By 1251 much of the land had come under cultivation and was subject to dispute with the Dean and Chapter of Lichfield, who also claimed the tithes. The monks claimed that the cathedral church had despoiled them of 124 lambs and eighteen woolfells and of a total of 723 thraves (one thrave is twenty-four sheaves) of oats, as well as of 1028 thraves of oats in the autumn and twenty-six geese. The complete absence of any other corn, and the importance of sheep, are likewise most interesting.

Amongst the Glapwell Charters is a taxation assessment of 1301 in Glapwell and Rowthorn. Thirteen tenants were in the survey. The absence of swine is quite in line with previous evidence. Oats, wheat and barley was the order of precedence for grains, and there was no rye or legumes. Milch kine came before draught animals, and oxen before affers. Horses were fewer than cattle. Sheep were the most prolific animal.

Derbyshire split into three farming regions which had their sub-divisions. The southern lowlands included the Trent Valley, the Derwent Valley and the Pennine foothills; there were further eastern Derbyshire (an active new-settlement area) and the Pennine area, which included the northern moors. In the southern lowlands swine and sheep were common, but in the Pennines, though evidence is rather thin, cattle seem to have been numerous. Even so there were plenty of sheep everywhere in the whole county. Information about crops is scarce for all parts of Derbyshire and there was no hint of an interest in legumes. As in other highland areas goats were popular, but limitation's upon pasture rights for them seem to suggest that sheep were ousting them from the affections of the English peasantry.

Turning to Gloucestershire, John Smith of Nibley revealed a great deal about the farming methods of the lords of Berkeley. The second Lord Thomas (1281–1321) sowed wheat, barley, peas, oats, rye, vetches, dredge, pilcorn (pilled or naked oats), mixtilon (maslin) and brotcorn (bread corn). Every second or third year he exchanged seed between manors and took the vale corn to an upland soil and the upland and cotsall (i.e. Cotswold) corn to the vale and low grounds. He set his beans by hand and did not sow them. At certain times of the year he moved his cattle from one manor to another, according to soil and other conditions. He singled out the oldest sheep as cullions to be fatted for the butcher. He kept the rams and ewes apart some of the time and brought them back together in October, but kept some in reserve for fifteen to sixteen days until the first lot were worn out. Thus all his ewes were fertile. In Smith's day there were more than 200 medieval account rolls in Berkeley Castle. There were barn accounts, and records of the sale of stubble, withies, osiers, offal wood from the hedges, butter, cheese, milk, dung and soil, bran, nuts, wax and honey. At Slimbridge and Hurst Farm two orchards usually provided eighty quarters of apples and pears for making cider and perry.

The third lord, Thomas the Rich (1326–61), held thirty-four demesne manors in Gloucestershire, nine in Somerset, three in Essex and twenty-eight in other counties. In some manors he had flocks of 300–1500 sheep. At Bewstone, Gloucestershire, in 1333–4, he sheared 5775 sheep from his adjoining manors. In each manor and farm he had a pigeon-house, in many two, and in some, where he dwelt, three. From each house he drew 650–1300 young pigeons, and from one, in one year, 2151.

Gloucestershire was a highly arable county – one of the first to develop a common-field system. Even in the Cotswolds there was considerable ploughland. Temple Guiting, an upland

manor farmed out by the crown to the Bishop of Hereford, had
250 acres of demesne under crop in 1335, most of them under
barley. The variety of Gloucestershire made it the typical
woodland county and the counterpart of Norfolk.

Like Gloucestershire, Oxfordshire was highly arable but had
considerable pastoral, dairying and poultry-rearing proclivities.
Details of crops and stock have survived for one manor in 1272,
eight in 1280, two in 1288 and one in 1297. Wheat was the first
crop on seven manors, oats on two manors and barley and rye in
one manor each. Barley was the second crop on four manors,
wheat and rye on two manors each and oats and dredge on one
manor each. Three manors grew peas, one beans and one vetches
– and the crops were small. Two manors had particularly large
herds of cattle and swine and one of these was rich in cheese and
butter but also had 443 sheep. Two other manors were very
interested in dairying, and both had herds of cattle and flocks of
sheep. Four manors had 300–400 sheep. Five manors had
chickens, three geese, two doves and two peafowl. The
economy was varied, but not very progressive.

The Bishop of Winchester had two manors in Oxfordshire in
1210–11. Oats was the principal crop of both, followed by
barley at one and rye at the other and there were no legumes.
Oxen were many times more numerous than affers and swine
than cattle. On one manor the pigs outnumbered both sheep and
cattle, and there were many sides of bacon in stock. One manor
had comparatively few sheep and the other, which made quite a
large quantity of cheese, had a fairly large flock of sheep. The
lord sold most of the cheeses. Donkeys, capons and hens existed
on one of the manors.

Oxfordshire was on the whole a wheat and oats county with
here and there some signs of agrarian poverty but on the whole
good mixed farming with a lively interest in stock-rearing,
wool-growing, dairy- and poultry-farming. Legumes were
grown a little and their use increased steadily in 1275–1350, but
it was probably not sufficient to affect fertility very much. In
general pressure upon the resources of the soil seems not to have
been too great.[2]

3 TECHNIQUES – THE OPEN FIELDS

Headlands existed in Gloucestershire in 779, and in 1002 there was a block of ploughland 'common by popular allotment'. Oxfordshire and Worcestershire also had early open fields, and in Worcestershire, as in Gloucestershire, there were common woods. A two-course crop rotation probably existed in Worcestershire in 904 and 974. References to open-field, let alone common-field systems, in England in 974–1156 are very scarce. Garsington, in Oxfordshire, had open fields in 1086: 'There I hide of inland which never paid geld lying scattered among the king's land.' Early two-course rotations are known from Oxfordshire, where they existed at twenty-two villages. Gray recorded twenty-three early two-field villages in addition to these twenty-two, four first recorded in 1300–50 and two early three-field villages in addition to five discovered since he wrote. He mentions two three-field villages first recorded in 1300–50. Gray also has by far the earliest clear reference to a communal crop-rotation, from Piddington, in 1105–7, in a grant of tithes from two acres of demesne meadow: 'that is, when the west field is sown the first two acres of the meadow which is called *Westmede*, but when the east field is sown the breadth of two acres in the meadow which is called *Langdale*.' Two villages changed from a two-field system about 1240–1334 and in 1270–1337. Oxfordshire also provided a good early example of inter-communal arrangements for pasturing beasts on the fallow of two villages in 1221–9 and (like Buckinghamshire, a county with good early evidence of mature open fields) shows clearly that it almost certainly had communal crop rotations well before the Norman Conquest and that it practised communal grazing upon the bare fallow long before 1300.

There were early two-field crop-rotations in five Gloucestershire villages in 1182, 1189 and 1250–65. In 1182 Sherborne had a two-field ploughing custom to which a piece of land transferred from the neighbouring village had to conform. Gray adds seventeen early two-field systems to the six described, but none of his three-field villages were early and the only addition dates from 1322. There seems no doubt that Gloucestershire had a mature open-field system with a two-course crop rotation by the early-tenth century.

Worcesterhire had a good early two-field village in 1164–79 and 1182. There was a late three-field village in 1338. Gray adds two early two-field villages and one early three-field village. There seems no doubt that Worcestershire had a mature open-field system with a two-course crop rotation by the tenth century.

Warwickshire also has good early common fields with a two-course crop rotation at Little Wolford, in about 1205, where there was a virgate 'having 27 acres in one field and 18 in the other, since what is lacking in the one is supplemented in the other, since in each field $22\frac{1}{2}$ acres come to perfect one virgate of land.' The implication here seems to be that normally a virgate would be equally divided between the two fields, because there was a two-course crop rotation based upon the field as a cropping unit. Gray adds twelve early two-field villages and two early three-field villages.

Gray knew very little about open fields in the new-settlement counties of Derbyshire and Staffordshire. Rig and furrow and fossilized strips show that by the end of the open-field period they existed practically everywhere up to an altitude of 1300 feet above sea-level. There were many contiguous villages with open fields, but none in Edale, the extreme north or south-east of Buxton. Most of the three-field villages in the county were on a level with or south of Derby, in north-east Derbyshire round Chesterfield and in the Wye Valley. These were the more mature new-settlement areas of the shire. About 90 per cent of all open fields were below 1000 feet above sea-level, 80 per cent of the villages with three or more fields were below 500 feet above sea-level, and 36 per cent of the two-field villages were also below 500 feet above sea-level. Most one-field villages were on the high limestone plateau, but 60 per cent of all open fields were on clays. Some 90 per cent received less than thirty-five inches of rainfall a year and 55 per cent faced south. These geographical details of the distribution of the physical remains of the open fields tell nothing about their early history.

Gray knew no two-field villages in Derbyshire, but the earliest of all, and one of the earliest with certain two-course crop rotations is found on the manor of Burton Abbey in Mickleover, being dated late in 1114 or early in 1115. The phrases *in uno anno* (in the one year) and *in altero* (in the other) used in describing the holdings of the *censarii* imply a two-course crop rotation. The remaining five early open fields were in three-field villages. Nearly all these villages were close to Derby.

Only three-field villages were known in Staffordshire and seven of those unknown to Gray were from 1300–50. Staffordshire was predominantly a three-field county, but not until late in the period. One of Gloucester Abbey's manors had land in four fields, each of which contained several parts. The four fields were under a three-course rotation, so that here, as elsewhere in England, the furlongs were the real cropping areas, and each field contained one of each of the three courses. Out of the fallow third forty acres were enclosed in the first field and cultivated and twenty acres in the second field.

There were excellent *inhokes* in two-field villages in the west Midlands, especially in Oxfordshire, with two exceptionally early examples (1170–9); for the most part *inhokes* occurred after about 1250. In the two-field village of Little Tew, in Oxfordshire, there were *inhokes* whose existence has provided two most interesting agreements. In 1268 the lords and other free tenants of Little Tew sued the lord of Great Tew, who

had sown and made an *inhoke* from a certain culture, which is called Costowe, against the will of the said abbot and of the others before-named, and in addition had placed in defence the common pasture of the whole fallow between the way which is called Woodway and Little Tew.

Little Tew had a right to common of pasture 'as often as the corn is carried away from the said cultures and the land is not sown.'

Little Tew granted the lord of Great Tew the right to take away the crop when the draught animals were pasturing if he liked. In 1288 dispute broke out again between the same participants. The main interest in the resulting settlement is the elaborate description of the two-course crop rotation wth one field fallow and the other sown with winter and spring corn:

> They shall be sown for one and after the corn is gathered on the said culture the same year they shall enter with all their draught animals to feed until the time of the winter seed in the other following year if they ought to be sown with winter seed, or until the time of the Lent seed of the said following year, if they ought to be sown with Lenten seed; so, that is to say, that after the sowing, the corn harvest, the collecting or gathering of the corn, there shall be no deceit, but that the above-mentioned commoners shall have the aforesaid common at the convenient time: and let it be known that the said cultures shall be sown one year, and the other year shall lie fallow.

Anyone who made *inhokes* was to pay a ten pound penalty. On the other hand, some land in Little Tew must have been outside the rotation system, for in about 1275, at least one virgate of land there was 'to be sown every year'.

A few agreements about making *inhokes* survive for various other counties. In 1242 the Templars and Bruern Abbey, Oxfordshire, came to such an agreement. Sometimes there was trouble over such arrangements, as at Broughton Hackett in Worcestershire, in 1287, when the men of Upton Snodsbury and of half Broughton fed their cattle upon the young corn sown by the men of John Lovet upon an *inhoke* in the fallow field. A quarrel arose and there was a death. An agreement of 1200–25 at Bradbourne, in Derbyshire, also seemed to imply the cultivation of fallow, or at least, a very flexible crop rotation.[3]

4 TECHNIQUES – CROP NUTRITION

The one certain marlpit mentioned in the Gloucester place-name survey first occurred in 1327, but the Berkeleys were active earlier. According to John Smith of Nibley, Maurice the Second, the Resolute (1243–81), was the first of the Berkeleys to marl his land, in 1255–6. Thomas the Second, the Wise (1281–1321), made, in 1301–21, nearly 800 gifts in tail in which he usually included licence to take marl from marlpits in various villages. He also bought up many of his forefathers' feoffees in tail and regranted them, with liberty of taking marl and earth out of the ways and green places. In the later Middle Ages the marlpools became disused. Smith mentioned one, disused since 1422–83. In every hamlet of one village there had formerly been marlpits, seven or eight of which were large, but they had not been in use since the Wars of the Roses laid waste the Berkeley estates. There was one in Michaelwood from which Thomas the Second in 1281–1321 sold large quantities of marl. Lord Thomas first alienated a marlpit in 1281–1307, but reserved to himself enough marl for his own demesne lands.

Nine Staffordshire marlpits existed in 1242–1325. There were several marlpits on the waste of Needwood Forest in 1272–90 and a road at Sandon about 1300 led into the marlpits. Three of the marlpits were on or next to assarts, and one was a common marlpit in which a thatcher had a two-acre share.

Derbyshire had twelve unquestionably medieval marlpits and marled lands. The earliest was in 1238, and the remainder dated from 1286 to 1457. Of the twelve ten were from the fast-expanding, rapidly-settling areas of eastern and central Derbyshire and there were none from the well-settled lands south of the Trent. In addition to these well-attested marlpits there was marling in the far south of Derbyshire in 1252.[4]

5   THE LIFE OF THE PEOPLE – THE PEASANT'S RESOURCES

As in 1086, so later, the west Midlands had larger holdings than
the east Midlands, south-eastern and eastern England. In
Derbyshire in 1114–15 and 1126, there were large holdings of
one or two bovates, and middle-sized holdings of half-virgate
size. Late in the period in Baslow there were many smallholdings, but comparison is barely possible, since so many of the
Burton Abbey estates were in the more fertile south.
Staffordshire offers more copious material for comparison. In
1114–15 and 1126 the Burton Abbey estates were the more
settled manors of the Trent Valley, and the hamlets of the
Pennine fringe. The two resembled each other. Except in
Burton itself, holdings were large, usually of bovate or virgate
size. In 1250–1330, in most parts of Staffordshire, the typical
holding was of virgate, bovate or half-virgate size. The county
was still thinly inhabited in 1330, and although certain upland
manors, especially those with coal, iron and millstones, attracted
a great influx of landless squatters, on the whole tenements
continued to be large. Sometimes, as in Arden Warwickshire,
the median holding tended to be a quarter-virgate, and holdings
of less than five acres were very numerous, though not so
numerous as in the east Midlands, or south-eastern and eastern
England. The general standard throughout the lowland zone of
the west Midlands was a half-virgate, but in much of
Gloucestershire, Oxfordshire and Feldon Warwickshire many
villages had median holdings of one virgate. The half-virgate
standard was commonest where there had been a fair amount of
new settlement and virgates were split; extreme fragmentation
occurred (rarely in the west Midlands) where there had been
least new settlement.

The goods and chattels of a felon on a Staffordshire manor, in
1283, throw a little light on peasant agriculture. He had twenty
acres of oats, wheat and barley (presumably in that order), a
chest, a cow with a calf, a brass pot and eight pigs.

An assessment of 1301 in Glapwell and Rowthorn in

Derbyshire was of thirteen tax-payers, and each peasant family had, on average, fourteen bushels of wheat, nearly one quarter of barley, nearly three and a half quarters of oats, more than one ox, two other cattle, nine sheep, more than 1s.2d. worth of forage and utensils; every two families had nearly one affer and one other horse. These people were quite well off. They had more than enough surplus grain to feed a man for a year, mainly on oat-cakes, plenty of sheep, a good supply of milk, butter and cheese, but no bacon.

In 1279–80 the villeins of Mickleover in Derbyshire rebelled against their lord, the Abbot of Burton, and there was a famous law-suit between them. The abbot seized and confiscated all their goods and chattels which included forty oxen, fifty cattle, 104 swine and 506 sheep. Since there were thirty-nine serfs involved in Mickleover the typical villein family possessed one ox, one cow, three swine and thirteen sheep. Their possession of milch kine was important and an earlier rule of the abbey governing its villeins at Mickleover confirmed this. In 1114–15 the twenty-four villeins each of whom held two bovates had 'leave and time given when working for the lord to drive home and milk their cows'.

At Wessington, in Derbyshire before 1246, the pasture rights of five bovates given to Darley Abbey showed that a typical bovate-holder had two oxen, a cow, two calves, a horse or mare, two foals, five ewes, five lambs, eight other sheep, a sow and her litter.[5]

6 THE LIFE OF THE PEOPLE – INHERITANCE CUSTOMS

Partible inheritance probably existed in Derbyshire in 1126. On Burton Abbey's manor at Winshill in 1126 there were eleven villeins, three *cotseti* (cottars), eleven *censarii* (rent-paying tenants) and seven sokemen. The sokemen of 1114–15 were the same as those who held *ad malam* (for a payment) in 1126. Sokemen and molmen were privileged villeins who held by money-payment, not by week-works. In 1114–15 they already practised partible inheritance as this remark suggests: 'When any of these shall die their heirs owe 16 shillings for heriot.' Thus the sokemen were unfree and divided their holdings between their heirs. There were *tenentes ad malam* (tenants for a payment) at three manors in 1126. At Winshill the *censarii*, also in 1114–15, corresponded with the *tenentes ad malam* of 1126. There were six sokemen at Winshill in 1086 and they had previously owed services at Repton. They may well have had different inheritance customs from those of the molmen, both in Derbyshire and in Staffordshire. Sokemen existed all over Staffordshire before 1350, but there is no information about their inheritance customs.

In the west Midlands new settlement continued very late in Derbyshire, Staffordshire and Arden Warwickshire. This continued late new settlement fuelled the late, fast population increase of 1293–1315, which succeeded the decline of 1273–93. The stagnation of 1114–1211 suggests an unusually late start to assarting in the new-settlement regions, coupled with little advance in the rest of the west Midlands. Much of the region had been a smallholder zone with many slaves in 1086. Their manumission, as in southern England, created a peasantry which, except in Arden, had sufficiently large holdings for subsistence. Especially in the southern counties partible inheritance was rare and the economy comparatively inelastic and unprogressive. Even field-systems were backward and depended upon *inhokes* for greater production. Legumes were rare, oxen very much in vogue, sheep very common, and used for dairying as well as wool-production. In the highland zone forest products, goats, iron, coal and millstones helped the peasantry to a modest living.

CHAPTER 9

SOUTH–WESTERN ENGLAND

1 NEW SETTLEMENT AND POPULATION GROWTH

Place-name information on new settlement in south-western England is possible only from Devon, since Cornwall's Celtic place-names are not helpful. After 1350 five Devon new-settlement place-names appeared in the records for the first time and ten in 1281–1350. Like Somerset, Devon continued to develop late.

There are, altogether, 303 *leahs* or clearings recorded in the Devon place-name survey of 1931–2. Devon does not have an especially great density of clearings. Eighty-one clearings were already there in 1086, and 140 were first recorded after 1280, forty-seven of them after 1350. Devon was well-developed by 1086, did not begin to develop further before the thirteenth century, and continued late.

One very good indication of new settlement is the growth of daughter chapelries in the parish of an ancient mother church. Thus in 1225 Bishop's Tawton had a mother church with two dependent chapelries. These three villages are now three distinct parishes, but in 1086 they formed a great territory of 15,000 acres which was the bishop's estate of Tawton. The large parish of Tawstock had no known relationship to Bishop's Tawton, but it was probably the *stoc* (dairy-) or cattle-farm of Tawton. The original estate would therefore be 21,000 acres on both sides of the river. *Stocs* are very old and Tawstock must have grown big before the creation of the hundred boundaries in the mid-tenth century, since the two places are in different hundreds. The original name of the estate was perhaps the simple 'Taw'. North Tawton is not related, but was well-established by the eleventh or twelfth century. From here settlement continued, and by the late-twelfth century there was a settlement on the fringe of the moors. This was a good corn-growing area in the thirteenth century, as the corn-drying oven and griddle excavated there witness. North Tawton itself had thirty ploughlands and thirty ploughs in 1086, and its title Chipping Tawton in 1199 shows it had a market. In 1315–16 forty quarters of wheat from Chipping Tawton left Teignmouth for Carlisle. Plympton and Plymstock are similar examples of this development. Plympton included three chapelries on the coast and one on Dartmoor. The parish of Plympton covered all the land between the lower Plym and Yealm and far up on to the moor – an area of 29,000 acres. Similarly West Alvington was the mother of all the land between Kingsbridge and the sea. Also near Kingsbridge, Chillington was the centre of a large estate in 1086. Similarly Paignton, Brixham and Sidbury each included two other settlements. The first two were settled as fishing hamlets from Sidbury, which is inland, before documentation.

Colyton is one of the best examples of this type of early settlement. The village is three miles inland, and the parish, which now comprehends nine parishes, originally covered 22,000 acres. Its daughter villages grew up at different times between 1005 and 1216. The way in which the modern parishes interlock suggests that three other villages were also part of the original settlement of Coly.

Most of these ancient village centres were nucleated, open-field villages. The church of Ugborough was actually inside 'a small but well-defined oval earthwork'. Many became hundredal centres, and most were either royal estates or given to the bishop by King Athelstan.

In 1086 there were 1170 settlements recorded in the Domesday Book, and forty settlements are known to have existed but not been so recorded. There were only 470 parishes. The Sandford charter of 930 mentioned eight places already settled, none of which are in Domesday. The bishop's great manor of Crediton included them all together with a wide tract of settled and occupied country to the west and south. Other places not in Domesday were recorded in a Crediton charter of 739. A true picture of the number of scattered hamlets in

1086 might require doubling the 1170 recorded settlements.

By 1086 cultivation had gone up to the 1200-foot contour line on Dartmoor and Exmoor, but only to 900–950 feet on the wetter western slopes. The inner wastes of Dartmoor – six settlements – were not settled until about 1300. Paring and burning moorland and heath took place in 1204–20 on the flanks of Dartmoor.

Marsh-reclamation was also fairly widespread. The Sokespitch family, which lived on the farm of Marsh Barton, a little above the tidal marshes of the River Clyst, is a good example. They obtained their farm in 1170–80, with the salt-marsh and any gains they could make from the sea and improve. In about 1234–5 Robert Sokespitch granted the Hospital of St Mary Magdalen at Exeter sixty acres of newly-enclosed marsh pasture. The Exminster marshes were probably reclaimed about 1086–1300. Braunton Marsh is a reclamation from the Taw and the Otter and the Axe have similar estuarine marshes.

Woodland clearances were the single most important form of reclamation. Farmsteads at the end of narrow lanes with a radius of hedge-bank fields around them are a well-known feature of Devon, which paid King John 5000 marks for a charter of disafforestation in 1204. The Abbey of Buckfast had already assarted 1340 acres in 1159–60. At Hackpen in Uffculme in 1249, the Abbot of Dunkeswell agreed with a neighbour to have common pasture in lands, woods, meadows and pastures, except on Hackpen Hill, which the neighbour might assart. This latter should be open to the abbot's beasts after harvest and the abbot made a reciprocal grant. The extent of new settlement in Devon was therefore moderate and we should expect its impact upon society to be commensurate.

New settlement in Cornwall is not well-known. The late life of the sixth-century Cornish St Brieuc says:

> All gird themselves to work, they cut down trees, root up bushes, tear up brambles and tangled thorns, and soon convert a dense wood into an open clearing ... then the soil was worked carefully with light hoes, and being ploughed

with very small furrows, its various produce was placed in due time on the threshing floors.

This is not good evidence for sixth-century new settlement but it is a good description of the later practice.

We know that Cornishmen were interested in assarting, for in 1204 they paid King John 2200 marks and twenty palfreys to be rid of forest law. We know a little about the areas in which expansion took place – Bodmin Moor and Twelve Men's Moor in North Cornwall. Temple is more than 800 feet above sea-level, on the desolate track across Bodmin Moor. The hamlet took its name from the Templars, who built it in the twelfth century and from whom it passed to the Hospitallers in 1312. By 1241 settlers from Temple had built Merrifield Farm, and other farms sprang up in yet more distant spots. Of these the most remote was Fernacre, or Fernaise, more than 900 feet above sea-level, far up the De Lank River, underneath Rough Tor. There are Bronze Age hut-circles beyond the farm boundary and the settlement was first recorded in 1327. A little distance away there is an earthen bank faced with moorstone, probably from this period, high up on Brown Willy.

Caradon, in one of the valleys on the eastern fringe of the moor, was carved out of the estate of Rillaton in 1161–75, by Reginald, Earl of Cornwall, and given to Launceston Priory, together with some five square miles of wild moorland. In the fringing valleys lived twelve tenants to whom, in 1284, the Prior of Launceston made over part of the moor, saving to the prior's tenant at Caradon right of summer pasture. The moor is still Twelve Men's Moor and on the bank of the Withey Brook, 900 feet above sea-level, surrounded by bronze age hut-circles, lies Trewortha Farm, the home in 1284 of William of Trewortha. A few shadowy foundations are all that remain of the hamlet excavated in the 1890s. The excavator found rectangular huts of a pastoral settlement which grew no corn and worked no tin.

From the point of view of the agrarian historian, Cornwall is one of the most obscure counties in England. It is not particularly mountainous – about half is over 400 feet above sea-level – but in 1086 it was very thinly inhabited and highly pastoral. This was still its condition in 1350, and indeed in 1500. Carew's statements about Elizabethan Cornwall bear this out. In Devon new settlement moved a long way up the hills, and continued very late, but was not very active compared with new settlement in the West Riding of Yorkshire. On the other hand, nobody should confound Devon with Cornwall. New settlement is hard to trace because the evidence is scanty, but the economy of Cornwall made great strides well before the sixteenth century. Mining and fishing are scarcely agrarian activities, and communities can be rich yet unable to grow a lettuce. Kalgoorlie and Coolgardie had hotels with marble staircases and could afford to drink champagne out of buckets after the gold rush of 1893, but the nearest food grew 200 miles away. Today the rich iron-mining towns of the Pilbarra, in Western Australia, fetch nearly all their food in road trains of refrigerator-vans from Perth, 1000 miles away. Carew's description of sixteenth-century Cornwall as agriculturally backward must therefore still stand, despite the other documented wealth of the county.

Nothing significant is known about population movements in Devon during the twelfth century, and nothing at all about population growth in Cornwall during the twelfth and thirteenth centuries. During these periods rapid population growth probably took place. Very slow growth took place on two Devon manors, which increased their recorded population by half in 1086–1326. On the other hand, the fourteenth-century population was double or treble the 1086 population on ten Devon and ten Cornish manors. This seems to have been (at the bottom end of the scale) the normal growth rate in south-western England. There is no real evidence of declining population in Devon and Cornwall in 1280–1350. One Devon manor grew by a quarter in 1235–1326. There is nothing spectacular in south-western England, and no signs of a crisis of over-population.[1]

2 CROPS AND LIVESTOCK

Something is known about demesne agriculture in Devon, especially on the estates of Tavistock Abbey. In 1086 on ten of the abbey's manors there were 28 ploughteams, 114 cattle, 918 sheep, 167 goats and 58 swine. None of these totals is remarkable, but the herd of goats is noteworthy, for goats only occasionally played a part in the agrarian economy of medieval England. Oats was the main crop in the thirteenth and fourteenth centuries and down to 1332 pill-corn – naked oats – was the only kind of oats grown. Staffordshire and Yorkshire grew the same corn, as did Cornwall down to the nineteenth century. In 1332 the reeve of Hurdwick bought large oats and sowed it on land dressed with seasand, but in 1342 he reduced the sowing of the new oats. In 1332 Hurdwick tried barley for the first time and sowed it in the following spring. The crop failed, but three years later two other manors sowed barley. For six years they persevered with barley before giving up. Rye existed in the county very early, for in 1100–7 there were dues paid in rye. Wheat grew from the first, but it played only a small part in the economy before the fourteenth century. Werrington sowed no wheat in 1298, and Hurdwick sowed very little in 1332. Its first appearance at Ottery was in 1338. Typical grain crops were, at Werrington in 1298, small oats and rye; in 1350, small oats, large oats, rye and wheat; at Hurdwick, in 1332, small oats, rye, wheat and large oats; in 1347, rye, wheat, large oats and small oats.

In the thirteenth and fourteenth centuries there were no goats at Tavistock and in 1328 no goats on the Bishop of Exeter's estates. Yet in 1338 the Hospitallers had pastures for 100 goats. The output of cheese was very large in 1298–1337. The cheese production at Hurdwick in 1332 and 1347 came respectively from seven cows and sixty-nine ewes, and from three cows and eighty ewes; that at Ottery in 1337 from eight cows and fifty-eight ewes. Since one cow produces as much as three or four ewes, most of the cheese was ewe's milk cheese. Butter production was much smaller than cheese production. According to the anonymous *Hosebonderie*, a cow should produce from May to Michaelmas 981 pounds of cheese and fourteen pounds of butter. The cows at Werrington and Hurdwick produced only thirty-two pounds of cheese per annum, and their productivity was therefore very low. Sheep were not especially important on the estates of Tavistock Abbey. At Werrington there were 154 in 1297 compared with 150 in 1086; at Hurdwick there were 185 in 1332 compared with 200 in 1086. There had therefore been a slight decline in the number of sheep during the new-settlement centuries.

There is excellent information about the crops and stock on the manors of the Courtenay Earls of Devon on five manors in 1286–7. Except at Plympton, where wheat predominated and barley was significant, oats was overwhelmingly the chief crop by acreage sown and legumes scarcely existed. At Tiverton in 1307–9 no legumes grew and oats was the chief crop but rye was becoming more popular. By crops grown Plympton was the largest wheat manor, but even here oats exceeded wheat as the main crop. Plympton was also the largest barley manor but Exminster led in oats. Rye was not a very major crop but it was most prominent at Barton. The smallest oats crop in the shire, except that of Topsham, occurred at Barton and on the same manor there was comparatively little wheat and no barley. In poor conditions therefore rye acted as a substitute for other grains. Most of the grains received the lord sold on the market. Wheat and rye the earl grew largely for the market; barley and, even more so, oats he used himself.

The grain yields for 1225–6 show a very different situation sixty years earlier. There was no wheat on four manors, but Plympton and Exminster bought wheat for seed. At Topsham there was a small wheat yield. Wheat looks like a new, experimental crop of which the manors grew much more in 1286–7. In 1225–6 there was no barley which was also a later introduction. Oats was small oats only and the yield was about two-thirds of the 1286–7 yield on four manors. Oats, though the first crop, cannot have been very productive in 1225–6. Over half the crop went back into the land as seed compared with a quarter in 1286–7. This marks a considerable improvement in agriculture during the intervening sixty years. In 1225–6 figures for the yield of rye show that only about one-seventh of the rye went back as seed, and in 1286–7 rather more than one-fifth. Oats had become more profitable than rye, which produced a rather smaller crop in 1286–7 than in 1225–6. Topsham led in oats and rye in 1225–6. In general grain production was a good deal less than sixty years later and much less profitable.

There were great fluctuations in the size of the principal grain crops of the peasantry. Unlike on the demesne, wheat was the principal crop and in 1295–6 it represented more than half of the total grain grown. Barley and rye dropped out after the first year, but rye reappeared at Tiverton in 1308–9. Maslin largely replaced barley and rye; pill-corn was usually well-favoured. Plympton, which was the leading demesne wheat-farm, also grew most peasant wheat; Exminster, which was the leading demesne oats-farm, yielded first place to Tiverton as the leading peasant pill-corn manor; Tiverton was the second wheat and second rye farm on the demesne, but its peasants produced more oats and rye than those of the other manors. Thus demesne and peasant figures differ somewhat but not unduly and the general tendency is plain: the economy was largely arable.

The figures for oxen and other cattle in 1286–7 for all manors show that at both ends of the financial year draught animals outnumbered milch kine. The lord made cheeses at all manors except Topsham. He sold most of them, but no figures of production per cow are possible because the weights of the cheeses differed from manor to manor. All manors except Topsham produced butter, most of which the lord sold. At Michaelmas 1286 there were nineteen horses, 303 oxen and cattle, 729 sheep and two swine on these five manors. By standards in southern England these Devon estates were not exactly great sheep-farming manors. Substantial flocks undoubtedly existed, as Domesday witnesses, but they were sporadically distributed and there were places where sheep were not a prime factor in local husbandry.

Devon was rather different from southern England since its interest in growing grain increased greatly in the course of the thirteenth century. It never became a great wheat county before 1300 but in 1086 it was a notable breeding ground for sheep, goats and horses. By 1300 it was predominantly arable and was becoming more proficient in growing cereals.[2]

3 TECHNIQUES – THE OPEN FIELDS

There was an open-field system in Devon and Cornwall. These open fields, as was true of other highland zone counties, arose late and ended early. It is ninety years since the antiquarians of Devon first noticed the Great Field of Braunton, but in recent years several writers have been at work interpreting maps and the landscape. Since the Second World War fossilized hillside strips have aroused interest and further work on Braunton Great Field has shown that it existed as far back as 1324 but nobody has been able to elucidate the crop rotation. Fossil strips and Norden's map of 1598 have proved that there were two open fields at Crediton. The Great Field and the hillside open field of Great Braunton, with their strips divided by balks called *landsherds*, are still in use. Nine open-field villages existed between the thirteenth century and 1393. In three villages, in 1377, there was a two-course crop rotation, and in four a three-course crop rotation. Open fields were therefore very common in Devon and the only difference between them and the Midlands open fields seems to be the lack of symmetry in the disposition of strips between the fields. This fact has been disguised by early enclosure, from 1303 onwards. This produced numerous examples of fossilized strips, particularly in a belt of country in East Devon, on light, fertile, easily-drained soils. On low ground, scattered between Exmoor, Dartmoor and Bodmin Moor, there are over a hundred similar localities, of which five are particularly convincing.

In Tudor times, twelve Cornish villages had open fields. The Lanhydrock Atlas of 1696 shows infield-outfield villages, and open-field villages of the run-rig type at Land's End, on the western shore of the Lizard and four other places. The fields of Tinten in North Cornwall were enclosed only recently. Carew's remarks are worth quoting in the context of the early enclosure of open fields:

> But since the grounds began to receive enclosure and dressing for tillage the nature of the soil hath altered to a better grain. . . . These in times not past the remembrance of some yet living rubbed forth their estate in the poorest plight, their grounds lay all in common, or only divided by stitch-meal.

Henderson says:

> Gweal Hellis on the north side of the town is Cornish for the open field of Henlis, or Helston, and takes us back to the time when the town was surrounded after the Anglo-Saxon fashion by great common fields, in which each burgess had a number of strips or stitches. Nearly all the Cornish towns of the Middle Ages had such fields surrounding them.

Traces of open fields are visible in north-east Cornwall, in east Cornwall and Helston. Historians have suggested English influence and have written of hybrid villages and names, where a Celtic hamlet has converted itself into a nucleated village with open fields. In 1086 large villages with more than twenty ploughteams were found mainly in east Cornwall, but four lay in the west. Some of these large villages contained independent *trefi* (hamlets). The ancient pasture *trev* generally had no ploughs or plough-oxen. Five examples are known and some settlements were small arable farms. Just over 100 manors had two ploughlands or less.

Some Cornish villages had an infield-outfield system. Near the homestead was 'the Gew' or 'hedged-in place', the first intake of the settlement; then came a *parc* and then the *Gweal*, a larger, 'open' field which represented the outfield. The field boundaries sweep in continuous curves.

But open fields were by no means universal, even in the earliest periods. In Penwith there were small and irregularly patterned fields surrounded by granite boundary walls of Bronze or Iron Age origin. Great granite bounders or grounders have small stones on top, surmounted by a layer of turf. These walls are associated with prehistoric sites and at Amalveor in Towednack there was a Bronze Age hoard *in* the field bank.[3]

4 TECHNIQUES – CROP NUTRITION

In Devon, the assize roll of 1249 speaks of one Richard Harding of Leigh, who was suffocated to death in a marlpit. Nearly all the evidence shows marling peculiarly attached to assarting, even in parts of England where assarting was not very common.

In south-western England several other methods of fertilizing the soil were in use, the commonest being the use of sea-sand and beat-burning. Richard Carew wrote, in 1602, in *The Survey of Cornwall*:

> Then do they bring in sea sand of greater or lesser quantity, partly after their nearness to the places from which it is fetched, and partly by the good husbandry and ability of the tiller. An ordinary horse will carry two sacks of sand, and of such the borderers on the sea do bestow sixty at least in every acre, but most husbands double that number. The inland soil requireth not so large a proportion, and in some places they sow it almost as thick as their corn, for if they should strew the same very thick the ground would become over-rank and choke the corn with weeds.

The earth cast up by the tin-miners also found its way to the Cornishman's fields:

> for after the sea hath seasoned it with his salt and fructifying

moisture, his waves work up to the shore a great part thereof (together with more of his own store, grated from the cliffs), and the tillers, some by barges and boats, others by horses and wains, do fetch it and therewith dress their grounds. This sand is of divers kinds, colours, and goodness: the kinds, some bigger, some lesser, some hard, some easy. The colours are answerable to the next cliffs. The goodness increaseth as it is taken farther out of the sea. . . . Some have also used to carry up into their grounds, the ooze or salt water mud and found good profit thereby, though not equalling the sand.

In former times 'the shire, through want of good manurance, lay waste and open' but 'since the grounds began to receive enclosure and dressing for tillage, the nature of the soil hath altered to a better grain'. The lands near the sea were therefore richer than those inland, and the main inconvenience was that the people used their horses to carry sacks of sand when they were two-years-old, 'which boweth down and weakeneth their backs.'

The former times of primitive agriculture of which Carew wrote must have been at least 350 years before his time, for Henry III, in 1261, confirmed a grant of Richard, king of the Romans,

> for the common advantage of the land of Cornwall, allowing all the inhabitants to take seasand without payment and to heap the sand on their lands, and to cart it throughout Cornwall for the fertility of their lands by a proper road assigned or to be assigned. . . .

The original grant was made in about 1250.

Devon had the same practice. In 1270, the steward of a castle of the Earl of Cornwall set up a ferry with tolls at Saltash on the Tamar and charged twelvepence per annum on every barge. There were bitter complaints about this from the hundred jurors during the great inquest of 1275. In 1332 at Hurdwick the Abbey of Tavistock sowed wheat and oats on sanded land, and in 1350 at Werrington there were no foals born 'by reason of great toil in fetching sand'.

Carew also described the use of sea-weed for fertilizer:

To this purpose also serveth orewood, which is a weed either growing upon the rocks under high-water mark, or broken from the bottom of the sea by rough weather and cast upon the next shore by the wind and flood. The first sort is reaped yearly, and thereby bettereth in quantity and quality; the other must be taken when the first tide bringeth it, or else the next change of wind will carry it away. His use serveth for barley land. Some accustomed to burn it on heaps in pits at the cliffside, and so converted the same to a kind of wood, but the noisome savour hath cursed it out of the country. This floteore is now and then naturally formed like ruffs, combs, and such like, as if the sea would equal us in apparel, as it resembleth the land for all sorts of living creatures.

According to Carew the Cornish practised beat-burning with sanding.

For first, about May, they cut up all the grass of that ground, which must be newly broken, into turfs, which they call beating. These turfs they raise up somewhat in the midst, that the wind and sun may the sooner dry them. The inside turned outwards drieth more speedily, but the outside can the better brook the change of weather. After they have been thoroughly dried, the husbandman pileth them in little heaps, and so burneth them to ashes.

The husbandmen then fetch their sand.

A little before ploughing time, they scatter abroad those beat-boroughs and small sand-bags upon the ground, which afterwards, by the plough's turning down, give heat to the root of the corn. . . . The charges of this beating, burning, scoding and sanding, ordinarily amounteth to no less than twenty shillings for every acre, which done, the teller can commonly take but two crops of wheat and two of oats, and then is driven to give it at least seven or eight years leyre, and to make his breach elsewhere.

Yet in spite of its costliness it had been in use in Devon since 1225–50. In 1246, the lord of the manor of Leigh in Milton Abbot granted a fifteen-year lease of his demesne to the Abbot of Tavistock. The lessee was to limit the area of beat-burning to that for which he could provide manure, an indication of the possible harmfulness of the custom, and of the shortage of manure. Beat-burning was a technique for bringing marginal land into cultivation.

Beat-burning was also used in routine agriculture on the inlands of established farms to prepare ley ground for seeding. Beat-burning took place at Werrington in 1298, Hurdwick in 1332 and 1347, and Ottery in 1335–8 and 1342–4. The work was piece-work and included paring, burning and scattering. The average area burnt was nine acres, but twenty-seven acres were burnt at Hurdwick in 1347. Its usefulness was limited, for it could be harmful. Beat-burning was a particularly suitable preparation for rye. In 1298 at Werrington, 1332 at Hurdwick, and 1343 at Ottery land sown with rye was partly beatland and partly manured land.[4]

5 THE LIFE OF THE PEOPLE – THE PEASANT'S RESOURCES

In Devon and Cornwall most holdings seem to have been of half-virgate size, and what is known about farming in south-western England in the thirteenth and fourteenth centuries suggests that there was no fear of want.

CHAPTER 10

NORTHERN ENGLAND

1 NEW SETTLEMENT AND POPULATION GROWTH

Development was latest in the north. The exception to this rule is the East Riding of Yorkshire, which recorded no new-settlement place-names for the first time either after 1350 or in 1281–1350. For the rest, after 1350, Durham, the North Riding of Yorkshire and Westmorland each recorded two such names for the first time, Northumberland four, Cumberland five, the West Riding of Yorkshire twelve and Lancashire twenty-two. In 1281–1350 Westmorland recorded three for the first time, the North Riding of Yorkshire four, Northumberland six, Cumberland eight, Durham and the West Riding of Yorkshire twelve each and Lancashire no fewer than thirty-four. Lancashire was by far the most active county in the whole of England in new settlement after 1280, more than twice as active as its nearest competitors, Cheshire and the West Riding of Yorkshire. Apart from the strange inactivity of the East Riding of Yorkshire, the least active parts of northern England, considering the large area involved, were Westmorland and the North Riding of Yorkshire. This is the wildest part of England and contains great tracts above the highest practicable altitude for new settlement in Northern England, which is about 800 feet above sea-level. Thus some of the greatest areas of expansion were in northern England, and we know a good deal about them. Settlement had already begun long before 1086 in Lancashire and Yorkshire but it had a long way to go and there is little evidence of a pause in this activity.

By 1086 most villages in the plain of south-west Lancashire were firmly established but some important places in the lowlands were not yet recorded. To argue from the silence of Domesday, especially the exiguous Lancashire Domesday, would be foolish but we must note the first mention of Ormskirk in 1194 and of Liverpool in 1196. Round Liverpool a fringe of nucleated villages and dispersed hamlets grew up, such as Hale and Halewood. Hale was recorded in 1086 but Halewood was mentioned for the first time about 1200 and was a clearing in the wood belonging to Hale. Knowsley, 'the clearing of Cynewulf', first occurred in 1086. In 1161–75 there were frequent references to assarts. In 1199 John granted the knights, thegns and free tenants dwelling in the forests of the Honour of Lancaster licence to cultivate their woods, and in so doing confirmed an earlier grant of 1189–94 for which they had paid £500. By 1200–25 eight villages on the plain of south-west Lancashire had assarts. In 1288 Sir Adam of Hoghton granted a relative a piece of land and waste for pasture while they were not enclosed, and received in return the right to enclose entirely provided that the relative 'shall be kept indemnified for defect of closure unless he have insufficient cattle and this shall be judged according to the custom of *byrlaw* of that vill and country'. (The land was for pasture, not for arable, and the reference to by-laws is very early.) Some of the most interesting reclamations were taking place on the coastal marshes and carrs at Alt and Ince Blundell. On South Moor at Alt, after 1241, Richard Blundel granted Whalley Abbey half of Alt Marsh which Robert, a citizen of York, had first dyked. The investment of moneys perhaps gained by merchandise in draining marshes is unusual and significant. At Ince Blundell in 1241 the abbey and Richard Blundel exchanged land, marsh and meadow by the river Alt. The rest of Ince Marsh was to remain common pasture and uncultivated. In fact further small enclosures did take place, but by 1288 the general intention was to preserve the fen economy.

Some Cockersand assarts were on the south Lancashire plain. At Ainsdale, in about 1220–50, Lawrence son of Thomas, granted the abbey 'all my part of the whole marsh next their buildings, that is from Siward's croft as far as Blackmoor, however much of it they can "conquer", by reducing it to use with sand'. The technical use of the word 'conquer' for reclaiming marshland occurs elsewhere, especially in the fenland. Less common is the use of sand to make heavy wet land, newly drained, drier and lighter. Assarts existed in four other villages in 1190–1225, about 1190, 1200 and 1260.

The estates of Edmund, Earl of Lancaster, in 1296, contained substantial assarts. At West Derby four qualities of assarts approved from the waste existed, with a total area over 766 acres. The average value was well above the normal for late-thirteenth century arable. But this did not last. By 1346 the rent of the riddings was only twelve pence, since the whole was in decay: in all 142 acres, most of it assart land, was waste. Three other manors had 146 acres of approvements and eight bovates 'of former conquest'. In spite of the assarting the Forest of Derby and its woods were still at least 675 acres in area. We find assarts on the manor of Manchester and developments of a more pastoral kind in the forests of Rossendale and Pendle.

Whalley, an ecclesiastical centre of very great antiquity, has left an interesting post-Conquest tradition about its origins. In the churchyard of All Saints' church at Whalley there were, about 1300, certain stone crosses which the people called St Augustine's crosses, and the church was formerly called the White Church under Leigh. Whalley was an ancient chiefly and tribal centre. All Blackburnshire and Bowland had been for many years in the parish of Whalley Minster, but as the population grew they built three new churches in Blackburnshire which became the centres of new parishes. At first there was no castle at Clitheroe, and each rector possessed the church of Whalley as an endowment which he could give to his children or his friends, subject to the lord of Whalley's approval and institution by the Bishop of Lichfield. For a long time the rectors of both Whalley (which included Rochdale) and Blackburn were married men and lords of villages, and the rectors of Whalley were called not parsons but deans. This was because for a long time the population was so sparse and the country so wild and woodland, and there were so many wolves and wild animals, that the bishop had to allow the jurisdiction of the ordinaries or common deans to the rectors of Whalley. This state of affairs lasted 470 years to the time of William the Conqueror, and from then to the Lateran Council (presumably the Council of 1216). Before 1066 there were as many lords as there were villages, manses or men's manors, and all held directly from the king. In 1296 the monks of Whalley succeeded the deans of Whalley.

The foundation of chapels marks the growth of settlements in the hundred of Blackburnshire. Three already existed by 1100–35. Four came into existence in 1188–99 and before 1284. In 1284–1400 there were no new chapels in the parish. Nine others came into existence in 1461–2, 1461–85, 1511–12, 1540–1, 1543–4, 1577 and 1788. The foundation dates of these chapels reflect the economic tendencies of the periods.

Between the Ribble and Bowland Forest the countryside is very like Devon. Beyond Longridge, near Preston, the country is scattered with isolated farms named after trees – Ashes, Oakenclough, Hazelhurst and Birchen Lee. Below Wolf Fell is Wolfen Hall, a reminder of the savagery of this neighbourhood. By 1203 settlement was advanced because in that year a market arose at Chipping, near Preston, and by 1278–90 there was a ridding which grew wheat. St Mary of Sallay had an assart there in 1232–40. In remote country, Bleasdale was first recorded in 1228. Active settlement seems to have taken place between the late-twelfth and early-thirteenth centuries in this region.

Our account of the land between Ribble and Lune starts with the area around Preston. Most of the new settlement there was to the north-east in or near Fulwood. In 1252 Henry III legalized 324 acres of old and new purpresture under Fulwood. The men of Preston were to cultivate this land or not, as they wished, and in 1257 they had not only these 324 acres but had cleared more of Fulwood. The resulting enclosure was eighty acres in extent. There were further improvements in Fulwood in 1326 and in 1346 there was quite a healthy little settlement. In seven other villages in 1230–1327 there were seven riddings, nine assarts and a breach, and in two of these settlements the existence of a new field shows that the people had incorporated the assarts into the open fields. The rest of the region provides much evidence of thirteenth-century expansion.

The new settlement area north of Preston on the Lancashire Plain was around Garstang, with much late assarting. The Abbey of Cockersand had considerable properties in Amounderness, between Ribble and Lune. Assarts existed in four villages in 1206–46, 1212–42, 1212–46, 1230–68, 1238–59 and 1246–59, and in one of these there were both *Avenames* (intakes from the waste) and a new field. At Carlton, in 1212–42, assarting was active and if more should happen the abbey was to receive the share due to four bovates. Also at Carlton, in 1261, the abbey received one-sixteenth of the wasteland and of the arable land, all approvements to be made from the wastes, and the donor was to keep the approvements made in his and his father's lifetime. There were apparently enclosures in the mosses, marshes and carrs of Hackensall in 1246–62. By 1268–84 the coastal marshes between Preesall and Pilling were extensively dyked.

One of the most informative late assarting agreements is that for Wyresdale. In 1320 the Abbey of St Mary de Pré, Leicester, and Lady Christiana de Lindsay, agreed that she should have common of pasture in all lands assarted from the waste beyond Wyre, eastward and southward, except Wyresdale Park, which was enclosed. She might nevertheless assart beyond Wyre, and might enjoy all lands assarted on this side of Wyre except about six acres in five named assarts. These she had assarted since 1280, and together with the woods and wastes this side of Wyre they were to be open to the abbey's cattle and the cattle of the men of Cockerham all the year round, and the assarts there after hay-time and harvest. There were to be no further assarts this side of Wyre, westward and northward, but the abbot might make pigsties there of elm or willow deadwood. In 1327, the abbot agreed that she might assart beyond Wyre. This agreement is especially interesting because it distinguishes between the land inside the bend of the Wyre, which was well-settled and was to have no assarts made after 1280, and the land towards the Pennine foothills east of Wyre where assarting still continued in 1327.

Further north again there was assarting round Lancaster and in the Lune Valley. At Caton, cultivations extended into the moors and wooded valleys bordering Quernmore. In Furness there was very extensive new settlement in the twelfth century and continued enclosure in the later Middle Ages. Furness Abbey was founded in 1127, and in 1163 the monks added Furness Fells to their territory. Furness evolved into Plain Furness and High Furness – the mother territory and its colonies. Reclamation must have been very considerable, for in 1205–6 the monks paid £2669 (the equivalent of 53,380 acres) for pleas of the forest. The place-names mark two stages of settlement. The 'park' names date from 1127–1540 and represent the enclosure of open fell and the clearance of woodland for sheep-runs. The process reached its apogee in the fourteenth century. The second stage of settlement was the opening up of 'grounds' after 1540 and does not concern us here. The north of Lancashire was very wild country. In 1276 at Ulverston Furness Abbey and a neighbour agreed that the latter might keep most of his assarts in Ulverston. In return the neighbour confirmed the abbey's own assarts, and agreed that both parties and their men should common in turn every open time in the assarts. In 1333 other estates at Ulverston contained assarts.

Lancashire was extraordinarily active in new settlement in medieval times, particularly in the thirteenth century, and assarting continued until well after 1300. Here and there, and especially in south Lancashire, there were signs of regression by the 1340s. The mosses, carrs and marshes of the Lancashire Plain from the Mersey to Furness were everywhere favourite areas for assarting, but the region between Mersey and Ribble was perhaps the most active. Lowland Lancashire was very wet, with much turbary and large woods, especially in the Manchester region, but by the 1320s much of the turbary had gone and many of the trees were felled. Upland Lancashire, below the 1000-foot contour, was also very active in settlement from forest. Much of this land is in the Pennine foothills where there were many cattle ranches. Lancashire differs very much from the sandy heaths of Cheshire. Of highland Lancashire little is known. As in Staffordshire, Derbyshire and Cheshire land over 1000 feet above sea-level was not generally assart land. Lancashire was not an easy county to develop, and its development was very late, but it had a great variety of development, from the sea-dykes of Preesall to the upland assarts of the great parish of Whalley.

We turn to Cumberland which had a high density of clearings. No pre-Conquest clearings were recorded, and seventy-five out of 189 *leah* or *thwaite* names appeared after 1500, especially in the sixteenth and seventeenth centuries. Forty-seven names were first recorded in 1280–1500, nine of them in 1350–1500. Cumberland therefore settled most vigorously from the waste in 1200–1350 and after 1500. The country was very like Lancashire, but had more highland. Assarting in the Lake District was practically non-existent, but on the mosses and marshes of the coastal plain extensive. Round Solway Firth there were sea dykes and there was also extensive settlement in the Eden Valley.

Little is known about the state of Westmorland in 1086 since all but a small portion of the county is missing from the Domesday Survey. Westmorland was at no time a great new-settlement county. In spite of its undeveloped condition in 1086 it had only three *leahs* and four *thwaites*, that is, five clearings recorded in 1086–1280, and two in 1280–1350. Westmorland is one of the most purely mountainous counties in England and Wales and lack of forest may have affected its poor performance by the criteria chosen, but the same putative lack had no apparent effect upon other mountainous parts of England and Wales. The history of assarting there is very simple. It had begun by Henry II's time but it was scanty and found mainly in the northern and southern lowlands – the Eden valley and the Kendal region. The mountainous heart of Westmorland was untouched, and there was insufficient lowland for us to class it as a new-settlement county.

Evidence of new settlement is not plentiful in Durham and mostly comes from the late-twelfth century. Before 1195 the Bishop of Durham gave away 120 acres of land to be prepared and measured. At Finchale, probably in 1189–95, there was an assart, and before 1196, the hermitage of Finchale received land. If the hermit wished to break or plough anything new from the moor, he required the donor's permission. Soon after 1196 there was assarting from woodland in Chester-le-Street, and in about 1233–44 Finchale Priory received a wood to enclose and assart. This grant set some limit to the period of settlement.

Some of the earliest and most instructive references to assarting occur in 1183 and are particularly interesting because of the claim that the twelfth century was a period of economic regression. Assarts existed in seven villages, and in at least one of these they were recent. Four of these assarts contained 116.5 acres, but in three of the villages thirty acres and nine bovates, four which the bishop had bought and five of the villeinage, were waste. Assarting may have taken place in Darlington where the villeins held forty-eight bovates 'both of the old villeinage and of the new' and there were twelve rent payers on twelve bovates. Alternatively the new villeinage might have occupied demesne land. At Redworth a new village had recently come into existence. A tenant held 'the new town next Thickley' and there was 'Old Thickley, which was made from the territory of Redworth'. Assarting and agrarian decline were present simultaneously in 1183. In about 1190 sixty acres of assarts were in a peninsula of agriculture which was pushing westward into the waste in the upper reaches of the Derwent Valley. About 1190–5, the bishop granted away 'the towns of Cornsay and Hedley' which must have sprung up from the waste after 1153. Durham was very busy creating new villages, and all the evidence points to late but extensive new settlement.

Not much is known about new settlement in Northumberland, but it must have been fairly extensive after 1086. In 1189–90 the sheriff paid for the farm of 942 acres of purprestures and accounted for three acres of wasted wood. In 1286–7 the Cistercians had sown 600 acres of purpresture. Brinkburn Priory and others had a number of assarting interests in five Northumberland villages in 1242 and the priory had enclosed eighteen acres as early as 1153–95. In 1297, Hexham

Priory had mill-suit of all newly assarted lands and lands to be assarted. Here assarting was late.

After 1086 there is abundant evidence for new settlement in all three Ridings of Yorkshire. The great Cistercian abbeys of Yorkshire were reclaiming large quantities of land during the twelfth and thirteenth centuries. Rievaulx Abbey had assarted 880 acres by 1155–6, and in 1150–60 the monks had an assart near Barnsley for making smithies. In 1154–89 the abbey received a grant in the forest of Pickering with the right to cultivate at will. Below Pickering was then all waste and pasture, but by 1275–6 there were 300 acres of arable in the Vale of Pickering. Byland Abbey had assarted 500 acres by 1169–70. In 1230 the monks had eighteen and a half acres of assart sown with oats. In 1275 they had assarted forty acres in the forest of Galtres. Kirkall Abbey, had even more extensive ventures. In 1169–70 the monks had assarted 3000 acres, in 1174–5 700 acres, in 1177–8 6 acres and in 1184–5 3000 acres. Fountains Abbey was also assarting, and their grange at Marton le Moor was confirmed in 1162. Fountains also had an acre in arable and assart on the edge of Marston Moor in the twelfth century. Almost all the assarts in the forest of Pickering were sown in 1334 by which time seventy-four assarts had come into existence since 1217, mostly of five acres each, but some of twenty acres. The nunnery of Rosedale had enclosed and sown thirty-eight acres and the Abbey of St Mary at York had taken in eighty acres of meadow in the marshes near Pickering.

The West Riding of Yorkshire was in many ways the supreme new-settlement county. The eight volumes of the West Riding place-name survey recognize 324 place-names in *leah*, eighty-two of which are in the Domesday Survey, and sixty-four of which are names of villages. Most of these clearings were on the coal-measures – that is, on upland rather than highland. They were chiefly west of the Great North Road with clusters round Doncaster, Kellingley and Selby. Outside Calderdale, there were not many over the 800-foot contour. They were particularly rare in Upper Nidderdale and Craven, but also in the south-eastern marshland. To these we must add field-names in *leah* as well as place-names and field-names in *thwaite*. The grand total of all clearings in the West Riding is 1379. This makes one clearing every two square miles – the greatest density in England.

The West Riding divides into six geographical regions – the Vale of York, the Humberhead levels, the limestone hills, the sandstone hills, the Pennine Moors and Craven. Except in the valleys of the Nidd, Wharfe, Aire, Calder and Don there was not much new settlement in the Pennine moors, and, except in and on the slopes of the valley of the Ribble, even less in Craven. There were plenty of cattle-ranches in these areas but little cultivation over 800 feet above sea-level. This is in contrast to Devon. The greatness of the West Riding as a new-settlement county came from the enormous number of assarts in the four other regions. Woodland and moor in the sandstone and limestone hills made massive contributions to the clearances but woodland and fen ('moor' in the other sense) made even greater additions. The most ambitious reclamations were in the Vale of York and the Humberhead levels, especially round Selby, and for an overall impression the reader must ignore the county boundaries with the East Riding and Lincolnshire.

Assarting was often individual but sometimes communal, especially where dyke-building was necessary. Whole villages sometimes assarted from the waste together and, in some places, the bovate was the unit of assarting, shareholders receiving their allotments from the common assarts. But the appurtenance of assarts to bovates does not necessarily mean communal assarting. Sometimes individual commoners or groups of commoners took their share of the waste but other commoners did not. In these villages there were some bovates which had appurtenant assarts and some which did not. Occasionally, too, the assarts themselves were divided into bovates, but this was uncommon. The appurtenant assart was also sometimes a purchase or inheritance.

Assarts were frequently part of the open fields, and the open-field system itself grew up as a result of large-scale assarting. On the other hand, in upland wooded regions, full of becks, rivulets, streams and torrents, there were scattered twelfth- and thirteenth-century riddings, which often bore the names of owners with Old English or Old Scandinavian personal names and were therefore earlier than 1200. Isolated riddings in the waste were common in all the northern counties.

The West Riding must crown the account of new settlement. The characteristics of vigorous new settlement, begun late from a backward condition and continued late into the Middle Ages, sometimes after the Black Death, are common to all the new-settlement counties. Two periods of regression are known. In the West Riding, Derbyshire, Cheshire, Shropshire and parts of Lancashire there were many wholly or partly waste villages in 1066, 1086 and at various times between the two dates, and these villages had probably become waste earlier in the century. On the whole such villages were on upland or heath: a few were in marshland and some in highland. Most were below the 800-foot contour but above the 400-foot contour, and were therefore marginal land settlements. One reason for their comparative lack elsewhere in England may be the lack of land over 400 feet above sea-level. The lands of Burton Abbey showed in the time of Henry I some signs of decay too in east Staffordshire and south Derbyshire, and at least two West Riding villages had thoughts of regression in the 1130s and 1140s. At the other end of the period a few Staffordshire villages suffered from regression in the first half of the fourteenth century but elsewhere in the new-settlement counties there is little such evidence. Moreover, both in the first half of the twelfth century and in the period 1280–1350 there was good evidence that precisely those areas which had land falling out of cultivation were also, simultaneously, assarting from the waste. To claim, therefore, that at either of these periods full-scale decline had set in is scarcely possible, but there seems little doubt that, at any rate in the West Riding, the pre-Conquest regression was substantial, and that it took place on all types of land. Here the combination of a perhaps too-rapid growth in the tenth century and the political and military breakdown of the days of Ethelred Unraed produced a substantial setback, but the West Riding recovered rapidly in the early years of the twelfth century and continued the long, swift march it had begun long years before the West Saxon dynasty foundered in treachery and guilt. The North and East Ridings were different.

The whole of the immense North Riding of Yorkshire, in 2128 square miles, has only 47 names in *leah* and *thwaite*, including all field and farm names. This means only one clearing every forty-five square miles, but the county place-names survey, which dates from 1928, may be inadequate. Fifteen clearings existed in 1086, and the thirteenth century produced thirteen. Twelve clearings first appeared in the records after 1280. The chronological distribution of *thorpes* is even more significant. Their number is small – only thirty-six – and fewer than the number of West Riding *thorpes* which appeared for the first time in the thirteenth century (forty). The difference in size between the surveys does not account for all this. There are still 130 *thorpes* in the West Riding if we exclude thirty-eight field-names and still 136 if we exclude all those names which did not appear until the seventeenth to nineteenth centuries. If we put together North Riding names in *leah*, *thwaite* and *thorpe* they show that the great settlement period was before 1086 – much of it probably in the tenth century – and that there was not much after. We must look for a long slow development, perhaps continuous to the end of the period.

The North Riding divides into seven geographical regions. There was comparatively little new development in the Pennines and the North Yorkshire Moors, apart from cattle ranches in the dales. Some assarting took place in the Vale of York and some on the coastal fringe. Most was in Cleveland, the Howardian hills and the Vale of Pickering – especially the latter. As in the West Riding, the greatest amount of assarting was in the carrs and fens round the lowland rivers; next in importance came the uplands; higher than 800 feet above sea-level there was little. The Pennine Moors of the West Riding, outside Craven, contain more upland and less highland than the Pennines and the North Yorkshire Moors of the North Riding. The marshes of the Vale of York and the Vale of Pickering form a smaller proportion of the North Riding than the marshes of the Vale of York and the Humberhead levels form of the West Riding. Progress there certainly was in the North Riding and assarting continued after 1300, but it was not so fast or so extensive as in the West Riding. The North Riding was altogether more wild and intractable.

The East Riding had many of the characteristics of the North Riding, but it is a county of marsh and wolds, devoid of highland. The county place-name survey is fairly new – 1937 – and more complete than some, but it lists, amazingly, only twenty-one *leahs* and *thwaites* in 1172.5 square miles – one every fifty-eight square miles. This is an even smaller density than that found in the North Riding. Eight clearings were first known in 1086, and six after 1280. The predominance of early settlement is not so obvious with the clearings as with the element *thorpe*. The East Riding has sixty-nine examples and fifty-six of these are in Domesday. *Thorpe* is twice as common as in the North Riding and more common than in the West Riding and Lincolnshire. Out of these sixty-nine names, forty-nine have personal names, mostly Old Scandinavian, as their first elements. There can be no doubt that the East Riding developed far during the tenth century. Similarly, there can be no doubt of the extent of the wasteland in 1066 and 1086. Holderness was practically exempt, and most of the waste villages were in the Yorkshire Wolds, but there was a large group in the Humberhead levels, and a few in the Vale of York. Compared with the West Riding, the East Riding was not a great new-settlement county. Very little evidence of assarting is known from the Yorkshire Wolds which occupy one-third of the county, rise to only 808 feet, but are practically devoid of villages. Holderness, the Vale of Pickering, the Vale of York and the Humberhead levels are all very low-lying, often carr or fen, and in these regions most of the assarts were fen intakes. Progress there undoubtedly was, right down to about 1300, but it was slow.

The North and East Ridings exhibit similar characteristics. Like the West Riding and some other new-settlement counties they had much wasteland in 1066, but recovery was much slower than in the West Riding. The fenland regions of all three ridings became rich by 1350, but not so rich as the Lincolnshire Fenland. The highland regions of the Pennines and the Yorkshire Moors, and the upland zone of the Yorkshire Wolds, remained poor and undeveloped.

Nothing positive is known about population movements in northern England in the twelfth century. The greatest population growths of all in the two centuries after 1086 occurred in the highland zone, especially in northern England. In the East Riding of Yorkshire the growth was nine or ten times, in the North Riding eleven and a half to thirteen and a half times, and in the West Riding three and a half times. The parts of Yorkshire which created fewest new settlements experienced the greatest surge of population. However, all over northern England Domesday surveys manors without recording the presence of any inhabitants, and without mentioning waste. This absence of people may reflect the ignorance of the commissioners and the difficulty of carrying out King William's instructions in such wild country, rather than the ravages of the royal army sixteen years before, and the subsequent rapid recovery of a devastated countryside. The population increase in 1086–1300 may be more apparent than real.

On the other hand, in the East Riding of Yorkshire, three out of the four manors for which there is comparative material declined in 1280–1350, but there is no evidence for a like decline in the North and West Ridings. In the North Riding of Yorkshire there is some evidence of stagnation in 1280–1300, and a group of ten Lancashire manors shrank by more than a third in 1323–46. Seven Lancashire manors expanded in population in 1280–1350. There is no population evidence which would make comparisons possible at all in the four northernmost counties.[1]

2 CROPS AND LIVESTOCK

Lancashire presents, throughout the thirteenth century, a spectacle of unreclaimed wildernesses of woodland, moss and fell. Even the Manchester region had comparatively little settlement and preoccupied itself with cattle-rearing and hunting. In 1282 there was pannage of the wood at Heaton Norris, and in the Forest of Hopeworth pannage and an eyrie of hawks. In 1322 Blackley alone had pasture for 240 cattle and 240 deer and in Horwich there were eight vaccaries. Alport Wood was one mile round, and had pannage, honey, and eyries of hawks, herons and eagles, as well as many oak trees. In four villages in the Lancashire lowlands in 1219–1304 there was pasture for 500 sheep, 213 cattle, 186 pigs, 83 horses and 60 goats.

Whalley Abbey had many of its estates in and around the Forest of Rossendale, which was a notable assarting region on the flanks of the Pennines. Cattle were supreme in the forest. In 1194–1283 in four places, the abbey received pasture for 348 cattle, 120 sheep, 60 pigs and two horses. Possessions in the marshes of Amounderness were better adapted for sheep than cattle. The mosses in the south of Lancashire were also good for breeding horses. The Abbot of Chester's men of Whitby had common for forty horses in the marsh (1277), and on Gonolf Moor Whalley Abbey had pasture for eighty.

Most of the possessions of Cockersand Abbey were in Amounderness. In 1190–1268, in thirteen villages, the abbey received pasture for 412 pigs, 306 cattle, 251 sheep, 50 goats and 45 horses, as well as unstinted pasture for sheep in two villages, goats in one village, pigs in another village and a vaccary. In 1190–1250 St Mary of Sallay in Craven received pasture rights for 620 pigs, 240 sheep, 148 cattle and 60 horses in five villages. There were comparatively few sheep, many swine, a great many cattle, some horses and here and there herds of goats. The northern lowlands of Lancashire were not remarkably different therefore from the highlands.

The economy of Blackburnshire and the Forest of Rossendale

was also highly pastoral. Already in 1194 Wyresdale had fifteen
vaccaries and a century later there were twenty-nine in four
forests. The number of cattle in them remained much the same
in 1296 as in 1305 and was over 2500. In addition to the vaccaries
there were two ox-farms and a place for cows. The herdsman
lived in a booth. By 1324 there were only 415 beasts in twelve
farms, but in 1341–2 there were new cowhouses and repairs on
six farms. In 1342 the lord let out four of them and he had
previously let four others. On the other hand, at Haslingden, in
1311, there were at least 2000 acres of arable. The Earls of
Lancaster and Lincoln had vast estates in the Lancashire Pennines
and lowlands which specialized in cattle-rearing, with increasing profits from the sale of beasts and hides. In 1323–4 the lands
of Thomas, Earl of Lancaster and Robert of Holland had
extensive interests of this kind. The grange at Standen mainly
grew oats, and kept affers and 31 cattle. Twelve vaccaries were
in hand and housed 425 cattle. All these vaccaries were also on
the list of vaccaries farmed out 'besides the sustenance of the
lord's stock' so that the real size of the herds must have been
much greater. In addition twenty-four vaccaries, each with
eighteen cows, were in the hands of farmers. There seem
altogether to have been thirty-seven vaccaries of this lordship in
Blackburnshire. Two manors grew mainly oats, with some
beans, peas, barley, and wheat, and there was hay, horses, 114
cattle (including sixteen milch kine), and thirty swine. The
estates of the de Lacy Earls of Lincoln also included a large
number of vaccaries. In 1304–5 the cattle in stock in
Blackburnshire were 387 in Trawden, 848 in Pendle, 849 in
Rossendale and 328 in Accrington. There were five vaccaries in
Trawden, ten in Pendle, eleven in Rossendale and five in
Accrington. The grand total of cattle in 1305 was 2518. The Earl
was therefore a mighty cattle-rearer with the number of cattle
he kept remaining fairly steady in 1296–1305. He sold a very
great number every year of both cows and oxen, but especially
oxen. The forests of Lancashire must have been one of the main
producers of draught cattle for the long-settled arable plains of
the south and centre. As to crops produced on these granges, oats

was overwhelmingly more important than anything else, but the amount of grain grown altogether was not large. In 1311 there were still five vaccaries in Trawden, eleven at Pendleton, eleven in Rossendale and four in Accrington.

The county of Lancashire contains a good deal of land over 800 feet above sea-level, especially in the hundreds of Salford and Blackburn (the Forest of Rossendale) and in the narrowing coastal plain north of the Ribble and the fringes of the Lake District in Furness. The coastal plain was very wet, with numerous mosses, and there were coastal marshes in the Fylde and elsewhere. Nowhere was there much arable and as a rule oats was the most important and sometimes practically the only crop grown. Here and there, especially in Furness, there were major flocks of sheep, goats were not unknown even in the thirteenth century, and there were swine in the woods, sometimes in quite large numbers. Nevertheless cattle reigned supreme. Doubtless other highland regions had equally large numbers of cattle, but in Lancashire the record of their numbers is extant; thus we know that the Lancashire Pennines contained scores of vaccaries by the middle of the thirteenth century, and that right down to 1350 there were thousands of cattle. Many were cows and produced milk and calves, but many more were oxen intended for sale as draught animals.

In Westmorland evidence is good for four manors. At Beetham in 1254 the demesne included the hall, the garden, pannage for about eighty swine, demesne pasture for eighty cattle and two ploughteams of oxen. The lord let the two mills, there was a demesne fishery and an eel fishery. At Langdale there was herbage in the forest for about 600 cattle, a watermill and a fishery in Rothay Mere; at Lyth and Crosthwaite a watermill, a brewery and pannage for about twenty-four swine. Nine grants of pasture stints are known. All the swine were in one village but otherwise the various animals were fairly evenly spread. Beef and milch kine were more numerous than draught animals, and there were few horses. There were numerous sheep. Westmorland did not differ very much from Cumberland in its preference for livestock. One region has left details of sales of corn and livestock in 1294–5. Oats was overwhelmingly more prominent than any other grain – ten times more plentiful than wheat and eighteen times as popular as barley. Dredge and beans were insignificant. Cattle and swine sold were clearly of major significance, but no sheep were sold.

Pasture stints for twenty-four Cumberland manors are known. Not surprisingly for a mountainous area sheep were the most favoured animals and flocks were very large. Swine were the next most popular animal and nearly half of these were the 360 swine which could feed in Walton Forest. Goats were the most novel feature of the Cumberland scene and their presence indicates its mountainous nature. Their distribution was narrow but the herds were large. Milk and beef cattle were only slightly more plentiful than goats and were more widespread. Other cattle were over three times as abundant as oxen but there were nearly three times as many oxen as horses. Cumberland was old-fashioned in the matter of draught animals, but pasture was more significant than arable. Sheep (many of them in coastal marshes), swine, goats and cattle were the livestock most favoured in Cumberland. In 1217 or 1220 wheat was the prime grain, followed by maslin, with barley and oats third. Sheep outnumbered cattle.

At Temple Thornton, in Northumberland, in 1308–10 the manor sowed oats and wheat and cut twenty-one acres of hay. In stock were oats, wheat, barley, barley and oats mixed, and rye and maslin. Temple Thornton was a comparatively under-developed pastoral manor which had in stock, in 1308, a large herd of cattle, 485 sheep, a few goats, swine and geese. Newminster Abbey and Hexham Priory had pasture in Clifton for six horses, 280 sheep, twenty oxen, and twelve cattle. In 1297 Hexham Priory had common pasture on the moor for 100 cattle in a shieling. The number of sheep was moderately large, but there were fair numbers of cattle and horses, especially in the hills. Brinkburn Priory had stints for 170 swine, 132 cattle, sheep horses and oxen. There was considerable variation in Northumberland between different villages according to their geographical positions.

In Durham in 1183 many of the estates of the Bishop of Durham were let to farm for a corn rent. On eight manors, the farmers of the demesne paid rents in grain. Wheat, oats, barley is an interesting order of precedence for a new-settlement county. The mill at Cralton rendered wheat as a rent, which reflects the grain the peasants grew. A farmer of one of the demesnes could have 100 sheep there.

In 1337–8 the great manor of Bishop Auckland apparently did not produce its own grain or livestock, but received them from elsewhere on the bishop's estates as need dictated. Barley malt was overwhelmingly the most important item in the food-rents, followed by oats and wheat; beans and peas were insignificant. Cattle and swine were the only meat eaten, with cattle coming before swine. In 1348–9 oats and wheat were by far the favourite grains with oats very considerably in the lead. Barley was insignificant, rye scarcely existed and legumes were negligible. Oxen were often the most numerous livestock and always exceeded milk or beef cattle. There were very few sheep – often none at all – horses were few and only swine at all plentiful. On the whole the arable quite decidedly outweighed the pastoral on the Durham estates.

In 1303–48 there was a clear excess of oxen over affers and no affers at all in 1310–21 and 1348. Draught cattle were also always more prominent than milch kine, but the number of milch kine was greater in 1326–48 than in 1303–26. Horses were scarce, but swine were fairly plentiful, and both tended to diminish in numbers in the second half of the period. Sheep were far more popular than one might expect in a highland zone county. Their numbers fluctuated greatly but increased steadily in 1303–13 and 1326–38. The movements in the numbers of sheep and swine tended to follow each other. Sometimes there were a few birds – ducks, fowls, geese, and capons. Some of these creatures lived to a ripe old age, like the fourteen geese which were 'old' in 1326. In 1313 there were also cheeses in stock.

The stock of grain varied from one year's end to the other. In 1310–38 the acreage of wheat sown fluctuated. All the wheat was sown by 6 November in 1326; in 1338 forty-six acres were sown and twenty acres remained to be sown on 6 October. On 15 August 1310 the wheat was still not harvested, and the amount in stock was down to three quarters. At the same time thirty-six acres was still unharvested, but 300 traves of barley had been harvested. There was no barley sown yet on 6 October 1338, 6 November 1326 or 22 December 1331, but on 15 February 1313 twenty-two acres of barley had been sown. At this last date beans, peas and oats still remained to be sown, but beans and peas were sown by 17 May 1321. The acreages of the various crops differed from year to year. Oats was generally much less widespread than wheat, but in 1313 there was rather more sown of the former than the latter. Barley was seldom even one-quarter as popular as wheat. Peas and beans were surprisingly the second crop.

The monks kept a careful check upon their food supply. On 17 May 1321 there was one tun of wine in stock for lack of malt. On 1 October 1326 there was sufficient wheat in the barn, less the seed, for the support of the house until the new harvest, and there were enough beans and peas. There was scarcely enough barley and oats for malt until Christmas. On 21 August 1303 the harvest was still in the fields and the inventory remarks: 'Item in the barn of wheat nor of any other corn nothing at present, but the Lord will shortly give us abundantly of his grace.' 'Of oats, beans and peas nothing before autumn.' The economy was highly arable with wheat and legumes prominent and a fair number of swine and sheep.

In the Pennines in the West Riding there were many vaccaries, but we know less about them than about those in Lancashire. The best documented are the de Lacy cattle ranches in Sowerbyshire. In 1309 five vaccaries had three ox-houses, three hay-barns and a small house for the farmer, and there were 124 acres of meadow whose hay would support 192 cattle in the winter. The lord moved his cattle to summer pastures, one of which would take 38 fat beasts. In 1314 one of these vaccaries had 100 cattle, but in 1315 the lord leased at least three vaccaries. Three others were linked with the pasture on Mankinholes Moor. At Knaresborough and Aldborough in 1296–7 there were extensive woods for the peasants' pigs, which exceeded 1000 in number. The moors were sufficiently extensive to take 306 cattle and 57 horses in the summer and 44 cattle and 30 horses in the winter. Henry de Lacy, Earl of Lincoln, had estates in the West Riding in 1296. On three manors much of the land was on lease. On the whole sheep were quite significant, but the sale of 13,900 faggots illustrates the wooded nature of much of the West Riding. Oats, wheat, dredge, barley, rye, maslin and peas was the order of magnitude of crops threshed.

In ninety-three different places in the West Riding of Yorkshire in 1160–1332 sheep were overwhelmingly the first animals, but none are recorded in fourteen villages in 1175–1301. Goats were not very common but elsewhere in England were even rarer. The destructive power of goats seems to have been well-known in medieval England, and there are several examples of agreements which ban them. Cattle were more plentiful, even in the less mountainous parts of the West Riding, than in the Midlands. Specialization in cattle to the exclusion of sheep is apparent only in Bowland, Bolton, Rushton and in the Forest of Gisburn. Horses were more than 50 per cent fewer than cattle, but they appeared in multitudes in those regions where there were many cattle, chiefly in the more mountainous parts. Swine were rather less prominent than horses, their occurrence was more scattered but the herds were larger because the pig is more fertile.

The pastoral nature even of the lowlands is very clear. Thus cattle exceeded sheep in the wapentakes of Ewcross and Aggebrigge, but sheep outnumbered cattle slightly in the Liberty of Ripon and the wapentake of Strafford. The largest village herds of cattle were all near high moorland but some of these higher areas also carried considerable flocks of sheep. In some of the more highly arable villages oxen were more numerous than other cattle. The balance between cattle and corn was very fine in Strafford Wapentake, Ewcross was highly pastoral and the Liberty of Ripon and the Wapentake of Aggebrigge betwixt and between. The West Riding was conservative in its choice of draught animals compared with

Bedfordshire. Oxen greatly outnumbered affers as a rule but twenty-four villages preferred affers to oxen. Compared with the southern counties the West Riding of Yorkshire had a good number of affers at work. The greatest arable wapentake was Strafford. Oats were everywhere predominant, but the largest crops were on the high marginal lands. The major wheat and rye crops were all in Strafford wapentake at five wheat villages and three rye villages. Strafford wapentake therefore specialized in oats, rye, wheat and sheep; cattle and horses were everywhere popular, but Ewcross was the great cattle-rearer.

A truer picture emerges if we take out the lords. Few of the twenty-seven lords had very substantial holdings. The only great sheep-farmers were all monasteries: the Prior of Worksop, the Porter of Fountains and the Abbot of Roche. The gentry used three times as many oxen as affers, had five times as many sheep as cattle, followed the rest of the countryside by growing mainly oats, but grew more wheat than rye. These differences from the peasantry are not unexpected. The peasantry had a little less of everything than the whole populace, and particularly of sheep and oats, except that it owned more affers. The gentry were not a major part of the taxable population of the West Riding of Yorkshire.

Elsewhere in the West Riding of Yorkshire oats was the main crop. In 1296–7, at Rockcliff in Aldborough, by yields the crops were oats, wheat, rye, maslin (rye, peas, and barley), barley and peas. There were affers and oxen.

There were early vaccaries in the East Riding of Yorkshire. In 1179–89 Bridlington Priory received pasture for a vaccary of fifty cows, thirty mares and oxen in summer. In 1170–5 the Hospital of Lepers at Newton Garth received 500 sheep, the 24 oxen of 3 ploughs, 6 bulls, 12 cows, 20 swine, 100 hens and 60 geese. Pasture stints are known for thirty-four villages in the East Riding which was a considerable sheep-rearing region, though sheep did not occur everywhere. Cattle were the next most prominent animals and draught cattle were a third as numerous as milk and beef cattle. Swine were nearly twice as plentiful as oxen, but there were few really large herds. Horses were comparatively few and there were no goats. The East Riding was on the whole much more largely arable than the rest of northern England. Conditions varied widely from place to place from the less well-developed to the better-developed areas.

At Howden, in 1296, barley was the main crop followed by wheat, oats, rye and maslin. In Holderness, over all seven manors and the whole period 1262–91, oats were about one-sixth ahead of wheat, and barley and beans were of equal significance. Over the period 1262–76 the yield of oats was more than one-third as large again as the yield of wheat; the crops of barley and beans were equal in size and insignificant. In 1277–90 oats had lost nearly all its lead over wheat; barley and beans were equal and had increased their yield ten-fold. The area under the plough had increased by only 5 per cent but the yield had increased by more than one-half. An oats and wheat economy was gradually giving way to a barley and beans economy, with highly beneficial results for the output of grains and legumes.

In Holderness a great decline in pastoralism accompanied this change. In 1264–78 and 1279–91 the area of meadow shrank to three-eighths, and in 1263–74 and 1284–92 the number of sheep likewise shrank to under three-eighths of the first total. In 1279–91, compared with 1263–78, the butter production fell by two-thirds and in 1279–91, compared with 1263–78, the cheese production fell by three-quarters. Holderness was becoming a more highly developed area by 1300, and was turning away from pastoralism and oats to growing wheat, barley and beans; it was coming to look more like some of the long-settled counties of eastern England.

The North Riding of Yorkshire was much wilder, and given more to cattle-rearing and oats than the East Riding. There is no real evidence whether or not there was agrarian progress in the 250 years after the Norman Conquest. The Riding had very large interests in pastoralism, and numerous vaccaries are known to have existed both in the Pennine Moors and in the Yorkshire Moors. Like the East and West Ridings the North Riding of Yorkshire is geographically very varied. All three Ridings have a good deal of lowland and marsh which often accounts for the large flocks of sheep (large by the standards of the new-settlement counties). The only regions without sheep were the Forest of Teesdale, Swaledale, Pickering Waste and seven villages elsewhere. Flocks were often large. Cattle were less numerous than one might expect outside the moorland regions with large vaccaries. Many of the pasture stints for cattle recorded were in the Forest of Teesdale. Oxen were less than a quarter as many as beef and dairy cattle. Horses fell behind oxen and almost half of these were in the Forest of Teesdale. Swine exceeded both horses and oxen, but only fourteen villages had swine stints. Swine were concentrated in the wooded regions. There were 100 goats at West Witton.

Altogether the North Riding of Yorkshire was wilder and more pastoral than the East Riding of Yorkshire – perhaps wilder and more pastoral in the Pennine Moors than the West Riding. In special areas like the Vale of Pickering and Holderness a more advanced agriculture was developing by the fourteenth century, not unlike the agriculture of eastern and east Midland England.[2]

3 TECHNIQUES – THE OPEN FIELDS

In northern England there were many more open-field villages than Gray imagined, but their origin may be very late. Of the thirteen open-field villages which he found in Durham only one was early (1325). In Northumberland too the evidence is late.

The Lancashire open fields were divided into furlongs or groups of ridges, which were in turn divided into holdings called *butts* or *doles*, which varied considerably in size. These again were ploughed into ridges called *lands* or *selions*, which were also sometimes called *butts* or *doles*. The common arable and meadow of a settlement consisted of one large, or a number of small, open fields. The tenants held *oxgangland* in strips, which were unevenly distributed between the fields. In lowland Lancashire there was a system of 'half-year land', land which

was six months under tillage and six months fallow, with little
or no wheat; Furness had an infield-outfield system. Lancashire's
open-field system was unlike the Midland two- or three-field
systems, since there were no symmetrically located strips. Gray's
criterion does not exclude Lancashire from the list of open-field
counties, for unequal distribution existed in manors of Evesham
Priory, Glastonbury Abbey and Shaftesbury Abbey in
unimpeachably open-field country. Lancashire was an open-
field county by the thirteenth century, when on the coastal plain
between Preston and Lancaster several manors of Cockersand
Abbey had open fields. By the end of the medieval period there
were 164 examples of open fields in this county, mostly in the
Lancashire plain. They also existed in Lonsdale and Furness,
both along the coastal plain and in the Lune Valley. In the deep
valleys and on the high fells in Wyresdale, Bleasdale and
Longridge there were few open fields south of the Ribble in the
land of pastoral farming and many vaccaries. But there were
open fields in the valleys of the upper Ribble and Calder in four
villages. After the division of the vaccaries, in the sixteenth
century, there were also open fields in the Irwell Valley. The
mosslands of Amounderness and the south-western Fylde, such
as Marton Moss, were without open fields, but the settlements
on the edge of Over Wyresdale Moss had them. There were also
few open fields in the lowlands and mosses south of the Ribble.
South of Preston the boulder-clay country had open fields down
to the seventeenth century, and the same was true of the Shirdley
Hill sands and boulder-clay country round Ormskirk and
Liverpool. There were also open fields east of Chat Moss. In
general the Lancashire open fields were small. The real fields
were the furlongs, which were the units of production.
Lancashire seems not to have grown winter corn at all during
the Middle Ages, for the main crop was oats, highly suitable in a
cold, wet, sunless, climate. When there is no winter corn there is
less need to clean the land with a yearly fallow and the yield
of oats is so low that it is better to have all the land in production.

Study of the open fields of Cumberland began in 1893, when

balks or raines still existed in some villages. In 1704 Great Orton had rigs, raines, a fieldway, meadows and closes round the homesteads. In 1908 there was still evidence of open fields at Hayton. In 1909 balks and raines were still to be seen elsewhere and in 1591 Holme Cultram possessed by-laws, often the accompaniment of full common-field practices. The townfields of Cumberland apparently had no fallow course. Rig and raine were their normal divisions, and one field was generally under permanent cultivation or infield, with the others forming a sort of outfield. At Holme Cultram there were formerly three open fields and two on the lands of Wetherhal Abbey. In 1795, there had recently been open fields in seven villages. Enclosure acts mention common fields in nine villages. By 1913 there still survived at least four arable enclosures held in rig and raine, seventeen enclosures wholly or partly in grass, with raines, and fifteen old share-meadows. The focus of the old open-field country of Cumberland was Carlisle, but there were open-field strip lynchets in three other villages elsewhere. Halltown in Rockcliff was by then extinct as an open-field village. It was cropped continuously and there was no common pasture. There were also townfields in former times in seven other villages. The open fields of Cumberland were at their greatest extent in the sixteenth century. Before 1500 they were still growing and coming into existence, for assarting was still continuing, but after 1600 they began to decline in numbers and extent. There were apparently no open fields in the Lake District, the Fells or the Border mosslands. The exceptions were Wasdale Head and the Vale of Lorton, in 1567, where there was very extensive waste. In six open fields grazing rights on the stubble existed in 1518–1709. The peasants tethered their cattle to graze on the balks or raines in the summer during the day-time, and in the evening brought the young stock to the common and the milch kine to the closes. There were pasture stints on the open fields. Such fields consisted of an infield and an outfield. The infield grew peas and beans, and received sea-weed as a fertilizer. The so-called tangle dales are a remnant of this practice. The outfield, which received only the dung of animals, produced either five years crop with five years fallow, or three years crop and nine years fallow. The unit of cultivation and fallowing was the internal division calling the riving, and uncropped rivings were a part of the waste.

Three types of settlement went with the open fields in Cumberland. First, certain nucleated settlements had open fields. Aspatria is a large settlement on the boulder clay shelf above the valley of the Ellen. In 1567 two-thirds of its open field were in the outfield, which consisted of eight rivings. Over a quarter of the infield was under hay. At Mockerkin there was additional enclosed land which the tenants shared for grazing. At Hayton there were open fields and four daughter settlements.

Secondly, there were certain small hamlets with open fields. Westward is a large parish on the northern fringe of the Lake District. It was very pastoral and received summer animals from the outside. In the mountains there were scales (or shielings) and by the sixteenth century some of these had become permanent hamlets. Late medieval settlement was piecemeal here and led to the growth of closes. Eventually there were nine hamlets and eighty-six individual farms, and the closes contained more than three times as much land as the open fields.

Lastly, there were the Cistercian open fields of Holme Cultram. These were unique. In 1538 nine hamlets had shares in the four rivings. Long leys were customary and there were pasture stints upon the leys. Besides this there was the former monastic colt pasture, which after 1540 contained open-field strips. There were no rivings in this new field, and the inhabitants grew corn for three years and laid the land down to pasture for six years. By 1537 there were also small hamlets round nine granges, some of which had open fields. During the sixteenth century reclamation was very active and still largely communal. In 1538–1637 the inhabitants added new open fields, and during the sixteenth century the open fields of Cumberland increased by 1700 acres.

Historians have known of the existence of an open-field system in Yorkshire for many years, but hitherto there has been little attempt to distinguish between the field-systems of the upland parts of Yorkshire, especially the Pennine Dales, and those of the Great Vale of York. About 1650 Yorkshire was not an entirely open-field county, but more than half of the 403 villages recorded were open-field villages. In the West and North Ridings there were more villages without open fields than with them. Only in the East Riding was there a great excess of open fields over closes. This was because open fields existed mainly in the highly arable lowland areas round the Great Vale of York and in the East Riding. Closes predominated in the upland deaneries of the West Riding, and in Cleveland in the North Riding.

The study of the open fields in Yorkshire seems to have begun in 1888. The open fields of Wibsey, near Bradford, were still extant in 1884, and were mapped in 1829. The complicated field-system of Wakefield was already apparent in 1438, when there were selions or lands in the open fields and doles in the common meadows. In 1279–80 there were already nine open fields. This arrangement was typical of the hillier parts of Yorkshire. Even on the fringes of the upland there were villages with many open fields. Pontefract had seven.

Most Yorkshire villages in the lowland zone had two, three or four open fields. Six possible two-field villages are known from 1216–1346. Seven three-field villages are known from 1309–44. The existence of two, three or four fields implies nothing about the crop rotations or the existence of any form of communal husbandry. Nevertheless, from time to time the distribution of the holdings becomes apparent. Without some form of communal regulation such a distribution would have made life difficult.

The northern open fields probably developed late because settlement was late and really large villages did not grow up until modern times. Assarting probably created the open fields, all over England, but at different dates in different parts of England and Wales – in the late-seventh to early-ninth centuries in southern England and the east and west Midlands, and in the twelfth and thirteenth centuries in northern England. These same late-developing counties also tended to lose their open fields early, producing the typical *bocage* countryside. The most recent view of the open fields takes their origin and nature back where Vinogradoff found them, when he wrote of the medieval village as a community of shareholders who parcelled out the land as equitably as possible. Each part of England and Wales has furnished evidence of this process and the study of assarting has added greatly to our understanding. For a while enthusiasm for the open air and the Orwins' famous book have clouded this understanding, but the modern student of the open fields now perceives that the unspoken assumptions about the nature of rural society which our forebears possessed, rather than the action of the plough, shaped and perfected the field systems.[3]

4 TECHNIQUES – CROP NUTRITION

Northern England frequently used marling. The place-name survey of the West Riding of Yorkshire has two examples from 1341 and 1496, and several later ones. The Earl of Cornwall's estates in Aldborough bought a new cart for carrying marl in 1296–7. In Ilkley, about 1263, common rights included the opening up of the land for marling. At Constable Burton after 1290, there was a private marlpit. Nor was marling unknown in Lancashire. At Walton in 1263 Whalley Abbey received land in Walton Wood inside the assarts the monks already held and an assart Brother Richard of the Woolshed had enclosed. The lord gave the abbey the right to take marl upon his land wherever they liked to marl all the assarts they held from him in his wood. In 1348–9 on an estate of the Bishop of Durham there was nothing from the sale of marl, since none was sold, by order of the seneschal. In the thirteenth century on three manors in Northumberland, the Abbey of New Minster received the right to take marl.

Sanding took place in the north of England. The earliest example is from Hackensall in Amounderness, Lancashire, where, in 1246–62, Cockersand Abbey received land and the right of taking sand from the nearest pool, and of drawing it to the land. At Millom in Cumberland in 1260–80 sanding went with saltmaking. Here Furness Abbey received a saltern and sand for improving the lands belonging to the saltern.

Sea-weed was also a fertilizer in Cumberland in the sixteenth century, and there are certainly medieval examples of its use in the north. In 1292 the Abbey of Holm Cultram had rights to seawrack on the island of Holm Cultram. During the thirteenth century the monks of Newminster received land and the right to take sea-weed for fattening their land at Chopwell in Northumberland.

Liming also took place in the north of England. At Auckland, in Durham, the Bishop of Durham made liveries of wheat to a certain person burning one limekiln in 1337–8. At Wetherhal in Cumberland in about 1220–1 Wetherhal Priory received common in a wood, and the right to cart stone, dig ditches, make kilns for making and burning lime and construct buildings in the wood whenever they needed to store the lime. At Castle Carrock in Cumberland in 1236–47 the priory received stone for making lime to be taken outside the ploughed land. In 1226, at West Bretton in Yorkshire, Byland Abbey took stones to burn at their grange in the land between two riddings as long as the quarry lasted. All these examples are from poor marginal soils, and the last directly associated with assarting from the waste.[4]

5 THE LIFE OF THE PEOPLE – THE PEASANT'S RESOURCES

Evidence of the size of holdings in northern England varies greatly in quality, quantity and date. About Cumberland and Westmorland there is little to say because of shortage of material, but holdings in the Lake District were probably small. Lancashire was in many ways strikingly like eastern England by 1350. Much assarting, and rapid growth of population, coupled with the lords' desire to let the demesne to farm, had encouraged the growth of a numerous tenantry who practised free inheritance customs or took holdings at will from the lord whilst their parents were still alive. Especially in south Lancashire, in an environment not unlike the Lincolnshire Fenland, the typical holding was well under five acres, and sometimes under one acre. As in the Fenland, the peasants lived on the produce of the waste. Durham in 1183 had an economy still with much slack in it, and more than one-third of the tenants were rich peasants. Finally, there is Yorkshire. There may have been a tendency for holdings to become smaller in 1246–1307, and the middle and rich peasantry were stronger in the West Riding than in the North and East Ridings, but the median holding remained stubbornly fixed at half-virgate size. The strength of Yorkshire lay in its middle peasantry, but by 1307 a cottar class was beginning to grow up.

The Lay Subsidy of 1297 in the West Riding of Yorkshire covered areas in the western half of the Riding, in the sandstone hills and the Pennine Moors, but much of the land surveyed is under 800 feet above sea-level. The 1003 taxpayers (excluding twenty-seven lords) had each over two bushels of wheat, under a bushel of barley, thirty bushels of oats, over three bushels of rye, and just over one-fifth of a load of hay. This is enough to feed one man for a year, mainly on oat-cakes. Each family also had just under one ox and just under two sheep; every three families had two affers and four cattle; every ten families a pig; and every twelve families one other horse. These peasants were some of the poorest met. On the other hand the typical northern bondman could be a substantial tenant, well above the subsistence level. A widow who died at Durham in 1349/50 left two copper vessels, one dish, one lead vat, two affers, one plough, three beasts, five horses, three oxen, one cow, twelve two-tooths, fourteen acres of winter corn and twenty acres of spring corn.

Amongst the early records are two statements of the goods which two individuals held in Yorkshire, both peasants and not rich. In 1317 the property of a ward consisted of two acres of wheat, sixteen quarters of winnowed oats, eight oxen and one affer. Another peasant who died in 1279 left seven quarters five bushels of barley, three quarters five bushels of *pulmentum* (perhaps peas), five and a half quarters of oats, five shillings worth of hay, and 2s. 9d. in straw. His stock consisted of two affers and fifty-five sheep.

The size of the bovate varied greatly in the West Riding of Yorkshire and as elsewhere it was a complex of rights and duties. At Stapleton in 1160–70 a twenty-two-acre bovate gave the right to have 100 sheep on the feedings (viz. on the stubble after harvest time). At Hampole in 1175–90 the Hospital of St Peter at York received a *mansus* (homestead) eight perches by thirty-seven perches, 12.5 acres of land, half an acre of meadow, pasture for 100 sheep and common rights. This also was a bovate. At Stainford before 1265 twelve knights measured the pasture and declared that each bovate, of five acres, should carry the right to pasture four oxen and four cows with their two-yearlings, four mares and their two-yearlings and forty sheep and their one-yearlings. In 1262 at Barningham there was a measuring of pasture, and each bovate there could sustain nine beasts, twenty-four sheep, six goats, three horses, one pig with one year's litter, two ducks and one goose. The size of the bovate is not known, but the number of animals, especially of cattle, was considerable. The North Riding was probably not short of manure. All these examples attribute a remarkable head of stock to even the humblest bovate, and suggest that the West Riding peasantry may not have been too badly off.

Lastly, in 1333, Robert of Clitheroe took from Adam of Clitheroe goods which included eleven oxen, ten cattle, one affer, two quarters of barley, ten quarters of oats, two sides of bacon, one and a quarter carcases of salt beef, three stones of onions, four great stockfish, 2s. 11d. worth of saltfish and 160 herrings. Robert was a clerk and therefore not a wealthy man. His possessions probably reflect the typical resources of the more prosperous freemen in Lancashire.

6 THE LIFE OF THE PEOPLE – INHERITANCE CUSTOMS

Partible inheritance existed in Lancashire. There was a joint holding at Widnes in 1311. The fullest information comes from the south Lancashire estates of Robert of Holland in 1323. Here was an area already very like the Lincolnshire Fenland. Altogether there were 515 tenants, of whom 433 were tenants-at-will in West Derby in 1323. The bovate was only 4.5 acres and the commonest and median holding was one to three acres. Seventy-six per cent of the tenants had less than five acres of land and the holdings included seventy-two acres of assarts which five tenants held.

About 84 per cent of the tenants were tenants-at-will, and their condition of tenure had an extraordinary effect upon the opportunities available to the younger generation. In no fewer than thirty-one families, which contained seventy-eight landholders, the younger generation was holding land at the same time as their parents. Two of the seventy-eight landholders were wives whose marriage portions were mentioned separately from their husbands' property. Of the thirty-one parents two were widows and twenty-nine fathers. Since the percentage of widows was small the age at which fathers produced sons who could take land whilst the fathers were still alive must have been rather lower than elsewhere. Of the forty-seven men of the younger generation, Adam Brain was probably the brother of Henry Brain, William of Thingwall was probably the brother of Robert of Thingwall. This leaves forty-five of the younger generation. If we include the two wives with marriage portions thirty-one parents held twenty-one messuages, one and a half burgages and one and a half cottages, which was insufficient, but forty-five of the younger generation had only four messuages, one curtilage, one burgage and a barn. Perhaps nearly all the younger generation lived at home with their parents, for then there would be thirty households in twenty-five messuages, two and a half burgages, one and a half cottages and a curtilage, which is just right. The parental holdings were larger than the children's holdings. The commonest holding was of one to three acres, but the median holding was of three to five acres. In eighteen families a son held land concurrently with his parent, of whom one was a widow. In two families a daughter held land concurrently with her father. In one family both a son and a daughter held land concurrently with their mother. In nine families two sons held land concurrently with their mother. In nine families two sons held land concurrently with their father. Finally – and this is said not to have happened at all – in one family there *may* have been grandchildren holding land at the same time as father and grandfather. The grandchildren, four in number, held partibly and there were other examples of this, such as the Tarbock and Warrington families. There were also three other pairs of brothers, two of whom may have sub-divided their father's property because they held equal holdings. Two pairs are said to have been brothers and the third pair were probably brothers too.

The names of these tenants are also very interesting. Seven families bore assart names, for the parents were: Robert of the Breach, Richard of Longleigh, William of Longleigh, Richard of the Heath, John of the Moorhouses, Robert of Thingwall (of Thingwall Ridding) and Richard of the Moor. Henry the Reeve was an official, and the following practised trades: Richard the Fuller, Henry the Crowder (fiddler), John Cordwainer, Robert the Walker, John the Dairyman, Adam servant (or serjeant?) of Hamon, Dicoun son of John the miller and Agnes wife of John the Potter.

Lastly, a word about the Palmer family. Here the name had clearly become a true surname and the ramifications of the family were important. Their relationship is not quite certain and is deduced and grouped from the names. We may interpret the family as five brothers – Simon, Thomas, William, Robert and Hugh – of whom the last was dead. The brothers originally held five messuages and six and a half burgages, and at the time of the survey the four oldest Palmers held all but one-third of a burgage. Simon had sons, Adam and Richard, both of whom held smallholdings while Simon was still alive; Richard had a son, William, who held land at the same time as his father and grandfather. Thomas, the next brother, had sons named Thomas and Richard, who also held land whilst father was alive. Thus eleven families had grown up where there had originally been one ancestor and the younger generations held only tenancies-at-will.

Hale was similar but less complex. All tenants were tenants-at-will and out of 114 holdings the commonest and median holding was of three to five acres. There was one joint holding and four examples of sons holding land whilst father was still alive. There was no real difference between the two generations in economic status and again fathers and sons seem to have lived together, because there were just enough houses to go round.

At Crosby the bovate contained five acres and out of thirty holdings the commonest and median holding was of quarter-virgate size. There were two examples of joint holdings. Some of the tenants who had disappeared from West Derby in 1323–46 may have turned up at Great Crosby in 1346. At both dates the bovate contained five acres, but in 1323 there were, at Crosby, only thirty tenants, and in 1346 Great Crosby had ninety-two tenants. There was one free tenant, *nativi* (villeins), tenants-at-will and tenants of riddings. The bulk of the *nativi* held from one to three acres but the size of the holdings ran up to just short of thirty acres. The tenants-at-will were less numerous than the *nativi* and their weight was in the category of under one acre. The majority of tenants of riddings held from one to three acres. The commonest and median holding in the whole manor was of one to three acres; in 1323 it had been of five to ten acres and all the growth (sixty-three holdings) had taken place amongst the holdings under five acres. This increased state of fragmentation was associated with partible inheritance among the oxgangers (bovate-holders). The bovate, though only five acres, was split into very small fragments, of which the smallest was one-forty-eighth. Thus both partible inheritance and the creation of tenancies-at-will encouraged the growth of population and the proliferation of smallholdings.

The lesson of the Lancashire extents is not unlike that learnt in eastern England. In an 'open' society where there was much assarting and rapid population growth there were also free customs of inheritance and transference of property before the older generation died. This was certainly possible under East Anglian partible socage, but it was also possible under Lancashire tenancy-at-will. The major factor was the attitude of the lord to his demesne. If he kept it all to himself and farmed for the market the village remained static, unfree, small and 'closed'; if he let it out or created socage tenures out of it the village was dynamic, free, large and open.

Inquisitiones Post Mortem for the West Riding of Yorkshire are very numerous and show that a good deal of proliferation had taken place on estates like the Soke of Snaith where, in 1258, thirty-two out of thirty-nine tenants of nineteen and a half bovates held partibly. Yet partition had not gone very far even here, for in the Soke of Snaith the commonest and median holding was ten to twenty acres.[5]

CHAPTER 11

WALES AND THE MARCHES

1 NEW SETTLEMENT AND POPULATION GROWTH

Late new settlement was commonest in the highland zone of the Welsh Marches and northern England. Shropshire had no new-settlement place-names first recorded after 1350, but Herefordshire had two and Cheshire three. New-settlement place-names first recorded in 1281–1350 consisted of four in Herefordshire, ten in Shropshire and twenty-two in Cheshire. By the middle of the fourteenth century Herefordshire was the most developed of the Welsh Marcher counties, followed by Shropshire, with Cheshire last and this was their order of development in 1086 too.

Wales and the Marches were on the whole very poorly developed in 1086. Cheshire developed little newland in the twelfth century, but by the fourteenth century the Domesday population of about 12,000 had doubled. The story of settlement really began with Earl Ranulf's grant to his barons in 1215–16 of the right 'to assart their lands within the arable area of the forest and to grow crops on lands formerly cultivated and free from wood, without payment'. The greatest and best-known of the assarts which followed were in Wirral, the most highly-developed part of Cheshire in 1086. The process was far-gone by 1267–70, for already lords were questioning the right to assart without payment. By 1265–81 the people had ploughed up the heaths in various Wirral villages. In 1265–91 the Abbot of Chester cultivated over 140 acres of heath and waste in Wirral, and by 1295–6 there were another ninety-seven acres under the plough. By 1272–1307 the prior of Birkenhead was cultivating a newland, had enclosed waste and assarted twenty acres. He obtained permission to enclose another thirty acres, and the Abbey of Whalley had to pay a fine for enclosing a small wood and ploughing land near his grange. In 1282–92 the house of lepers at Bebington received a licence to enclose and cultivate five acres of their own waste. In 1305 the Abbot of Chester agreed to divide his heath near his manor of Eastham with others. If they were to cultivate the heath the others were to enclose one acre for every two the abbot enclosed. By 1333 the abbot had assarted 400 acres of waste in Wirral and in 1349–62 his successor paid for 'fresh ploughing' and digging marl in Wirral. In 1357 he received a pardon for making an enclosure in Wirral. The Black Prince extorted large payments from some lords in his eyre at Chester in 1347 when one tenant produced a charter of Hugh, Earl of Chester, 1162–74 and 1177–81, about assarting in Wirral.

Outside Wirral assarting in the thirteenth century was particularly extensive on Rudheath, in the mid-Weaver basin, and round Delamere, Mondrem and Macclesfield Forests. The Prior of Norton enclosed land near Rudheath in 1272–1307. In the thirteenth century Hulse super Rudheath and Cranage were the main centres of this process, and the latter village had some 270 acres of pasture to be put into cultivation. In 1324–49 the Abbot of Chester obtained licence to enclose and cultivate all the waste of Hulse on Rudheath, some 270 acres. In 1301–60 three Vernons and a Grosvenor jointly obtained licence to approve 453.5 acres of land on the waste of Rudheath. These licences were one of the causes of the rising of 1353. On Delamere Forest the tenants had always assarted their own woods where, by the oath of the foresters and twelve lawful men, it could be done without nuisance to the forest. There was also a great deal of enclosure from the marshes at Frodsham and Ince, by the tenants of the Earl of Lancaster and the Abbot of Chester. By 1312 there was already a dyke 'towards the Weaver and the Mersey' and in 1312–13 the quantities of timber and branches to repair it cost £11. In 1315–16 the inhabitants cleared out and repaired four dykes, one of them the big seadyke. In 1325 the lessees of the manor of Frodsham undertook the contruction of a dyke to protect certain lands liable to inundation. In 1351–2 an artificial channel for the waters emptying into the Mersey was in disrepair and was flooding the surrounding pastures. The Black Prince removed the stoppage and used timber from Delamere Forest to repair the gate. The Abbot of Chester defrayed half the cost. None of the assarts were early and some were very late.

Vale Royal Abbey, which had a famous revolt of the bondmen of Darnhall in 1329 and 1336, was a late assarter. At Darnhall in about 1338, the peasants complained that Warin le Grosvenor had assarted eighty acres, bit by bit, in Darnhall Woods. In 1334 six hamlets seem to have had a common-field system in which they shared. Altogether there were sixty-two fields and twenty-eight of these contained the lands of more than one hamlet. Churchtown had the largest number – thirteen – of unshared fields, and was perhaps the oldest settlement. Some of the fields were clearly assarts. In addition there were assarts in some of the fields, but individual assarts were small.

Assarting was very widespread in Cheshire on heaths and in marshes, but on the whole there was little in the Cheshire Pennines. There was plenty of late assarting, practically on the eve of the Black Death, and curious field-systems grew up with several hamlets sharing open fields.

Shropshire was thinly settled and servile in 1086 but showed many of the characteristics of Cheshire. Buildwas Abbey had assarted 1340 acres in 1169–70. At Bishop's Castle, in 1295, the free tenants held twenty acres of assart and tenants in the borough sixteen acres. The lord of Myndtown held an assart under Long Mynd and four other tenants held assarts. At Prees in 1285–6 there were nine acres of land on the heath and the Bishop of Lichfield was approving his waste above Hynford Heath. At least two assarts existed at Actun Scot in 1328.

Herefordshire was the only county whose assarts were recorded in 1086. In four manors assarts from woodland consisted of 58 acres, assart for two ploughs worth 16s. 3d., and assart worth 17s. 4d. Settlers (*hospites*) were probably assarting from the waste on four other manors land worth 24s. On one of these manors seven settlers had one plough. At another two men rendered 4s. for hire of land. All these assarting villages were in good lowland, in contrast to the hills of Herefordshire.

Settlement seems not to have proceeded fast between the Norman Conquest and the end of the twelfth century. Over in the Golden Valley the Abbey of Dore was assarting the forest of Trevillen. In 1198–9 they had assarted 300 acres of it and in 1199–1200 a further 107 acres. They continued to assart woodland in 1215 and 1223. By 1225–50 assarting was fairly general in Herefordshire. In 1228 Hubert de Burgh received all Archenfield, the hundred of Wormelow, the wood of Aconbury and Aistons Wood, with licence to assart, enclose and cultivate the woods. On five estates of the church of Hereford, in 1253–68, 163 free tenants held land and pieces of assart. 'Worth', 'stokkyng' and 'croft' – testifying to new settlement – appeared several times in Herefordshire villages. Individual assarts were plentiful, but there may also have been communally controlled assarts absorbed into the open fields.

Apart from the short section of Domesday attached to the Cheshire folios there is no early survey of Wales. In 1086 Flintshire and Denbighshire were largely pastoral. Though there is little direct evidence of expansion during the twelfth century, rapid expansion of settlement is known to have taken place then in North Wales. The study of settlement morphology has done much to cast light upon the darkness of the period before the Edwardian Conquest, particularly in Anglesey, and in some parts of Wales the traditional idea of an entirely pastoral society needs modification.

However, the only properly known case of assarting in North Wales comes from the manor of Kilforn, in Denbighshire, in 1334. Here there was a stubbing of forty-four and a half acres and a new ing of thirty-five acres. There was also low and wet arable land full of young alder-groves suitable for assarting and making meadows and various pieces of broken-up land. There were apparently over sixty-five acres in the new meadow which, if assarted, would be worth half as much again. There were nearly four acres of broken-up land and over thirty-two acres of old broken-up land. The countryside had plenty of room for expansion in 1334.

In south Wales, where English penetration was deeper, new

settlement was early. In Glamorganshire the Bishop of Llandaff and the Earl of Gloucester agreed in 1126 that the bishop should have 900 acres of marsh between the Taff and the Ely, to plough. At Brecon in 1205–6 a lord granted his man six acres of land by the water of *Toui* which the man had assarted at his own expense. He was to hold the land for seven years rent-free. When the lord's heir should be unable to warrant the man the land (i.e. confirm his tenure) he should give him twelve acres of cultivated land of the same quality. The proportion of assarted land in a typical holding in Brecon appeared when Brecon Priory received thirty-six acres of cultivated land by seven divisions, of which five acres were assart which two tenants had made. The assart seems to have been a marsh assart. At Trewalkin by 1234–47 the monks of Brecon Priory had disputed pasture attached to assarted land. There were late assarts in Monmouthshire. At Usk in 1325–6 there was land assarted from the thorns and brambles and the lord hired a man to assart a piece of land above the castle for fallow. At Caerleon they were assarting a piece of pasture in the marshes near the River Usk.

In both Wales and the Marches there was very extensive new settlement, but in Wales early information is very hard to come by and there is little help from place-names. In all three Marcher counties there was little Saxon settlement in the fifth and sixth centuries, and the indigenous population apparently expanded little before the last quarter of the ninth century. In 870–1086 Cheshire, Shropshire and Herefordshire were amongst the most rapidly settled counties in all England, and Cheshire continued until late in the Middle Ages. Settlement throughout Wales and the Marches was not confined to one type but occurred practically everywhere. Only the north of England could vie with it in rapidity and extent.

We altogether lack information about population movements in Wales and the Marches in the twelfth century. Wales may have been prosperous before 1066, for in the time of Llywelyn ap Seisyll, supreme king of Gwynedd c.1005–25 and king of Deheubarth c.1018–23, the old men of the kingdom were wont to say that his territory from the one sea to the other was replete with an abundance of wealth and men, so that it could not be imagined that there was a man either poor or needy in all his lands, nor an empty village, nor a place of want. Improvement was certainly the order of the day for the Norman kings. In 1092 the Red King took an army northwards to Caerleon, restored the town, built and garrisoned the castle, and sent many peasants from the south with their wives and livestock to settle there and till the soil. This was the first English plantation. The second was in 1102-8 when Henry I settled the men of Flanders, whose land the sea had covered with sea-weed and sand, in the *cantref* of Rhos, near the estuary of the Cleddyf in Dyfed. They drove out the original inhabitants.

Even for the period 1200-1350 evidence on population movements in Wales and the Marches is poor. The Hereford-shire figures suggest a five-fold growth in 1086-1300. In the Marches one manor declined in 1280-1350, and three others in 1086-1350. There is no comparable evidence for Wales. In 1086-1350 forty-four manors in Herefordshire and twenty in Cheshire expanded very fast indeed. This may have been true of most of Wales and the Marches.[1]

2 CROPS AND LIVESTOCK

In 1206-23 Giraldus Cambrensis made plain his view of Snowdonia and of Anglesey:

As the mountains of Eryri [Snowdon] could supply pasturage for all the herds of cattle in Wales, so could the Isle of Mona [Anglesey] provide a requisite quantity of corn for all the inhabitants.

His famous description of the wild inhabitants of the Welsh mountains draws a colourful picture.

They neither inhabit towns, villages, nor castles, but lead a solitary life in the woods, on the borders of which they do not erect sumptuous palaces, nor lofty stone buildings, but content themselves with small huts made of the boughs of trees twisted together, constructed with little labour and expense, and sufficient to endure throughout the year. They have neither orchards nor gardens, but gladly eat the fruit of both when given to them. The greater part of their land is laid down to pasturage; little is cultivated, a very small quantity is ornamented with flowers, and a still smaller is sown. They seldom yoke less than four oxen to their ploughs; the driver walks before, but backwards, and when he falls down, is frequently exposed to danger from the refractory oxen.

In 1256–7 the lordship of Abergavenny in Monmouthshire consisted of six manors. On four manors oats was the principal crop, but on one maslin and one rye. On three manors wheat was the second crop, but on the others respectively barley, oats and rye. Beans was a major crop on one manor; on another the peasantry also grew maslin. The surprising aspect of the livestock figures is the small numbers of animals (except at one manor). This, the presence of goats, and the mention in one case of honey, obtained by the primitive method of killing the bees, prove that South Wales was still very under-developed in 1256–7.

The Templar manor of Llanmadoc in the Gower Peninsula in Glamorganshire was let to farm in 1308. The farm was small, barley and oats were the principal crops, beans were quite plentiful, oxen were preferred to affers, milch kine came before oxen and, on the whole, in spite of the absence of cattle and swine, this was a fairly pastoral economy.

The estates of the Cathedral Church of St David's had livestock stints on ten demesne manors in 1326. Altogether the bishop could keep 354 cattle and 2540 sheep, but only 40 horses and 12 pigs. The greatest pasture was the Isle of Ramsey and the richest meadow an acre which could pasture 12 bullocks. Although the Forest of Loydarth was 300 acres in extent, and although there was a wood in one park, there were few swine.

In Cardiganshire there were six forests and five localities in which the lord could keep 278 cattle, 424 sheep but only 24 pigs. The Forest of Crynnenith also provided honey, and, occasionally, lead. In Glamorganshire in Gower the lord ploughed with one plough and kept 8 oxen and 120 sheep upon the rest of the land. In Breconshire on four manors the lord could keep 68 cattle and 325 sheep. Cattle (often bred for the plough) were a major interest, but sheep were rather more popular.

Crops and stock in north Wales are better known, but not at a very early date. At Lanmays in Anglesey in 1291–2 the crop of oats was nearly seven times greater than the wheat crop and oxen eleven times as numerous as affers. In 1291–2 there were no swine or sheep in Caernarvonshire on the royal estates, and of the other cattle seventy-five were cows. This was large-scale cattle-raising. The Welsh peasantry grew largely oats *bragalis*, and smaller quantities of maslin, wheat-malt, barley and oatmeal. The oats was perhaps used to make *bragwd* or ale. Cattle and oats were clearly the leading products of Anglesey and Caernarvonshire at the end of the thirteenth century. The stock of food in Criccieth Castle in 1294–6 confirms the picture. Oats, wheat and beans were locally grown foods, and the castle had to buy its malt from outside. Beef, mutton and fish were all local products; honey and cheese came from Bristol. In the Colwyn lordship in 1264–5 'Castle Maud could have in pasture 1000 oxen and cows and 2000 sheep, 500 mares, horses or studs, swine as many as they wished without number.'

The Lleyn Lay Subsidy Account for 1293 tells the surplus stock of cereals, and the stock of animals in fifteen villages in the Commote of Gafflogion and town of Nevin. The flour was oats-flour and oats was therefore vastly predominant over all other grains. Wheat followed and barley and peas were insignificant. Oxen were more popular than affers, but not so overwhelmingly more than they were in southern England. In two villages affers exceeded oxen, while in four villages the relationship was just the other way round. Milch kine were about two and a half times more plentiful than oxen, and oxen were fewer than all horses. Sheep were only seven-eighths as many as milch kine, and there were no swine. The Lleyn Peninsula was therefore a region of cattle, chiefly milch kine and horses and was interested in fishing.

The separate survey of Nevin, also in the Lleyn Peninsula, fills out this picture. Oats was greater than all the other grains put together, and wheat and barley followed in popularity. Rye and peas were insignificant. Oxen were more than twice as many as affers, but affers plus other horses came before oxen. Milch kine were twice as popular as oxen, but sheep were about one-sixth more plentiful than milch kine. Thus the relationships of the various grains and stock were slightly different from elsewhere in Lleyn, but the general picture was much the same.

Some time prior to 1334 there was a different state of affairs in the village of Aberffraw, with its outlying hamlets, in Anglesey. Here oats, though still ascendant, mattered less compared with wheat and barley than in the Lleyn Peninsula; cattle predominated over horses by the same comparison. The real difference lay in the status of sheep. In Anglesey they were nearly twice as many as cattle but in Lleyn sheep were only nine-tenths as common as cattle. Anglesey therefore placed more emphasis upon oxen and sheep. Neither survey mentioned swine. With this exception Anglesey was more like southern England than Lleyn, but the great emphasis upon oats, horses and cattle and the comparatively small number of sheep made it emphatically a county of the new-settlement type so far as grain and stock are concerned.

In Shropshire in 1197 the Abbot of Shrewsbury paid for easements in Hawksley Wood in wheat, rye, hay and cheeses. In 1203 Hugh of Leigh had sixty cart-loads of dead-wood and sixty pigs quit of pannage in Kinley wood. Hugh's men of Leigh were to pay pannage but to have pasture.

On three manors of Leominster Priory in Herefordshire in 1332 there was apparently twice as much wheat as oats and few legumes. At Huntington the land was poor. Herefordshire was the richest of the new-settlement counties by 1300, but it had large areas of very high upland which was not good for agriculture.

Of Cheshire William of Malmesbury remarked in about 1125:

> It is barren and unproductive of cereals, especially of corn, as are many parts of the north, but abounding in beasts and fish. The natives delight in milk and butter; the richer people live on flesh, and think much of bread made of barley and wheat.

Higden remarked later '[It] has a plentiful supply of all kinds of foods, grain, flesh and fish, more especially the better kinds of salmon.' About 1200 Lucian said that it imported corn from England, and Malmesbury's remarks about bread made of barley and wheat suggest strongly that the local grains were rye and oats. The stock of Cheshire, particularly in the Pennines and the Pennine slope, consisted of many swine and cattle. At Macclesfield in 1237–8 there were four vaccaries and the sheriff disposed of 231 swine. In 1238–9 he disposed of 195 pigs and had 178 left. In 1240 he received 144 pigs and sold 197 sides of bacon and 266 pigs. In 1240 he still leased out four vaccaries and sold 76 cattle. Similarly in 1241–2 he sold 411 pannage pigs, 311 in 1242–5 and stored the castle of Dyserth with 200 sides of cured bacon. A generation later the sheriff was still selling pannage pigs. Cheshire and the neighbouring parts of Flintshire and Denbighshire also provided stores for the castles at Flint and Rhuddlan. They received predominantly oats, followed fairly closely by wheat, smaller quantities of barley, beans and peas, and a plentiful supply of bacon, cheese, honey and salt.

Vaccaries existed in Pennine Cheshire in 1214–23 when the rectors of Leek and Dieulacres Priory gave up their rights to tithes from the vaccaries of Hugh le Despenser and the Countess of Chester. The Cheshire lowlands also had their share of pastoral activities. On one manor in 1274–80 the Abbot of St Werburgh, Chester, received the right to keep fifty pigs free of pannage.

Wales and the Marches present a considerable variety of regions, some of which, for example Herefordshire, were considerable wheat-growing regions. On the whole farming was as mixed in Wales and the Marches as elsewhere in England, but there was a great mass of oats, fish at the seaside, more honey from the woods than elsewhere, many swine (except in Caernarvonshire and Anglesey), thousands of cattle and remarkably few sheep. The area is large, and specific farming regions which were not of the pastoral, new-settlement type may have existed, but to prove their existence is impossible. In most of Wales the historian is deprived of the leading light of Domesday and the pre-Conquest charters. On the whole Wales and the Marches were strikingly different from England.[2]

3 TECHNIQUES – THE OPEN FIELDS

Giraldus Cambrensis, in his description of Welsh society about the year 1200, has given a picture of a largely pastoral people, but he was certainly describing the habits of the mountain people, and probably those of the free kindreds who lived on marginal lands. The Laws of Hywel Dda correct the picture. The prince organized his court at Aberfraw in Anglesey to suit a largely arable economy. 'The reason why the law shall be closed in autumn and spring, is because the land is cultivated during those periods; lest ploughing in the spring and reaping in autumn be impeded.' The *land maer* ordered the ploughing and all the necessaries for the court, the smith of the court made the blade of a coulter, and the chief falconer lodged in the king's barn, lest smoke should affect his birds. The Dimetian Code reflects the importance of corn in the early Welsh economy in the value it sets upon cats:

1 The worth of a cat, that is killed or stolen; its head is to be put downwards upon a clean even floor, with its tail lifted upwards, and thus suspended, whilst wheat is poured about it, until the tip of its tail be covered; and that is to be its worth; if the corn cannot be had, a milch sheep, with her lamb and her wool, is its value; if it be a cat which guards the king's barn.

2 The worth of a common cat is four legal pence.

3 The *teithi* of a cat, and of every animal upon the milk of

which people do not feed, is the third of its worth, or the worth of its litter.

4 Whoever shall sell a cat, is to answer for her not going a caterwauling every moon; and that she devour not her kittens; and that she have ears, eyes, teeth and nails, and being a good mouser.

This care of cats and corn argues an insufficient supply of both, and the equation between the value of a cat and of a ewe and her lamb suggests plenty of sheep. No doubt early Welsh economy was balanced far towards pastoralism compared with that of East Anglia, but there was certainly plenty of arable, especially in Anglesey. Whenever the laws need a suitable criterion they draw naturally upon an agrarian image, as in the following:

The *saraad* of the king of Aberfraw is to be paid thus: an hundred cows for each *cantrev* in his dominion, and a white bull with red ears to every hundred cows; and a rod of gold equal in length to himself, and as thick as his little finger; and a plate of gold as broad as his face, and as thick as the nail of a ploughman who has been a ploughman for seven years.

The Welsh society of the mid-tenth century was a new-settlement society. The Venedotian Code has the following law about clearance of woodland:

No brother is to clear woods belonging to another brother, without yielding him wood equal to that cleared by him; and, if he cannot obtain as good, let him yield of old field as much as the wood; and, if he cannot obtain old field, let him till the wood, which he cleared, for four years; and thenceforth let his brother have equal with himself from it.

Such a diminution of the rights of kindred must have been common, for in the Anomalous Laws the following also occurs:

Three things that are not to be done without the permission of the lord and his court: building on a waste; ploughing a waste; and clearing wild land of wood on a waste: and there shall be an action for theft against such as shall do so; because every wild and waste belongs to the country and kindred in common: and no one has a right to exclusive possession of much or little of land of that kind.

As in England, so in Wales new settlement went with an open-field system. The famous passage in the Venedotian Code shows the practice of co-tillage which often took place in the open fields:

1 Whoever shall engage in co-tillage with another, it is right for them to give surety for performance, and mutually join hands; and, after they have done that, to keep it until the *tye* be completed: the *tye* is twelve *erws*.

In England co-tillage was more casual than this and perhaps not obligatory. In another place the laws say that in Wales co-tillage was obligatory and set a penalty for its breach: 'No one from a *taeogtrev* is to plough until every one in the *trev* shall obtain co-tillage.' And elsewhere: 'Whoever shall break co-tillage willingly engaged in, let him pay three kine *camlwrw* to the king; and all his tilth to the co-tiller.' The *erw* was the English acre-strip or selion and the Venedotian Code defines it as follows:

2 The measure of the legal *erw* is, four feet in the length of the short yoke, and eight in the length of the second yoke, and twelve in the length of the lateral yoke, and sixteen in the long yoke; and a rod as long as that, in the hand of the driver, with his other hand upon the middle spike of the long yoke, and as far as he can reach with that rod on each side of him, is the breadth of the *erw* and thirty times that is the length. Others say, that it is to be a rod as long as the tallest man in the *trev*, with his hand above his head. . . .

Then comes the well-known passage about the scatter and

assignment of the acre-strips or *erws*. The whole arrangement is formalized in the usual spirit of ancient Celtic law in an apparently democratic share system, 'from best to best', but nowhere is there evidence that the acre-strip of arable had a different owner every year.

> 3 The first *erw* belongs to the ploughman; the second to the irons; the third to the exterior sod ox; the fourth to the exterior sward ox; and the fifth to the driver, and so the *erws* are appropriated, from best to best, to the oxen, thence onward, unless the yoke be stopped between them, unto the last; and after that the plough *erw*, which is called the plough-bote *eyrar*; and that once in the year.

Co-tillage was obligatory and

> 10 Everyone is to bring his requisites to the ploughing, whether ox, or irons, or other things pertaining to him; and, after everything is brought to them, the ploughman and the driver are to keep the whole safely, and use them as well as they would their own.

No horses, mares or cows were to plough. Oxen were proved from 9 February onwards, and their value increased up to their third year, and stayed at the prime until their sixth year.

The laws also make clear the reasons for the scatter of acre-strips, that is, so that each person should have a share of the easy and the difficult, the far and the near land, and make provision for the settlement of disputes about this.

> 17 If a dispute arise between two co-tillers, as to rough bushy land, and to other clear; the one willing to plough the bushy land, and the other not willing; unless there be an agreement to the contrary, it is right for him to plough for the other such land as he may have.
> 18 If a dispute arise about ploughing, between two co-tillers,

one willing to plough far off, and the other near, we say, that they are to go to such place only as that the oxen may reach their stalls, and their work, the weak as well as the strong, within their own *cymwd*.

Other laws bring the open fields yet more clearly before our eyes. The apparitor was to have, from a house in which a death had taken place,

> the meat in cut, the butter in cut, the lowest stone of the quern, the green flax, the lowest layer of corn, the hens, the cats, the fuel axe, and the headland of corn uncut in the field, or the skirts if there be no headland.

Provisions for the protection of the crops are also revealing. If a horse were found stretching his neck over a hedge eating the corn, no one should take him. Whoever made a fence about his corn might take animals upon the grass which might be in the enclosure, as well as upon the corn, because nothing was to depasture there. Whoever removed his corn from the stubble to the ley, and made his rick upon the ley, was not to receive compensation if someone damaged the rick. Flax, not in a garden, was subject to the same law as corn. There were laid-down penalties for the different animals – horses, cattle, swine, sheep, lambs, calves, and geese – found in corn, for hens and cocks found in a flax-garden or barn, and for a cat found mousing in a flax-garden. Between each pair of *erws* there were to be two furrows, but there were also examples of 'a stone cross, that is, a meer stone or meer timber or other specified thing which should preserve a boundary.' There were private as well as common meadows.

The Laws of Hywel Dda therefore imply a mature open-field system, but nowhere do they certainly proclaim that this open-field system was also a common-field system. There is ample reference to co-tillage and the bond hamlets were obliged to enter into partnerships of co-tillage, but there is no reference in the laws to communally controlled crop rotations or communally controlled pasture on the fallow. The Welsh open-field system, whatever its date of origin, seems not to have been fully mature.

Gray placed Wales and part of the Marches outside the area of open fields proper, but there is abundant evidence of open fields all over the country. The open field of Rhosili still exists complete to this day, balks and all, as the Vile of Rhosili and Middleton. Up to the mid-nineteenth century there were open fields in four villages in south Monmouthshire, and they were formerly widespread in the Vale of Glamorgan and the Gower Peninsula. Three open fields still survive at Laugharne, in south Carmarthenshire, and on the raised beach between Llan-non and Cardigan Bay, in Cardiganshire, is an open field called Morfa Esgob. In all three surviving open-field systems the strips are flat, not ridged, and have balks between them. There is also good evidence of open-field agriculture round Hawarden in Flintshire down to 1748.

There seem to have been open fields in Pembrokeshire in 1326. The arable lay in different fields at St David's and no open-field system is provable. At Trefdyn the arable was in two fields and at Castle Maurice in three fields, at Wolf's Castle in thirteen fields, one of which was 'beyond the wood', and at Lawhaden part of the demesne arable was at Lettardistoune with the rest in six fields. At Lantefey the arable was in five fields, and in this village the pasture on the fallows could feed 300 sheep in winter and 200 sheep through summer. Elsewhere on the estates of the Cathedral of St David's there is no proof of open-field systems, least of all in the Welsheries, but the evidence quoted squares with what we know already about open fields in south Wales, and the reference to grazing sheep on the fallow at Lantefey suggests that Pembrokeshire may have had some villages which possessed fully developed common-field systems.

In Denbighshire in 1334 certain manors had three seasons which may have replaced the continuous cropping of a former infield-outfield system. Henry de Lacy imposed the manor of Kilforn upon Kilforn and Astret Canon in 1282–1311 and the demesne there and at Denbigh and Dynorbyn Vaur was in three seasons. Astret Oweyn (like Dynorbyn Vaur) existed before 1282, and the demesne was in four portions, each in a different field. In Kilforn and Dynorbyn Vaur the seasons and the fields did not coincide, but were divided in a most complex manner. These examples suggest, once more, that some elements peculiar to the fully developed common fields, here a crop rotation which might have been communally arranged, existed in the open fields of Wales.

There were also open fields in Flintshire, but they mostly appeared very late. Altogether some seventy-six open-field parishes are known but only two offer any early evidence. Open fields occurred randomly in Welsh-speaking and English-speaking areas, and racialist arguments are therefore not appropriate.

Cheshire presents a complicated picture which is probably typical of the new-settlement counties, and which may have existed in the east and west Midlands and southern England in the days of Ine and Alfred the Great. Cheshire was a county of small settlements. In 1669 outside Chester there were still only seventy-five parish churches for 400 villages; composite parishes were frequent. A detailed consideration of Wybunbury parish, which contained eighteen villages, has produced a complicated analysis of settlement patterns and field-systems in which practically every stage of growth and development appears. Out of 293 Cheshire villages, forty-three are suspected open-field villages, sixty-seven show slight evidence that they were so, forty-three had open arable but not open fields, and twelve had open fields whose number is uncertain. Of those clearly open-field villages seventy-seven had one field, twenty-four had two fields, six had three fields, and twenty-one had four or more fields. In 1334 on the Vale Royal Abbey estates there were eight manors with land apparently intermixed in three fields. How soon open fields appeared in Cheshire is not known, but as in so many thinly populated counties with a larger amount of pasture, meadow and waste than was usual in the Midlands, enclosure was early and the *bocage* characteristics appeared before the end of the Middle Ages. In 1334–1475, enclosure took place in

Over, and by 1475 only a small core of open field remained.

Cheshire was an open-field county, but not a three-field county. A one- or two-field system was most typical, but in a striking number of villages extended communal new settlement developed a multi-field system. The open fields of Cheshire were most densely distributed over the loam and boulder clay regions of the county. They were found most particularly in the Wirral (except in a small area east of Burton), in the Dee and Gowy Valleys, in the Weaver and Dane Valleys, and east of Northwich and Nantwich. They were sparsest in north Cheshire between the lower Weaver and the lower Bollin, east of the line through Stockport and Macclesfield between Alsager, Sandbach, Middlewich and Congleton, in central Delamere, and in the Mondrem Forest in south Cheshire between the Dee and the Weaver.

There is now more information about the open fields of Herefordshire, which again, as befitted a new-settlement county, were mostly not of the 'Midland' type. There are five certain examples of a two-course crop rotation in the more settled parts of the county. Much of the evidence for a three-course crop rotation is inconclusive, and it may have existed in villages with more than three open fields. The best example in 1326–44 implied a three-course system. The crops were winter-sown wheat, spring-sown oats and fallow. At least six villages had many fields. One had six, one at least seven and a possible three-course crop rotation; one had fourteen and in part, at least, a two-course crop rotation; one had fifteen and one thirty. In some of these villages the fields were perhaps grouped for the crop rotation. Herefordshire was far from the classical open-field pattern.

Historians have assumed that all these open fields in Wales resulted from English influence seeping in after the Norman Conquest, not from the natural development of a growing agrarian economy. Yet in north and west Wales the open fields were aboriginal, as the Laws of Hywel Dda have plainly shown, and the *bocage* countryside of closes and dispersed homesteads a phenomenon of the agrarian decline in the later

Middle Ages. Open fields still existed in some parts of north and west Wales, but for the most part by 1500 the system had largely broken down into isolated farms, and few nucleations have survived. The 'Celtic' dispersed settlement is not Celtic at all, and is certainly not an example of arrested development. It is the product, not of a particular 'race', but of economic forces at work in the later Middle Ages, and a proof that there is no inevitable progression from hunting to pastoralism, and from pastoralism to cultivation, but the ever-present likelihood of stepping back into less intensive ways of exploiting the soil.

Early settlements in Wales were either bond or free – small bond hamlets or dispersed homesteads of a free kindred. Every free kindred had a *gwely* or resting-place which centred upon the 'old settlement' of the clan founder. The arable was subject to partible inheritance and became open-field *shareland*. When the population grew the parceners founded new *sharelands*. Sometimes there was one resting-place confined to one village, but in 1315 the clan Elidyr held land in the old settlement of Trefydd Bychain and in eleven other villages. At Trefeddion, in Merioneth

the quillet outliers of the Treffeddion farms in later centuries were relics of such a shareland which had once consisted of a small patch of unenclosed arable land wherein quillets, separated only by turf baulks or overwidened furrows, were interspersed with an occasional headland.

In 1840 Trefeddion contained nineteen farmhouses; in 1592 there were at least twelve; in the late-thirteenth century there were at least seventeen households. Medieval Trefeddion was 'an open cluster of cottages surrounding one or more nuclear tracts of open-field arable'. By 1326 at least one coastal village in Merioneth had developed communal tendencies. It fined a villager 'because he kept his animals on the common pasture of the *Hendreve* (old settlement) after the community of the township had taken itself and its animals to the mountains.'

In Denbighshire in 1334 the Gwely Rhys ab Edred lived in five villages and two subsidiary hamlets where thirty-nine members of the clan held 1036 acres of land, wood and waste. Only eleven members of the clan held arable and winter pasture rights confined to the village where they resided and the rest had arable holdings which were still scattered through several *sharelands*. For example, Gruffydd ap Cynwrig held fifty-one acres in Abergele, forty-seven acres in Mostyn and forty-five acres in Hescyn, of arable, meadow, pasture and wood. In three settlements the clan rights were exclusive, but in Abergele the clan had only 689 out of 2908 acres and twenty-two members of Gwely Rhys mixed with 121 of three other clans and 112 of two other clans.

At Llysddulas in thirteenth-century Anglesey there were seven free clans or *gwelyau*. The ancestors of these seven *gwelyau* were two brothers, and they flourished about the middle of the twelfth century. All had land about Llanysddulas, which was their *hendref* or old settlement. In 1303 *gwely* lands were to be held 'openly and not otherwise'. The limit to appropriation of land from the *cyttir* or common waste by new clansmen had come by 1294, and secondary clusters or hamlets had developed because most of the land of new clansmen was in new enclosures.

There is no doubt, therefore, of the existence of open fields in the free settlements. By about 1300 each clansman had a homestead, five to ten acres of arable in two or more *sharelands* and a stint in proportion to the area of his arable in the common grazing. The *sharelands* were seldom larger than 100 acres and so there grew up a girdle-pattern of homesteads on the edge of the *sharelands* to conserve the arable. The Welsh freemen practised co-operative farming by entering into voluntary contracts of co-aration. Spring cereals, especially oats, were the favourite crops, and the *sharelands* were generally available for fallow in the winter, but some low-lying *sharelands* had fences and grew winter cereals. Summer grazing of the uplands and winter grazing of common pastures in the villages was the normal practice.

In each *Hendref* or old settlement division of land *per stirpes* (by families or lineages) led to the emergence of new *sharelands*. Gavelkind went with population expansion, and all was well as long as there was new waste to till. After 1300 increasing *morcellement* led to monopolization and enclosure brought the death of the Welsh open-field system. This system was not an English introduction but grew from the social system which developed in early medieval Wales, both in bond and in free communities. The open fields were fairly well-developed, and had some characteristics which would entitle them to the name of common fields. Wales was much closer to the Midlands than used to be thought and not unlike other highland zone regions in its settlement patterns and development.[3]

4 TECHNIQUES – CROP NUTRITION

Pliny says that the Greeks knew all about manuring but there is only one early reference to it. The laws of Hywel Dda, of which some portions may date from 942–9, lay down that 'The wife of a *taeog* can give nothing but her head gear; and lend only her sieve, and that as far as her voice can be heard, from the dung hill, requesting its return.' The Welsh had apparently many cattle and mountainous dung hills which could serve as rostra for anyone who wished to practise the *hwyl*. The same laws give rather complicated and somewhat enigmatic directions about ploughing as follows:

10 A fallow, two years it is to be ploughed. 11 Rotten-dung (i.e. land where cattle are accustomed to lie without folding) truly the same. 12 Ley-land, truly the same. 13 Yard-dung, three years it is to be ploughed. 14 Car-dung, four years it is to be ploughed. 15 Woodland, truly the same. 16 Manured fallow, four years also.

These laws make clear a big difference between a simple intermission of plough and fallow with a three-course system, and the long ploughing period of manured land on a four- or five-course system.

There was considerable marling in the highland zone as well as quite abundant use of it in Wales and the Marches. There was a marlpit in Chester in 1238–9, and in 1272–1307 the Wirral had scores of marlpits. One man had newly tilled two acres and made a marlpit. There are plenty of other instances to show that Cheshire was very conscious of the utility of marling. But not only Cheshire; in 1256–7 three manors in the lordship of Abergavenny had a spade for digging marl. At Usk, in 1319–20, the lord hired horses to carry marl and manure from the castle to the field and in 1325–6 marled nearly ten acres of land beyond the Usk.

Sanding was also well-known in Pembrokeshire in 1603, but no earlier examples have yet been found. Seasand was in use near Newport and in three other places. The peasantry carried the sand in sacks on horseback for three or four miles, and the good effect lasted for six or eight years. The use of sea-weed was also known in Pembrokeshire but its effects were very temporary, since it lasted for one year only.

> It is a saieinge amonge the Countrye men of the contynuance of these foresaied amendementes that a man doth sande for himself, Lyme for his sonne, and Marle for his graunde child.

Beat-burning was also a common practice in Pembrokeshire in 1603. Owen says that there were two sorts of beat land – clean beatland and pied beatland. In the latter the farmer beat only half of the land. Normally he used beat land to sow rye, but sometimes to sow barley and oats. The method was really useful only on marginal land and Owen was highly critical of its value:

> and thereof often cometh great proffitt, but this is said to be a great ympayringe of the grounds for after the rie and one badd Cropp of oates, there will noe more corne be had thereof for twentie or foure and twentie yeares after, and for a year or two scarse any pasture. . . . I have seane many poore

men vse this kinde of betting in lande, which otherwise
would have been tilled to better profit; wherein theye were
much to be blamed in doinge themselves, the lande and the
Countrie, harme.

After this forthright comment we must consider beat-burning
neither profitable nor wise.

One form of crop nutrition much used on acid, marginal soils
needs discussion – liming. Liming on the estates of the Cathedral
Priory of Canterbury near Romney Marsh in Kent has already
drawn our attention earlier. It was known in Wales, too; lime
burnt in a kiln and spread on the land met with great favour
from Owen in Pembrokeshire:

> This trade of lyminge hath ben more vsed within these thirtie
> or fortie yeares then in times past and it destroyeth the ffurse,
> fearne, heath and other like shrobbes growing on the land and
> bringeth forth a fine and sweete grasse and quite Changeth
> the hue and face of the grounde and hath greatlie enriched
> those that vsed it.[4]

5 THE LIFE OF THE PEOPLE – THE PEASANT'S RESOURCES

Cheshire, even as late as 1334, was a county of small hamlets.
The median holding was only a quarter-virgate and there were
practically no tenants with a virgate and more. In Shropshire
near the Welsh border, north-west of Shrewsbury, holdings
may have been quite small. There were some large manors, but
in the southern highlands by 1280 there were many small upland
hamlets. As in Derbyshire and Staffordshire, holdings were here
rather large, often virgates. Except near the castles, there were
very few cottars. Herefordshire was the most prosperous of the
Marcher counties. By 1280 there were many villages, and the
bishop had small, but thriving, boroughs at Ross, Bromyard
and Ledbury. Holdings were usually virgates or half-virgates.
Most of the bishop's estates were in eastern Herefordshire and

Archenfield, still Welsh, was probably different. In Wales itself
gwely-holders were sometimes rich, but perhaps more often
poor. The existence of sub-tenants, and the complicated
interlocking of *gwelyau* make such judgements virtually
impossible.

Three lay subsidy assessments give valuable help with the
problem of the wealth of the Welsh peasant. Two of these form
the Lleyn Lay Subsidy Account for 1293, which covers fifteen
settlements in the Commote of Gafflogion. The average tax-
payer had one-third of a crannock of wheat (a crannock was two
or four bushels), one-quarter of a crannock of barley and four-
fifths of a crannock of oats. The amount of grain they ate was
therefore very small. In addition, every household had two
sheep; every two households a horse; every three two fishing
nets; every four seven milch kine; and every five two affers and
four oxen. Nine of the ninety-three tax-payers were worth
three pounds or more. The rich had less than their due
proportion of wheat, barley, peas, affers, cattle, sheep and
horses, but more than their due proportion of oats, rye, oxen,
boats and nets. Oxen were the property of the rich everywhere
in thirteenth-century England, and it is perhaps surprising to
find that mixed arable and pastoral interests were the province of
the poorer classes, but oat-cakes and fish the province of the
richer classes.

The Lay Subsidy Roll for Aberffraw and Anglesey notes
seventy-one tax-payers. Each household had on average one and
a half crannocks of wheat, three-quarters of a crannock of
barley, four and a half of oats, and two-sevenths of peas and
barley. In Anglesey men had seven times as much barley, three
times as much wheat and twice as much oats per family as in the
Lleyn Peninsula. Every family in Aberffraw had on average two
oxen and eleven sheep, and every two families three horses and
eleven cattle. The men of Anglesey were well off compared
with the people of the West Riding of Yorkshire, or of
Bedfordshire, and had more oxen, cows, and sheep than their
compatriots in the Lleyn Peninsula.

The lay subsidies have many deficiencies which make them

very unreliable indicators of poverty or wealth. Like all tax records at all times, they are dishonest, and the historian cannot be sure that the dishonesty is spread evenly. Particularly in Suffolk, Essex, Sussex and Bedfordshire, there would be a long tail of very poor labourers who escaped taxation altogether. Their existence is clear from what we know about sizes of holdings.

6 THE LIFE OF THE PEOPLE – INHERITANCE CUSTOMS

On the estates of Vale Royal Abbey in 1334 there was a complete lack of any very rich peasants. The hamlets were tiny, but so were the holdings. The size of holdings may have been the result of the practice of partible inheritance: two pairs of brothers had joint holdings. Partible inheritance did not affect Cheshire very much because the county was still thinly inhabited in 1334. At Ellesmere in Shropshire in 1280 many of the tenants were Welsh and most carried out the traditional service of following the court and feeding the sergeants. There is also evidence of Welsh *gavelkind*. At Barton, near Hereford, in 1253–68, five freemen were 'heirs' and eleven named tenants held jointly two carucates.

The basic statement about Welsh *gavelkind* comes from the Laws of Hywel Dda and is as follows:

Three times is land to be shared among kinsmen: first among brothers; then among cousins; the third time among second cousins. Thenceforward, there is no proper sharing of land. When brothers share their father's *trev* among them, the youngest gets the principal homestead and eight *erws* and the whole stock and the boiler and the fuel hatchet and the coulter, since a father can neither give nor devise them except to the youngest son; and although they be pledged, they never lapse. Then let every brother take a principal homestead and eight *erws*; and the youngest son shall share, and from the youngest to the eldest they are to choose. No person is to demand re-sharing except him who has not obtained a choice, as there is no *gwarthal* with choice.

Elton noticed the relationship of this custom to borough-English, or inheritance by the youngest son and the similarity of early Welsh law to the custom of Kent. He quoted a thirteenth-century Kentish custumal, which he translated from a copy made by Lambarde and published in his *Perambulation of Kent*, and which he had compared with a manuscript at Lincoln's Inn and a copy published by Tottel in his *Consuetudines Kanciae* in 1556. The words in parentheses are absent from the last two copies.

1 If any tenant in gavelkind die, having inherited gavelkind lands and tenements, let all his sons divide that heritage equally. And if there be no male heir, let the partition be made among females in the same way, as among brothers. And let the messuage (or homestead) also be divided among them, but the hearth-place shall belong to the youngest son or daughter (the others receiving an equivalent in money), and as far as 40 feet round the hearth-place, if the size of the heritage will allow it. And then let the elder have the choice of the portions and the others afterwards in their order.
2 In like manner as to other houses which shall be found in such a homestead, let them be equally divided among the heirs, foot by foot if need be, except the cover of the hearth which remains to the youngest, as was said before: nevertheless, let the youngest make reasonable amends to his co-parceners for their share by the award of good men.

Elton further added that the 'best manuscript' remarks: 'These are the usages of gavelkind, and of gavelkinders in Kent, which were before the Conquest, and at the Conquest, and ever since until now.' Thus the thirteenth-century writer was describing a custom which he believed to be at least two centuries old. Unlike the Welsh custom, the Kentish custom seems to have placed no limit upon the extent of division.

The Laws of Hywel Dda have one other section which throws light both upon the size of the holding and the antiquity of the custom.

XII The Law of Brothers for Land

1 Thus brothers are to share land between them: four *erws* to every *tyddyn*: Bleddyn ap Cynfyn [Prince of Powys and Gwynedd 1063–75] altered it to twelve *erws* to the *uchelwr*, and eight to the *aillt*, and four to the *godaeg*: yet nevertheless, it is most usual that four *erws* be the *tyddyn*.

The size of the legal *erw* was somewhat vague but even if it were as large as a whole acre the standard holding of a *tyddyn* would be no more than the English *cotsetle* and the *uchelwr* would be a half-virgater. This particular law certainly does not encourage us to think that Welshmen were rich.

In the Honour of Denbigh in 1334 there were a number of clans, or *gwelyau*. The *gwely* was often the whole clan, but it could be a fraction of a major *gwely*. A good example of a *gwely* is the Gwely Edred ap Marchudd ap Cynan. It came from Strathclyde in the ninth century at the invitation of Rhodri Mawr (844–78) or Anarawd (878–916), and it radiated from Abergele and Llwydcoed all over North Wales. Its history shows that there was no automatic disruption of the *gwely* every generation, and pedigrees often went back fifteen or sixteen generations. The division of the *gwely* into sub-*gwelyau* did not itself disrupt the ancestral home as a matter of course every generation, for there was no division of land. The Gwely Edred ap Marchudd ap Cynan migrated from Llwydcoed to Mathebrud and dropped the original *gwely* name. From Mathebrud it migrated to Bettws-y-Coed and from there Rhys's family trekked south to Heskyn and Mostyn, and the line of Bleth went to Cilcein.

The history of this *gwely* shows that tribal consciousness could survive for several generations. The *gwely* continued in unity for more than four generations. The members of the migrating part of the *gwely* were nearly related to each other and when they settled they formed a new *gwely* or *gwelyau*. Political factors could develop quite separate *gwelyau*, but as a rule 'the word *gwely* meant merely a stock claiming some common descent, not necessarily in four generations, acting together and holding land together'. In Anglesey there were five *gwelyau* which had continued since about 1170. In 1538 the canons of the church of Caergybi implied the continuity of the *gwely*. In Dyfed in 1326 there were fifty-three and a half *gwelyau* in sixteen vills. In 1315 in Bromfield and Yale there were still sixty-one joint holders in Trefydd Bychain, but the *Progenies of Ken* had spread into six half-upland and five lowland vills. Altogether there were 141 holders in various groups. They had swept down from the uplands in William Rufus's day.

The *aillt* or unfree were tenants either of the king or of freemen and they held either in *tir gwelyawg* vills and followed the custom of the *tref*, or *tir cyfrif* vills, or in a *maedref*. They could hold unfree *gwelyau*, but most holders were individuals, and there were no tribal entities. These bond *gwelyau* did not expand like the free *gwelyau* since the unfree were not free to move. In some places there were *gwelyau* of servants or craftsmen, such as the *gwely* of the doorkeepers or the *gwely* of the smiths.

The *tir cyfrif* vill was one unit. Plots were assigned for the season only, and the *maer* controlled the allotments made for harvest. There were homesteads and homestead land, and every adult male save the youngest had a share. Apportionment to the harvest and to new cultivation was by individual male adults, not by families, but the youngest son remained his father's assistant until his father died, when he had a homestead. In the *maerdref* the *land-maer* was unfree and the tenants cultivated the demesne land.

The unfree had to find a number of renders and services. A relief or heriot, payable upon the father's death, was usual, but on *tir cyfrif* only the youngest son paid it. Free land paid the king's entertainment allowance and supper money for his servants twice a year. Every *tref* found bread made from a horse load of the best flour, and seven thraves of oats. With the bread went a cow or an ox, a three-year-old sow, a vessel of butter, and bacon. The drinks were a vat of mead, double of the finest ale, and quadruple of the common ale. The vat of mead had to be large enough for the king and a local elder to bathe in together. The unfree also found twice-yearly an entertainment allowance and maintained the king's officers on circuit. In winter they found a three-year-old sow, a vessel of butter, a vat of the finest ale, a thrave of oats, twenty-six loaves of the best bread, and a man to light the fire in the king's hall on the night of the tribute. In summer they found a three-year-old wether, a dish of butter, twenty-six loaves of bread, and the milk of every cow in the *tref*, for one day made into a cheese. The tenants of the *maerdref* had to supply the king in his palace.

The bond communities were older than the free communities. Anglesey had been a land inhabited predominantly by bond communities until the intrusion of free elements in the course of the twelfth century. The earliest free settlements were along coastal ridges and above the estuaries on the west coast of the island, the later in the low-lying interior. By 1282–4 there were about a hundred *gwelyau*, not more than 90–120 years old. There were also bondmen living in mixed communities as well as in communities of the three types – *tir gwelyawg, tir cyfrif* and *maerdref* vills. *Tir cyfrif* was the earliest form of tenure, and it existed by the time of Hywel Dda (904–50).

There is evidence of a change to freedom. *Gwely* tenure seems to have sprung from *tir cyfrif* and the dividing line between *tir cyfrif* and *gwely* tenure was less pronounced than formerly thought. The existence of bond *gwelyau* in Caernarvonshire is particularly significant since it shows the possibility of the ascent of bondmen to freedom. Originally all early Celtic churches were founded in bond hamlets, and dispersal was the later result of population pressure and enfranchisement. The division of territory between the *gwelyau* was so artificial that it suggests deliberate policy. Partible inheritance will not explain this phenomenon and in any case it arose too late (c. 1100) for such an explanation. Only a deliberate policy of new settlement started in north-east Wales will explain it, but the association of partible inheritance and new settlement is quite clearly there.[5]

Wales and the Marches and northern England were quite unlike the Midlands, and eastern, southern and south-eastern England. Both regions were highly pastoral, but had good arable areas, as in the Central Plain of Herefordshire, the Great Vale of York and Holderness. On the whole agriculture was backward, but in Wales and Lancashire peasant society was remarkably fluid, and the economy expanded fast. We are ill-informed about population, but field-systems and social structure are better known.

CHAPTER 12

THE MALTHUSIAN PROBLEM

'Perhaps, after all, we do not need to add this half-century to the periods of history when the death-rate and not the birth-rate has exercised the more profound influence on the population trend.' Speaking about the period 1300–48 in 1965 Miss Barbara Harvey ended her paper with this sentence. One of my aims has been to show the truth of this statement, but first I must once more pose the question: Did the population of England decline in 1300–48? Miss Harvey suggests that it may have stagnated; Dr Kershaw thinks it declined, but he would not be too dogmatic about it, and he recognizes the complexity of the problem.

We have good counts of heads of households in eastern, south-eastern, and southern England, and less good counts for the rest of England. In the north there are figures only for Yorkshire, and Domesday probably omits much of the population. In eastern England population increased in 1086–1300, but the increase was slower in 1229–1300 than in 1086–1229. The population of south-eastern England was stagnant in 1260–92, but grew very fast in 1292–1315. In the east Midlands there was considerable decline in 1244–80, but a new increase in 1280–1312 which failed to bring the population back to the 1279 level. In southern England a fast decline in 1287–1311 led to a rapid increase in 1311–28, which failed to bring the population back to the 1287 level. In the west Midlands a slowish decline led to a very rapid increase in 1293–1315. The Yorkshire figures suggest a great increase in 1265–90, followed by a large decline in 1290–1309. Stagnation or decline took place in five of the eight regions of England, but in south-eastern and southern England, and the east and west Midlands, a fresh, but slower increase followed stagnation or decline. Insufficient figures exist for 1325–50, and the poor representation of the late-settled highland zone, where expansion of the cultivated area (as well as contraction) was still going on in 1348, makes conclusions very shaky, but I shall risk a general statement about the population history of England in 1086–1318.

In 1086–1193 population increased quite quickly – by 72 per cent in 107 years – and if we suppose the highest arguable Domesday population of 2,000,000 by 1193 this had grown to 3,440,000 or so. In 1193–1230 – in 37 years – the population increased by half, from about 3,440,000 to about 5,120,000. The rate of increase in 1193–1230 was about 80 per cent of that in 1086–1193. In 1230–65 – in 35 years – the population increased by a quarter, from about 5,120,000 to about 6,380,000, which gives a rate of increase in 1230–65 about half that in 1193–1230. In 1265–94 – in 29 years – the population grew by 13 per cent, from about 6,380,000 to about 7,200,000, a rate of increase in 1265–94 a little over half that in 1230–65. Thus the population rise was continuous in 1086–1294, but the increases were constantly slower after 1193. In 1294–1318 the population declined, but the decrease – in 24 years – was considerably slower than the increase in 1086–1230, and it brought the population down from 7,200,000 in 1294 to about 6,740,000 in 1318. What happened in the period 1318–48 is not clear, since there are few surveys for this period. The figures do not cover the towns which may have absorbed some of the half million missing people, but they were perhaps not large enough to have taken them all. The decline is real and seems to have coincided with Dr Kershaw's agrarian crisis, but I have suggested in the chapter on eastern England that in the most thickly inhabited part of England, which contained nearly half the population, famine was not the cause of the decline.

If we suppose a lower Domesday population then the maximum population in about 1294 would be at least 4,500,000 or 5,400,000, which would still make the population before the Black Death as great as or greater than that of late-Tudor England. All possible population figures presuppose an average household size of 4.75 people but in some parts of England where peasant holdings were substantial five or even six people to the household would have been more usual. The larger the holding the larger the household. After the Black Death household sizes may have been nearer the 3.5 people which Professor Russell has always advocated, and this shrinkage may have started in some regions before 1348.

A high population of 7,200,000, which England was not to see again before the eighteenth century, depends upon the belief that Domesday missed out very many more people than the early Domesday scholars thought likely. The omission of the four northern counties and most of Wales, the very inadequate treatment of Lancashire, together with the omission of London and Winchester and most of the clergy, would alone make a 1086 population of only 1,250,000, and a 1294 population of only 4,500,000 seem insufficient. But there were probably other omissions. The time has gone when historians could class the apparently uninhabited vills of parts of Yorkshire with the *terra vasta* (wasteland) and lay both to the charge of King William's devastation of the north in 1070. Surely these vills seem to have no people because the king's commissioners never found out who lived there: they sent no representatives to the shire court. Similarly we are now fairly certain that sokemen are missing from the Staffordshire folios, and the mention of slaves in the Black Book of Peterborough (1125) suggests that their absence from the Lincolnshire Domesday may be an omission rather than an expression of the superior freedom of the Danelaw. In the regions remote from London and Winchester the great survey is much less reliable than in the heartland of Wessex. These considerations favour a Domesday population of 1,500,000 or 2,000,000 and a 1294 population of 5,400,000 to 7,200,000.

How did England manage to support so many people? England and Wales occupy roughly 37,280,000 acres, which gives to a population of 7,200,000 24.2 acres for every household of 4.75 members. Much of the highland zone was not arable but even in the lowland zone men did not live entirely from the products of the open fields. They had livestock on the commons and they practised crafts and trades. In East Anglia a family could live on eight acres of land. If the real population of England were not 7,200,000 but 5,400,000 each family would have 33.3 acres of land on average, which is surely enough by any medieval standard. There can be no doubt that England could physically support the high populations suggested.

Earlier I have stressed the importance of progressive agriculture in eastern and south-eastern England and some parts of the east Midlands. Most Englishmen lived in these regions. These parts of England, by the middle of the thirteenth century, tended to grow barley rather than oats or wheat, planted considerable crops of nitrogenous legumes, reared pigs and cattle rather than sheep (the sign of a backward economy), possessed no goats, laid stress upon cheese and butter made from cow's milk (not ewe's or goat's), and ploughed with small horses not with oxen. The possession of horses was itself a sign of a rich economy, for horses need to eat oats, else they die, whereas oxen can get along with hedge clippings in the winter. The possession of horses is the reason for growing oats, and the power to grow oats, which are not needed for human consumption, makes the use of horses possible. The horse eats twice as much as the ox but he works more than twice as fast and his adoption was an important technological advance. He is the sign of a successful economy and the pledge of its further success.

Further technological advances took place in field-systems, crop rotations and crop nutrition. Many authors have supposed that no such advances took place. In the past concentration upon the racial origins of the open-field system has obscured its economic characteristics. Open fields, whether common fields or not certainly existed by the tenth century in England and may very well have been present in the seventh century. Their association with the heavy plough, which the Orwins insisted upon, is not a necessary feature of their existence, for nobody really knows who used the heavy plough (*caruca*) in the medieval period, and its qualities and advantages were certainly different from those which the Orwins entertained. The action of the plough is no longer considered a necessary part or condition of the creation of the open fields, and modern students of the open fields are now back where Vinogradoff left them.

Land-sharing derived from the process of new settlement now seems to be the reason for the creation of open fields.

For the economic historian the open fields are best seen as various stages in the betterment of agriculture. The most densely settled parts of England formed, in 1250–1350, a three-course rotation which already existed widely in Cambridgeshire well before 1250. East Anglia went a stage further, to the more efficient fold-course common-field system peculiar to Norfolk and Suffolk, but practised in some neighbouring counties. In eastern England only Lincolnshire, except the Fenland, stuck fast to its original two-course system, save a few highland Lincolnshire villages which had the earliest recorded three-field systems in England. The east Midlands, except Nottingham-shire, used a two-course system, but Northamptonshire developed three-course rotation after 1300. South-eastern England, and especially Kent, had a peculiar open-field system of its own which was not a common-field system, yet was more advanced than that of the east Midlands, particularly in techniques of crop nutrition. The west Midlands and southern England, particularly Somerset and Wiltshire, mainly practised a two-field crop rotation, but in some villages two fields cloaked the existence of a three-course rotation, no doubt subsequent to the creation of two fields; in most of the two regions outfields were not uncommon and the practice of creating *inhokes* fairly frequent, especially in Gloucestershire. Hampshire and the Isle of Wight used three-course rotations and Wiltshire developed them extensively after 1300. Technically southern England and the west Midlands were less advanced than eastern and south-eastern England and the east Midlands and the growth of more complicated crop rotations and field-systems was later. In the highland zone open and even common fields existed at an early date, and in Wales perhaps by the mid-tenth century, and certainly by the end of the twelfth century. Staffordshire and Yorkshire had three-course rotations, Staffordshire mainly after 1300.

The connection between new settlement and the develop-ment of common fields is now plain. Fully-grown common fields probably existed in the east and west Midlands and southern England by the tenth century. The evolution of East Anglia and Kent still needs further clarification. Pressure upon the land by a growing population was less in the west Midlands and southern England than in eastern and south-eastern England and the east Midlands because they were less fully developed and still had space to fill in 1086–1280. Except in special areas the last three regions had little space for expansion, but their population continued to rise fast during most of the period. This population rise was possible because the east Midlands, eastern England (especially East Anglia) and Kent used superior agrarian techniques. It was necessary because they were also great practisers of partible inheritance.

The medieval English peasant maintained and increased the fertility of his soil by using a suitable crop rotation and by planting suitable crops, especially peas, beans and vetches, but he also made elaborate provisions for crop nutrition. This is one of the least known and most elusive aspects of medieval agrarian history, one of the most neglected, but also one of the most important.

Great lords frequently (perhaps always) practised manuring, and their serfs often carried out the arduous work of carting and spreading, for which the lord was sometimes glad to reward them with food. The dung used was normally cow-dung or sheep-dung, but there are fewer references to the latter because the sheep often folded on the arable. The East Anglian fold-course system was an especially thrifty way of using sheep-dung on the arable. Sheep were valued first for their wool, secondly for their dung, thirdly for their hooves which firmed the land in the spring, for the sheep 'had a golden hoof', and only fourthly for their meat. Occasionally pigeon-dung appears in accounts and dovecotes were extremely common in some parts of England. There are only a few ways of checking the amount of dung manorial lords used upon their land. Generally they used little cow-dung and manured the fields by hand infrequently. The peasantry also dunged their land but quantities are incalculable.

All forms of crop nutrition known to the medieval farmer, except sea-weeding, sanding and beat-burning, which were devices of the poorer parts of England and Wales, were in use all over the country, but marling was particularly associated with assarting in Gloucestershire, Cheshire, Staffordshire and Derbyshire, and all early agrarian literature advised its use as by far the most profitable long-term form of crop nutrition. But all agreed that it was laborious, and perhaps its use lapsed during the fifteenth century because of the cost and lack of labour compared with the thirteenth century. Its existence on a large scale – probably far larger than documentary sources can reveal – surely proves that the medieval farmer treated his land with careful thought for the future and was not desperate to secure a quick return to stave off famine. Neither did the lords take all the means of improvement for themselves. The peasantry used all forms of crop nutrition; though privileged, the lords had no monopoly.

There were great contrasts between the more pastoral, new-settlement counties of England and Wales and the more arable regions, but it is very difficult to decide whether any part of the country had enough means to fertilize its fields. Nowhere are there any statistics of the dung-producing powers of medieval sheep and cattle, but the animals were very small compared with modern breeds. In regions like the West Riding of Yorkshire and the Lleyn Peninsula the percentage of arable was small, and in some of these hill regions there were immense herds of cattle such as those which roamed the Forest of Rossendale and the Trough of Bowland.

The problem is complex and difficult, and there is at the moment no perfect answer to it. The study of crop nutrition adds something very important to the knowledge of medieval agriculture. It shows that it is wrong blindly to trust to straight Malthusianism as an explanation of what happened, and it suggests that we should not apply to the whole of England and Wales what may be true only of a part.

The rural proletariat – the fringe-dwellers – are really the key to the problem of English demographic history in the medieval period. They are interesting in two ways – because they were very mobile, and because they were the product of the medieval peasant marriage.

Several historians, notably those of the Toronto school, have written about emigration. Men could become clergymen, vagabonds or servants; women could become vagabonds or servants or could marry outside the village. In Lincolnshire in 1268–9 from a third to a half of the new generation emigrated in one of these ways.

Bondwomen often used marriage to leave their manor of origin. In Lincolnshire this form of mobility was not common before 1300, but the opening years of the fourteenth century saw a quite sudden rise in the number of women seeking husbands outside their own manor. In the half-century before the Black Death, when marriage itself was much more popular, and the population rising in numbers once more, fully a quarter of brides married outside their own manors. Most of them married within ten miles of home, but a few married in distant counties, such as Staffordshire, Northamptonshire and Hampshire.

The men had a greater variety of ways in which they could leave home. Even the sons of a reeve or a smith could take minor or holy orders. Some went into service. Then there were the illegal flights, sometimes of rich peasants from large holdings, but occasionally the grass over the other side of the fence was not so green as it had appeared and the vagabond returned. Besides these there were the legal emigrants who paid the lord chevage (or head money) for licence to live away from the manor, usually to practise a trade or craft. There were few of these before the Black Death. In Lincolnshire, Lynn and London attracted most emigrants. Emigration must have taken place since the time serfdom began, but after 1300, in Lincolnshire, the departure of brides was the biggest factor to keep down population, unless as many brides came into these villages as left them.

Emigration was going on all over England, and manorial lords tried to control it by enforcing the assize forbidding lodgers. The king was always concerned to put down robbers and the foot-loose were often criminally inclined. Violent crime was extremely common from about the time of King John, when we have the first assize rolls, and hangings correspondingly frequent. In 1287–1304 a Bedfordshire village had numerous criminal contacts with the outside world. Fifteen of the humbler people had their garden exits towards the fields and took in illegal lodgers. Some were malefactors, usually corn-thieves, and some of these were women. The villagers were also not supposed to lead their neighbours out of the parish into the service of strangers, or to employ unlicensed servants themselves.

The medieval villager was much more mobile than historians once supposed. Few families stayed in the same village for even three generations. As a rule, where surveys of the same manor exist for dates about thirty years apart not only the high death-rate and short life of the medieval villager are apparent, but also the speed with which the population dispersed into the surrounding countryside. If bondwomen were so mobile that, in 1301–50, one-quarter of them married outside their home village, bondmen and free tenants must also have been highly mobile, and what applied to the settled, landed peasants would apply even more strongly to the fringe-dwellers. Distant migrations, except to the towns, were less common. From as far back as records can show, that is, back to the misty second quarter of the thirteenth century, the peasant population of England was constantly on the move. Manorial lordship did not impede this constant ebb and flow. The various fines which, our masters taught us, prevented the bondman moving about did not do so in the period after the Norman Conquest. Whether they had that effect in the Dark Ages we shall perhaps never know, but in the period for which good records are extant peasant mobility was very great. This does not mean that no families remained in the same village for two centuries or more. Examples exist but they were not the norm.

The settled, landed families who stayed put in their village for at least one generation were quite closely in contact with the outside world. The villein had to do all sorts of carrying services for his lord, and the adult males often carted or carried loads on their back for distances over forty miles. The lord gave them subsistence if they had to stay away overnight. Many examples of such carrying services are known. The tenants of the Abbot of Bury St Edmunds carried many sorts of goods all over east Suffolk and Essex, and sometimes as far as Lynn and London. In 1221 and 1251 the men of the bishop of Ely, living in the Isle of Ely, carried the bishop's wheat by boat down the Great Ouse to Lynn where merchants exported it to feed the hungry cloth-towns of Flanders. The medieval peasant saw a good deal of the world – much less than his movement-mad descendants, it is true, but his was no closed or subsistence economy. He was also well aware of political affairs, especially in wide-awake East Anglia, and particularly from the time of the deposition of Edward II (1326) when he made his views known about some of the more conservative forms of manorialism. The great rebellions against the Abbeys of Bury St Edmunds, St Albans and Abingdon, and against Dunstable Priory, were only possible in a profit-making, individualistic society where manorialism was obsolescent.

All over England during the medieval period, and, with some modification until the 1940s, all classes of society except the nobility practised prudential marriage. In pre-industrial England young couples entered marriage only with the consent of their parents, and only when they could assure themselves of a home and adequate means of support. Since, in medieval England, land and the common rights which attached to a homestead were the prime means of support for a very large section of the populace, only when land became available could a couple become man and wife.

Land could become available in a number of ways. If a man's father died, and he were the eldest or (on many villein tenements) the youngest son, or (in regions of partible inheritance) one of several inheriting sons, he married at the same time as he followed his father in the family holding. If she was an heiress a women might find that the attractiveness of her

father's holding more than made up for her own deficiencies of
face and figure. Such a succession was always subject to the
provision of dower and lodging for the surviving mother of
either of the newly-wedded pair. Sometimes father retired to
the chimney-corner or made an agreement that his son should
have the holding, provided that his. parents might occupy a
retirement room and receive an allowance of food and clothing,
or live in a small cottage inside the son's curtilage. Some fathers
had spare holdings they could settle on their sons whilst they
continued, in ripe vigour, to work their yardland or oxgang. At
other times the manorial lord, always concerned to support the
status quo and to strengthen the prudential marriage, stepped in
and offered a suitable young man a vacant holding. Sometimes a
widow dwelt on that holding, and manorial lords, not always
too mindful of canon law's insistence that both parties to a
match must have a mind to it, tried to coerce a man into
marrying her. If she were old and ugly or had an evil temper,
young men would sometimes submit to several fines rather than
place their peace of mind in such jeopardy.

The prudential marriage also existed for women. To claim
that romantic love did not exist would betray rank ignorance of
human nature but the medieval peasant knew that it was less
frequent than his descendants have pretended, and he was loth to
exchange 'is' for 'ought'. The marriage portion and the dower
therefore played a large part in a marriage which the parents (if
alive) usually arranged with the girl's parents through an
intermediary. There was a mutual inspection of premises, and
the girl's father stated the nature of her marriage portion.
Whether formally celebrated before the priest or informally at a
handfasting before relatives, the wedding included, besides the
plighting of the troth and the exchange of rings, a ceremonial
statement from the groom at the church door that he gave
certain land as dower to his wife. Even if she had no dower
manorial custom gave his widow a half or a third of the holding,
provided that, if the heir were under age, she paid heriot and
relief for it. If she was free, she had absolute right to dispose of
her dower and her marriage portion as she wished, provided

that she remained a widow and did not fornicate. If she was unfree she could pay the lord for permission to remain unmarried, if she remained chaste. And so a land transaction accompanied every stage of married life.

The corollary of this is that marriage was difficult for those who did not have the opportunity to get land. Sometimes non-inheriting brothers, sisters or other relatives agreed to work for the landholder, provided that they did not marry, but celibacy does not suit everybody. Many landless men practised trades, and landless women became maidservants or casual workers. Of this sort were the *anilepimen* and *anilepiwymmen* – the 'alone-leaping' men and women – of the Ely surveys of 1221 and 1251. There are six references to them in 1221 and twenty in 1251, in Huntingdonshire, Cambridgeshire, Norfolk and Suffolk but not in Essex. In most of the references they are shown coming to work at the autumn boons. The lord usually fed them on bread and herrings or eels. The *anilepiman* was either a householder or not, and if not, was either in somebody else's employ or not. The *anilepiman* could also hold stock. Most unfree tenants on the bishop's manors paid cowpenny to avoid folding their beasts in the lord's fold. Otherwise the two-tooths of the cottars and *anilepimen* lay in the bishop's fold, because they had no fold of their own. Some, perhaps most, *anilepimen* were not established in homesteads. They were probably, many of them, unmarried, for they did not pay chevage if they were in the service of their fathers and mothers. The whole population of smallholders and landless men was very mobile. The landless were a significant factor in eastern England, where they could squat on the commons and do casual work. The working class was not a product of the Industrial Revolution, but one of the factors which made it possible.

All over England and Wales when a bondman married his daughter he had to pay a fine, usually called *merchet* or *gersuma*. Though later considered a test of villeinage by blood, and sometimes called 'buying his own blood', it was not conclusive evidence that even the tenement was unfree. As the *amobyr* in Wales the marriage of every girl saw its payment, and in

Scotland every woman, noble or bond, paid it in kine. The thegns and drengs of Northumberland, often lords of manors, paid it for their daughters.

Typical *merchet* fines are those which Ramsey Abbey levied upon its villeins. The villein usually paid what he could negotiate for marrying his daughter, whether she married inside or outside the town. A high fine was compensation to the lord for loss of one of his stock of villeins and her issue.

Lords very often controlled the marriages of villeins other than villeins' daughters. Sometimes workmen on full lands (twelve acres) paid *gersuma* for their own and for their sons' and daughters' marriages. Some lesser cottars also paid *gersuma* to marry themselves. They could not, when widowed, marry again without the lord's licence. A villein's widow could also not remarry without the lord's licence. If widowed a woman could take a husband and paid whether she had licence to marry or not, but her husband had to be suitable. If a man's heir was a woman she also could marry without the lord's licence, provided that her husband was suitable. On the other hand, if a man had a daughter and married her he paid *gersuma*. Elsewhere the holders of full worklands who had heirs could not marry them within the town or without unless they had the lord's licence, but they gave nothing for this; they paid heriot, but no relief for the holding. On the other hand, if the heir was a daughter, then he who took her to wife made peace with the lord for both her and the land as best he might. Licence to marry and payment of *merchet* or *gersuma* were clearly separate matters, and even in free Norfolk and Suffolk the lord scrutinized the suitability of the husband whether he had to license the marriage or not. A suitable tenant was one who would not drink and idle and waste the lord's goods. By keeping control over marriage the lord kept control over the land, made sure that every holding had a man to run it, and that suitable men had holdings and wives.

There was a similar intention in the imposition of the *leyrwite*, since the fornicator and adulterer lost the lord's goods by paying a fine in the court of the archdeacon or rural dean, where sin was justiciable. In Cambridgeshire, in 1251, a workman who held a full land paid *leyrwite* for his daughter if she had fornicated with anyone and had been attainted for it. When would she be attainted? The open fields of England, with their high rigs, sometimes planted with rye, which as Brueghel's *Harvesters* again reminds us, grows over six feet high in the straw, made a secluded, green, but perhaps rather damp, bed for lovers and delinquent wives and husbands. Field names like Cuckold's Headland and nicknames like Alice le Hore remind us of man's unregenerate nature.

> Between the acres of the rye,
> With a heigh and a ho,
> And a heigh-nonny no
> These pretty countryfolk would lie.

Love in the winter must have been difficult for those who evaded the blessed state of matrimony. In Cambridgeshire the cottar paid the Bishop of Ely *leyrwite* for his daughter if she fornicated with others and persisted in it. The lord on his side endeavoured to fasten the fine on the sinners' own necks. Elsewhere on the bishop's manors, if the daughter of one of the *censuarii* fornicated with someone and was attainted of the fault, he who had the thing with her (so says the custumal) had to pay the *leyrwite*, but if he defaulted she herself had to make fine with the lord, as best she might. But why did her father not pay the fine? The father paid *leyrwite* for her as best he could make fine with the lord if she had fornicated in his custody (i.e. in the parental home), but she herself became liable, or he with whom she had fornicated, if she fornicated outside her father's custody (e.g. in the fields). If he who had fornicated with her afterwards married her, he was quit of *gersuma* (the marriage fine), but not otherwise.

One is bound to wonder what evidence the archdeacon's or rural deans's court took for notorious fornication, and also to ask why an ecclesiastical lord should worry about the loss of money which found its way into the same church's pocket by a different route, that is, through church courts. The answer seems to be that all lords objected to bastards because a bondwoman's bastard was free, not bond, and escaped all servile duties, but was not entitled to inherit land. He was outside the law and, unless somebody made special provision for him, likely to become a vagrant. The fine the peasants paid for fornication was sometimes called the *childwite*. The customers and rent payers paid *childwite* for their daughters if they fornicated with anybody and had children. Sometimes the daughter had herself to make peace with the lord as best she could. On one Suffolk manor she paid *childwite* when it happened (i.e. nobody worried if she fornicated provided there was no child). Elsewhere in Norfolk the father paid his daughter's *leyrwite*, and after that however many times she became pregnant, or had manifestly fornicated, he only paid the same amount. And so, like the modern prostitute before the magistrate, she paid her taxes. Widows also had to be chaste. Even freewomen lost their halves or thirds if they fornicated. In hundreds of medieval charters widows disposed of their lands *in libera et pura viduitate mea* ('in my free and pure widowhood') and the purity was a condition of the freedom. At Bramford, in Suffolk, Roger de Lovetot's wife, if he had one, remained on the whole tenement as if on free bench all her life, unless she fornicated with anyone and was attainted for it. If his daughter fornicated and had a child within the town he paid for *childwite* either a superior cloth or two shillings. This fine applied not only to her but to every outside woman, whether rich or poor, if she entered the town and gave birth in it outside matrimony. So the lord vindicated morality and discouraged landless offspring.

The medieval peasant marriage can be studied in the record of *merchet* fines from the Lincolnshire manors of Spalding Priory. According to the agreement which the prior forced upon his rebellious bondmen in 1212–22 both sokemen and workmen had to pay *merchet*. This payment was made by or on behalf of the bondwoman when she married. The *merchet* was different from the fine paid for marriage without licence. It is the nearest record we have to a registration of the marriage of bondwomen. On these manors there was (though earlier than elsewhere) a late age of marriage and a disproportion between the number of marriageable males and females. The masculinity ratio of the marriageable was 118. There was an imbalance between the sexes on all three manors which is very revealing. Females were fewer than males, and the disproportion increased as people became older. This disproportion in the older people must indeed have been much greater, since our information does not tell us about widowers, who must have existed. Puerperal fever, that old enemy of women, must have been actively at work, but what about the unmarried, and, we must assume, chaste girls? More particularly, what about the infants? The only ready explanations are exposure of infants and abortion, but the latter will not fit the facts because our ancestors did not know what sex the baby was before it was born. Exposure is therefore the likely reason. Once more we return to the rye fields, where some babies were engendered.

> Jack and Gye went into the rye,
> And they found a little boy with one black eye.
> 'Come,' says Jack, 'Let's knock him on the head.'
> 'No,' says Gye, 'Let's give him some bread.
> You give him one loaf, and I'll give him two.
> And we'll bring him up as other folk do.'

Jack and Gye were perhaps childless, and the little boy lucky because he was a little boy. Had he been a little girl Jack might have had his way. We have therefore a rural society where age at marriage was late, that is, near the Western European standard of about twenty-five for men and twenty-three for women, but the lack of suitable women probably made the age gap between husband and wife greater than two years.

We can now see how far the information we can obtain from the *merchet* fines reflects these conditions. An interesting question is the number of times different people paid the *merchet* fine – husband, wife, father, mother or brother. Textbooks assume that father paid it. In reality father did not even pay half the *merchet* fines recorded. Perhaps father always paid in antiquity, before there were court rolls, but the husband tended increasingly to pay after 1295. Doubtless the husband was more willing to pay if the wife had a good marriage portion, or if she were an heiress. Land shortage would make the husband more eager to secure a wife whose face was not her only fortune as the countryside became more and more crowded. The low marriage rate and the tendency for women to remain unmarried in 1260–1300, would likewise explain the large number of women who were willing to pay their own *merchet* fines in 1252–80, and 1296–1340. After the Black Death, except in 1356–60, and apart from a few minor fluctuations, women tended less and less to pay their own *merchet* fines, presumably because the great cut in population made in 1348–9, and again in 1369, in these manors, had restored the balance of land and people, and marriage was easier and more frequent.

The study of widows' *merchets* confirms most of these generalizations. Besides a rise in marriage rate the period 1301–50 saw the percentage of widows' marriages double and the number treble compared with 1252–1300. The demand for land had become very great. The last three years of this period saw the introduction of a complicating factor – the great increase in the death-rate brought by the Plague. The removal of fathers and husbands produced many desirable marriages which the figures amply reflect. Out of six *merchets* in 1348, none were for widows; out of eighteen in 1349 four; out of thirty-five in 1350 seven. The effect of the Plague continued for a year or two and the high death-rate made the demand for widows, which had hitherto sprung from the demand for land, seem greater than it actually was.

Study of the comparative sizes of widows' and spinsters' *merchets* shows that in 1252–1300 the value of the former was more than double the value of the latter, and in 1301–50 more than treble, but after the Black Death there was little to choose between them, though widows retained a slight lead in value, in virtue of the land they bore with them. The significance of widows' *merchets* also appears in who paid. Normally it fell to the husband to do so, and if she was a valuable widow it cost him dear. In 1335 a Spalding husband paid £40 for a widow. This would have taken all the wages of a skilled worker for sixteen years. Payments of £1, £2, £3 and £5 were common. Widows who paid their own *merchets* paid at a considerably lower rate than husbands who paid for them. There must have been some special reason why a widow herself paid two *merchets* of £2 and £5 but, barring private arrangements, it seems that widows who paid for themselves were less attractive than those whose husbands found the *merchet*. A widow with little but her personal charm to offer her new husband made up for her lack of property by finding the *merchet*. The lord graded *merchets* according to the amount the parties could afford. Occasionally we find written in the register 'Nothing since she is poor', or payments of one shilling 'since she is poor'. Even the payment of a token penny is recorded. There was a careful assessment of means on these occasions. The rich had to pay heavily, but the poor were let off lightly, sometimes altogether. A small *merchet* therefore meant poverty, and widows who paid their own *merchets*, at a lower rate than usual for widows, were poor with little land.

The careful definition of *leyrwite* which the Ely custumals of 1251 allow brings great caution to the study of fornication, adultery and bastardy. According to modern ideas young men and women, condemned by the strict bond which the economy and the lord placed upon marriage and the land, to tie them together, would not be able to stand ten years, the best of their lives, in enforced celibacy, but would have to burst out, like so many Trobriand Islanders, in a riot of copulation and parturition. The stern pattern of our Western society, set for material gain and the satisfaction of the ego, ordered otherwise, and the doctrines of the Latin Churches, which taught that man was born in congenital sin, next to his mother's excretions, backed up the need for celibacy, which was better than marriage. Only frequent and notorious fornicators had to pay *leyrwite*, and as a rule there had been a bastard born. The *leyrwite* is not an adequate guide to the popularity of extra-marital love, but it is the best we have and suggests that the medieval peasant did not have sex on the brain (which is a very bad place to have it), unlike some of his descendants.

The practice of taking *leyrwites* seems gradually to have lapsed and become disused. The *leyrwites* show no effect from the Black Death – no breakdown of morality which the Church writers have taught us to expect. If we assume that each *leyrwite* represents an illegitimate birth, and each marriage a legitimate birth within a year (a big assumption), in the period 1252–1300 nearly 8 per cent of new sexual unions produced bastards, and in 1301–50 just over 7 per cent. A real bastardy rate would be much lower than these figures, because of the children born to previously married couples, but they are well within the maximum figures found in Western Europe in the sixteenth and seventeenth centuries, much lower than recent bastardy rates, but not so low as bastardy rates in eighteenth-century Brittany, modern Ireland or Malta. The Church was not so strong in the England of 1250–1350.

Such a tightly controlled society as these five manors of Spalding Priory is an irony in the comparative freedom of eastern England. The lineaments of England before 1350 are now laid bare. English customs and sentiment, from well before the Norman Conquest, encouraged new settlement and population growth, but never beyond reason. Economic expansion brought greater personal freedom and the encouragement of enterprise and hard work. Already in the thirteenth century prudence rather than self-indulgence in love was the rule, and in food and drink necessity imposed its own restraints. To the medieval villein one of the greatest pleasures in life was not free (if it ever truly is free). He had to skimp and save to make ends meet, to think of the morrow always, and provide for his children, and if he had the strength and ability he could use the rules to build up a modest competence. The laws of his life were the same as the drives of the Victorian industrialist, enhanced and purified as the latter were to be by the Reformation and Renaissance. The Protestant work ethic existed in many segments of medieval society long before Protestantism, and was rooted deep in the habits of centuries.

The monk, the merchant and the peasant were its custodians, but below and apart from them were the fringe-dwellers, the vagabonds, casual workers and the other landless men, also the product of the system, many of whom drifted to the towns or pitched their cabins on the commons of England. Their descendants would furnish labourers for the factories of the Industrial Revolution, and from them has sprung the urban proletariat of our own day. They were much less likely to work and save, and more prepared to enjoy, than their betters. The medieval establishment disapproved of the fringe-dwellers and did all it could to prevent their undue multiplication, but strict control of land and marriage, a control which the peasantry itself approved and exercised, was not sufficient to solve the problem. Unlike Sholokhov's Don Cossacks of Tsarist days the English peasantry did not live in enlarged households with several married siblings; the need to set up a separate household discouraged early marriage and created a working class, largely unmarried, with a tendency to beget bastards and expose infants, and to practise abortion and primitive forms of contraception, which found its way to the towns and the great marshlands of eastern England which offered 'overmuch harbour to a rude and almost barbarous, sort of lazy and beggarly people'. Such a society did not procreate itself, but depended for its renewal upon the middle and richer peasantry. When population density became too great marriage was hard to justify, so that even in the Lincolnshire Fenland in 1281–95 the number of marriages was only a third of what it had been in the most prosperous years. In these same villages there was a fresh surge in matrimony, particularly for widows, and much higher *merchet* fines, in 1326–35. Better harvests, a popular and stable government, and (perhaps) lower rents are the likely reasons for this change. This is not to deny the reality of the population decline, or to forget the famines or the climatic change. As Dr Kershaw says, the problem is complicated, but emigration and the prudential marriage are part of the answer to it.[1]

GLOSSARY

ACRE UNDER ACRE The scatter of strips in the open fields.

AFFER A draught horse.

AILLT Bond tenants of the king or of freemen.

ASSbART Land cleared of trees.

BALK, BAULK A ridge of land left unploughed.

BOCAGE A countryside of small hedges or walled closes, sometimes the result of early enclosure of open fields, sometimes of immemorial antiquity.

BORDAR A villein of the lowest rank, doing manual service for a cottage which he held at his lord's will.

BOVATE Latin for an oxgang or *mannislot*.

BRECK OR BREACH An assart.

BYRLAW, OR BY-LAW The local custom or popular jurisprudence of a village, township, or district, dealing with minor matters of dispute without reference to the law courts.

CAMLWRW A Welsh fine.

CANTREF A Welsh hundred.

CARR A fen, boggy ground, pool, or marsh.

CENSARIUS Unfree rent-paying tenant.

CLOSE A small enclosed field.

COTSETLE A cottar, cottager or tenant of cot-land.

COTTAR A peasant living in a cottage belonging to a farm and paying rent in the form of labour.

CROFT A piece of enclosed ground, especially adjoining a house.

CRONE An old ewe.

CULLION (or CULL) An animal picked out as inferior or too old for breeding, and usually fattened for killing.

CYMWD, COMMOTE An ancient Welsh local government unit, either larger than or the same as a *cantref*.

DREDGE A mixture of wheat or barley and oats.

ERIUNG, TENEMENTUM or PLENA TERRA. A standard East Anglian peasant holding.

ERW A Welsh acre or selion.

FERLING A quarter-virgate.

FLATT A level plain or low tract of land; a plot of ground laid down level. Still in use in Western Australia.

FOLD-COURSE The division of the fallow-pasture into sheep walks.

FOLDSOKE Suit of fold.

FREEDMEN Manumitted slaves.

FURLONG A group of strips of land in the open-field system of agriculture.

GAVELKIND A custom prevalent in Kent and Wales whereby the lands of a person dying intestate descend to all the sons in equal shares, or in default of sons, to all the daughters.

GODAEG The tenant of a *tyddyn*.

GORE, GORE-ACRE A triangular piece of land.

GRANGE A barn; a farmhouse with the outbuildings, especially if occupied as a country residence.

GWARTHAL A resharing of land held together.

GWELY, GWELYAU Clan or clans of freemen or fractions thereof.

HARDFISH Dried-fish or stock-fish, cod, ling, etc., split open and dried in sun without salting.

HEADLAND A ridge or strip of unploughed land at either end of a field where the plough is turned.

HERBAGE The right of pasture in the forest or on the grounds of another.

HERIOT A fine, such as the best beast, payable to the lord of the fee on the decease of the tenant.

HIDAGE A tax paid to the king for every hide of land; the assessment on which this was paid.

HIDE A certain portion of land (variously estimated at from 60 to 120 acres) originally enough to support a family and its dependants.

HOG, HOGGASTER or HOGGET A young sheep or bullock, usually of a year old.

HWYL The incantatory summit of a Welsh sermon or speech.

INFIELD-OUTFIELD SYSTEM A type of open-field system which has intensively cultivated fields near the village, home or base and extensively cultivated outfields cropped but not manured on the periphery.

ING A meadow.

INHECHINGES Inhokes.

INHOKE, 'INHOOK' Piece of fallow temporarily enclosed for cultivation.

INNING Lands recovered from the sea.

INTAKE Land enclosed, especially a tract taken in from moorland and cultivated.

IUGUM or *DOLA* Measure of land, quarter of a 'sulung' (Kent).

LAND-MAER A Welsh reeve.

LANDSCORE The scatter of strips in the open fields.

LEY Pasture land; fallow land.

MAERDREF A reeve's settlement: a bond settlement which adjoins a princely mansion and contains princely demesne.

MANCORN Maslin.

MANNISLOT A man's share, a family's share of arable with appurtenant common meadow and pasture, a bovate or oxgang.

MANSE A dwelling-house, tenement, manor, messuage or household.

MANUMISSION Release from slavery or serfdom.

MASLIN A mixture of grain, especially wheat and rye.

MAST The fruit of the oak and beech or other forest trees.

MEER, MERE A boundary; a boundary-stone; a landmark.

MEER BAULK A dividing ridge of land left unploughed.

MILL-SUIT The duty of grinding corn at the lord's mill.

MOLLAND Land on which a rent is paid.

MOLMAN A rent-paying tenant.

MOSS A bog, peat-bog, or wet, spongy land.

MURRAIN An infectious disease among cattle.

NATIVUS, NEVE, NIEF A villein, especially one born a villein.

NEWLAND New arable; an assart or new enclosure; the word is still in use in Western Australia.

OXGANG A bovate, a measure of arable land, one-eighth of a carucate, a *mannislot.*

PANNAGE The feeding or the right of feeding swine in a forest, or the payment for this; mast picked up by swine in a forest.

PARAGE Equality of condition, as among brothers holding part of a fief as co-heirs.

PARCENER One who holds property divided among joint owners.

PARTIBLE INHERITANCE The custom of dividing land equally between heirs.

PARTIBLE SOCAGE The custom of dividing land held in socage equally among the heirs.

PROGENIES A *gwely.*

PURPRESTURE An illegal enclosure or encroachment; an assart.

QUILLET An acre-strip, selion, or stitch.

RAINE, REAN, RHINE The double wet furrow between two rigs; rig and furrow is called cops and reams in Herefordshire. In Somerset a rhine is a large ditch or drain.

RAPE A unit of local government centred on a castle and peculiar to Sussex.

RELIEF A payment to the overlord by the heir on succession.

RIDDING or RODING An assart.

RIG A strip of ground thrown up by a plough or other implement.

RIVING A division of the open fields; a furlong.

RUNRIG Joint occupation of detached pieces of land, especially in Ireland.

SARAAD Insult money.

SEASON A sowing of grain, a course of cropping, land sown in a particular course.

SELION A strip of ploughland.

SEVERALTY Exclusive tenure or ownership.

SHACK Grain fallen from the ear and used after harvest for feeding pigs etc.; the right to send pigs etc. to feed on this, or right of winter pasturage on another's land.

SHIELING, SHIEL A hut used by shepherds, sportsmen, etc.; a small house or cottage; a piece of summer pasturage.

SHIFT A season.

SOKE The right of holding a local court; a district under such jurisdiction.

SOKEMAN A tenant by any certain and determinate service distinct from military tenure and villeinage.

SPRING CORN Barley.

STINTS OF STOCK An allotted number of animals allowed on the common usually by the oxgang or yardland.

STITCHMEAL The mixture of stitches (or strips) in the open fields.

STOCKING A clearing in woodland.

STOT A small, cheap horse.

STUBBINGS Land cleared of tree-stumps.

TAEOG A Welsh villein.

TIR CYFRIF Register or reckon land; land held by Welsh bondmen.

TIR GWELYAWG Land, whether bond or free, held by *gwelyau*.

TOFT A homestead; a place where a messuage has stood.

TREV A Welsh village.

TYDDYN A standard Welsh holding of 4 *erws*.

UCHELWR A Welsh freeman; usually a half-virgater.

VACCARY A vachery, cow-pasture, or grazing-farm.

VETCH A plant of the genus *Vicia* of the bean family, including several wild and cultivated species used for forage especially the common vetch or tare.

VILLEIN A feudal serf, a bondsman attached to a feudal lord or to an estate.

VIRGATE An old measure for land, a yardland, square-measure usually 20 to 30 acres.

WAPENTAKE A name formerly given in certain English counties to a division corresponding to a hundred.

WETHER. A castrated ram.

WINTER CORN Wheat.

WORTH, WORTHY A stockage or new settlement.

YARDLAND An old measure of area, varying in different counties from 15 acres to 40 acres.

YIELD RATIO The number of grains of corn produced for every grain sown.

CHAPTER NOTES

CHAPTER 1

1 For this chapter see: J. D. Chambers, *Population, Economy, and Society in Pre-Industrial England*, W. A. Armstrong (ed.), Oxford, 1972; J. Hajnal, 'European Marriage Patterns in Perspective', in *Population in History: Essays in Historical Demography*, D. V. Glass and D. E. C Eversley (eds.), London, 1965, pp. 101–43; Peter Laslett, *The World We Have Lost*, 2nd edition, London, 1971; Peter Laslett, *Family Life and Illicit Love in Earlier Generations*, Cambridge, 1977; Alan Macfarlane, *The Origins of English Individualism: The Family, Property and Social Transition*, Oxford, 1978; Lawrence Stone, *The Family, Sex and Marriage in England 1500–1800*, London, 1977; H. E. Hallam, 'The Medieval Social Picture', in *Feudalism, Capitalism and Beyond*, Eugene Kamenka and R. S. Neale (eds.), London, 1974; Peter Dronke, *The Medieval Lyric*, 2nd edition, London, 1978; Leon Battista Alberti, *I Libri della Famiglia*, trans. by Renée Nea Watkins as *The Family in Renaissance Florence*, Columbia, South Carolina, 1969; Pierre Bourdieu, 'Célibat et condition paysanne', *Études rurales*, nos. 5–6, 1962, pp. 32–135; Jean-Louis Flandrin, 'Mariage tardif et vie sexuelle: Discussions et hypothèses de recherche', *Annales*, XXVII, 1972, pp. 1351–78; André Burguière, 'De Malthus à Max Weber: le mariage tardif et l'esprit d'entreprise', *Annales*, XXVII, 1972, pp. 1128–36; Jean-Louis Flandrin, 'Contraception, mariage et relations amoureuses dans l'Occident chrétien', *Annales*, XXIV, 1969, pp. 1370–90; *Household and Family in Past Time*, Peter Laslett and Richard Wall (eds.), Cambridge, 1972; E. A. Wrigley, *Population and History*, London, 1969; *The Family in History: Interdisciplinary Essays*, Theodore K. Rabb and Robert I. Rotberg (eds.), New York, 1971.

CHAPTER 2

1 Professor Postan's most recent book is M. M. Postan, *The Medieval Economy and Society: An Economic History of Britain in the Middle Ages*,

London, 1972; but the reader will find the best of his original essays reprinted in M. M. Postan, *Essays on Medieval Agriculture and General Problems of the Medieval Economy*, Cambridge, 1973; J. Z. Titow, *Winchester Yields: A Study in Medieval Agricultural Productivity*, Cambridge, 1972; J. Z. Titow, *English Rural Society 1200–1350*, Historical Problems; *Studies and Documents, 4*, Professor G. R. Elton (ed.), London 1969. The best criticism of the Postan thesis is still Barbara F. Harvey, 'The Population Trend in England between 1300 and 1348', *Transactions of the Royal Historical Society*, Fifth Series, XVI, 1966, pp. 23–42, but trenchant criticisms of Postan's confusion between 'subsistence' and 'subsistence income' occur in Edward Britton, *The Community of the Vill*, Toronto, 1977. Also on the other side, and seldom mentioned in this context are Ester Bøserup, *The Conditions of Agricultural Growth: The Economics of Agrarian Change under Population Pressure*, Chicago, 1965, and Colin Clark, *Population Growth and Land Use*, 2nd edition, London, 1977. See also H. E. Hallam, 'The Postan Thesis', *Historical Studies*, XV, no. 58, April 1972, pp. 203–22 and reviews of Postan's collected essays and J. Z. Titow's 'Winchester Yields', in *Australian Economic History Review*, 15, 1975, pp.2 and 65. I. Kershaw, 'The Great Famine and Agrarian Crisis in England 1315–1322', *Past and Present*, no. 59, 1973, pp. 31–50 is excellent and moderate in tone. The latest writings of the Postan school are Edward Miller and John Hatcher, *Medieval England – Rural Society and Economic Change, 1086–1348, Social and Economic History of England*, I, Asa Briggs (ed.), London, 1978 and M. M. Postan and John Hatcher, 'Population and Class Relations in Feudal Society', *Past and Present*, no. 78, 1978, pp. 24–37. William H. McNeill, *Plagues and Peoples*, Oxford, 1977, is a relevant work by a very distinguished world historian.

CHAPTER 3

1 F. W. Maitland, *Domesday Book and Beyond*, Fontana, 1960; R. Welldon Finn, *Domesday Studies: The Norman Conquest and its Effects on the Economy; 1066–86*, London, 1971; H. P. R. Finberg, *Lucerna*, 1964; H. P. R. Finberg, 'Some Early Gloucestershire Estates', in *Gloucestershire Studies*, H. P. R. Finberg (ed.), Leicester, 1957; Frederic Seebohm, *The English Village Community*, 4th edition, London, 1890; H. P. R. Finberg, 'Anglo-Saxon England to 1042', in *The Agrarian History of England and Wales*, I, pt. 2, Cambridge, 1972; *The Roman Villa in Britain*,

A. L. F. Rivet (ed.), London, 1969; J. B. Whitwell, *Roman Lincolnshire*, History of Lincolnshire, II, Lincoln, 1970; S. J. Hallam in *The Fenland in Roman Times*, C. W. Phillips (ed.), Royal Geographical Society Research Series, V, London, 1970; R. V. Lennard, 'The Economic Position of the Domesday Villein', *Economic Journal*, LVI, 1946, pp. 244–64; 'The Economic Position of the Domesday Sokemen', *ibid*, LVII.

CHAPTER 4

1 The reader will find more detailed discussion of new settlement in eastern England, and appropriate references to primary and secondary sources, in the eastern England sections of volume 2 of *The Agrarian History of England and Wales*, H. E. Hallam (ed.). The remarks upon population growth in this and subsequent chapters are based upon the author's chapter on population in volume 2 of the same *History*.

2 For the sources upon which this section is based see the corresponding part of *The Agrarian History of England and Wales*, vol. 2.

3 Howard Levi Gray, *English Field Systems*, Cambridge, Massachusetts, 1915; H. E. Hallam, *Settlement and Society: A Study of the Early Agrarian History of South Lincolnshire*, Cambridge Studies in Economic History, M. M. Postan (ed.), Cambridge, 1965; *The Kalendar of Abbot Samson*, R. H. C. Davis (ed.), Camden third Series, LXXIV, 1954; *The Sibton Abbey Estates*, A. H. Denney (ed.), Suffolk Record Society, II, 1966; *The Domesday of St Paul's*, William Hale Hale (ed.), Camden Old Series, LXIX, 1858; J. Saltmarsh and H. C. Darby, 'The Infield-Outfield System on a Norfolk Manor', *Economic History*, III, 1935, pp. 30–44; K. J. Allison, 'The Sheep-Corn Husbandry of Norfolk in the Sixteenth and Seventeenth Centuries', *Agricultural History Review*, V, 1957, pp. 12–31; A. Simpson, 'The East Anglian Foldcourse: Some Queries', *ibid*, VI, 1958, pp. 89–96; M. R. Postgate, 'The Field Systems of Breckland', *ibid*, X, part II, 1962, pp. 80–101; Joan Thirsk, 'The Common Fields', *Past and Present*, no. 29, 1964, pp. 3–25; Joan Thirsk, 'The Origin of the Common Fields', *ibid*, no. 33, 1966, pp. 142–7; J. Z. Titow, 'Medieval England and the Open-Field System', *ibid*, no. 32, 1965, pp. 86–102; *Studies of Field Systems in the British Isles*, Alan R. H. Baker and Robin A. Butlin (eds)., Cambridge, 1973; A. R. H. Baker, 'Howard Levi Gray and English Field Systems', *Agricultural History*, XXXIX, pt. 2, pp. 86–91; W. O. Ault, *Open-Field Farming in Medieval*

England: A study of the Village By-Laws, Historical Problems: Studies and Documents, G. R. Elton (ed.), London, 1972

4 *Select Documents of the English Lands of the Abbey of Bec*, Marjorie Chibnall (ed.), Camden Third Series, LXXIII, 1951; Frances Gardiner Davenport, *The Economic Development of a Norfolk Manor 1086–1565*, Cambridge, 1906; W. M. Palmer, 'Argentine's Manor, Melbourn', *Proceedings of the Cambridge Antiquarian Society*, XXVIII, 1927, pp. 66–7; Lord John Hervey, 'Extent of Hadleigh Manor, 1305', *Proceedings of the Suffolk Institute of Archaeology and Natural History*, XI, 1903, pp. 152–72; John F. Nichols, 'The Extent of Lawling, AD 1310', *Transactions of the Essex Archaeological Society*, New Series, XX, 1933, pp. 184–7; G. F. Beaumont, 'The Manor of Borley, AD 1308', *ibid*, XVIII, 1928, pp. 254–69.

5 J. R. Maddicott, *The English Peasantry and the Demands of the Crown 1294–1341*, Past and Present Supplement 1, 1975; A. R. Bridbury, 'Before the Black Death', *Economic History Review*, Second Series, XXX, no. 3, August 1977, pp. 393–410; H. E. Hallam, 'Some Thirteenth Century Censuses', *ibid*, Second Series, X, 1958, pp. 340–61; 'Population Density in Medieval Fenland', *ibid*, Second Series, XIV, 1961, pp. 71–81; 'Further Observations on the Spalding Serf Lists', *ibid*, XVI, 1963, pp. 338–50; *The Agrarian History of England and Wales*, II, 'The Workers' Diet'.

6 H. E. Hallam, *Settlement and Society*; 'Some Thirteenth Century Censuses', pp. 344–9.

CHAPTER 5

1 *Early Charters of the Cathedral Church of St Paul, London*, Marion Gibbs (ed.), Camden Third Series, LVIII, 1939; R. A. Donkin, 'The Cistercian Settlement and the English Royal Forests', *Cîteaux*, XI, 1960, pp. 19 and 30; *Chertsey Cartularies*, II, Surrey Record Society, XII, 2 vols. 1958 and 1963; *Calendar of Charter Rolls*, II, p. 355; *Cartulary of the Priory of St Gregory, Canterbury*, Audrey M. Woodcock (ed.), Camden Third Series, LXXXVIII, 1956; T. A. M. Bishop, 'The Rotation of Crops at Westerham, 1297–1350', *Economic History Review*, IX, 1938–9, pp. 38–44; *The Cartulary and Terrier of the Priory of Bilsington, Kent*, N. Neilson (ed.), Records of the Social and Economic

History of England and Wales, VII, London, 1928; Robert Furley, *A History of the Weald of Kent*, Ashford and London, two volumes in three, 1871–4; John H. Evans, 'Archaeological Horizons in the North Kent Marshes', *Archaeologia Cantiana*, LXVI, 1954, pp. 103–46, especially Appendix B, pp. 132–9, and pp. 144–5; R. A. L. Smith, *Canterbury Cathedral Priory: A Study in Monastic Administration*, Cambridge, 1943; *Calendar of Charter Rolls*, III, p. 197; Eleanor Searle, 'Hides, Virgates and Tenant Settlements at Battle Abbey', *Economic History Review*, Second Series, XVI, no. 2, 1963, pp. 290–300; Eleanor Searle, *Lordship and Community: Battle Abbey and its Banlieu 1066–1538*, Studies and Texts, XXVI, Pontifical Institute of Mediaeval Studies, Toronto, 1974; L. F. Salzman, 'The Inning of Pevensey Levels', *Sussex Archaeological Collections*, LIII, 1910, pp. 32–60; *The Chartulary of Boxgrove Priory*, trans. and ed. Lindsay Fleming, Sussex Record Society, LIX, 1960; P. F. Brandon, 'Arable Farming in a Sussex Scarpfoot Parish during the Late Middle Ages', *Sussex Archaeological Collections*, C, 1952, pp. 60–72; Alan R. H. Baker, 'Some Evidence of a Reduction in the Acreage of Cultivated Lands in Sussex during the Early Fourteenth Century', *Sussex Archaeological Collections*, CIV, 1966, pp. 1–5.

2 *Ministers' Accounts of the Earldom of Cornwall*, L. M. Midgley (ed.), Camden Third Series, LXVI, and LXVIII, 1942 and 1945; *Select Documents of the English Lands of the Abbey of Bec*, Marjorie Chibnall (ed.), Camden Third Series, LXXIII, 1951; F. R. H. du Boulay, 'The Pipe Roll Account of the See of Canterbury, 9 December 1292 to 4 February 1295', in *Documents Illustrative of Medieval Kentish Society*, Kent Records, XVIII, 1964, pp. 41–57; *Chertsey Cartularies*, I. M. S. Giuseppi (ed.), Surrey Record Society, XII, 1933; 'The Pipe Roll of the Bishopric of Winchester 1210–1211', N. R. Holt (ed.), Manchester, 1964; T. A. M. Bishop, 'The Rotation of Crops at Westerham, 1297–1350', *Economic History Review*, IX, 1938–9, pp. 38–44; Ann Smith, 'Regional Differences in Crop Production in Mediaeval Kent', *Archaeologia Cantiana*, LXXVIII, 1963, pp. 147–60; *The Early Rolls of Merton College, Oxford*, J. R. L. Highfield (ed.), Oxford Historical Society, New Series, XVIII, 1964; R. A. Pelham, 'Studies in the Historical Geography of Medieval Sussex', *Sussex Archaeological Collections*, LXXII, 1931, pp. 156–84; 'The Exportation of Wool from Sussex in the Late Thirteenth Century', *ibid*, LXXXIV, 1933, pp. 131–9; 'The Distribution of Sheep in Sussex in the Early Fourteenth

Century', *ibid*, LXXV, 1934, pp. 128–35; 'The Agricultural Geography of the Chichester Estates in 1383', *ibid*, LXXVIII, 1937, pp. 195–210; L. F. Salzman, 'Early Taxation in Sussex', *ibid*, XCVIII and XCIX, 1960 and 1961, pp. 29–43 and 1–19; W. H. Blaauw, 'Remarks on the Nonae of 1340, as Relating to Sussex', *ibid*, I, 1848, pp. 58–64; E. M. Yates, 'Medieval Assessments in North-west Sussex', *Transactions of the Institute of British Geographers*, XX, 1954, pp. 75–92; E. M. Yates, 'The Nonae Rolls and Soil Fertility', *Sussex Notes and Queries*, XV, 1958–62, no. 10, Nov. 1962, pp. 325–8; A. J. F. Dulley, 'The Level and Port of Pevensey in the Middle Ages', *Sussex Archaeological Collections*, CIV, 1966, pp. 26–45; *Thirteen Custumals of the Sussex Manors of the Bishop of Chichester*, trans. and ed. W. D. Peckham, Sussex Record Society XXXI, 1925; *The Chartulary of the High Church of Chichester*, W. D. Peckham (ed.), *ibid*, XLVI, 1946; *Ministers' Accounts of the Manor of Petworth, 1347–1353*, L. F. Salzman (ed.), *ibid*, LV, 1955; *Custumals of the Manors of Laughton, Willingdon and Goring*, A. E. Wilson (ed.), *ibid*, LX, 1961; R. E. Glasscock, 'The Distribution of Lay Wealth in Kent, Surrey, and Sussex, in the Early Fourteenth Century', *Sussex Archaeological Collections*, LXXX, 1965, pp. 61–8; *A New Historical Geography of England*, H. C. Darby (ed.), Cambridge, 1973, pp. 136–85.

3 Alan R. H. Baker, 'Open Fields and Partible Inheritance on a Kent Manor', *Economic History Review*, Second Series, XVII, no. 1, 1964, pp. 1–23; 'Some Fields and Farms in Medieval Kent', *Archaeologia Cantiana*, LXXX, 1965, pp. 152–74; 'Field Systems in the Vale of Holmesdale', *Agricultural History Review*, XIV, part 1, 1966 pp. 1–24; E. M. Yates, 'History in a Map', *Geographical Journal*, CXXVI, part 1, 1960, pp. 32–51.

4 Smith, *Canterbury Cathedral Priory*; *Custumal of Battle Abbey*; *Ministers' Accounts of the Manor of Petworth*; *Select Documents of the English Lands of the Abbey of Bec*; *Cartulary of Boxgrove Priory*; Rev. William Hudson, 'On a Series of Rolls of the Manor of Whiston', *Sussex Archaeological Collections*, LIII, 1910, pp. 143–82; *Thirteen Custumals of the Sussex Manors of the Bishop of Chichester*; *Custumals of The Sussex Manors of the Archbishop of Canterbury*, B. C. Redwood and A. E. Wilson (eds.), Sussex Record Society, LVII, 1958; *Custumals of the Manors of Laughton, Willingdon and Goring*.

5 *The Agrarian History of England and Wales, 2*.

CHAPTER 6

1 *Danelaw Charters; Abstracts of the Inquisitiones Post Mortem relating to Nottinghamshire, Vol. II: Edward I and Edward II, 1279 to 1321*, John Standish (ed.), Thoroton Society, Record Series, IV, 1914; *Newstead Priory Cartulary, 1344, And Other Archives*, trans. Violet W. Walker, Duncan Gray (ed.), *ibid*, VIII, 1940; *Abstracts of the Inquisitiones Post Mortem and Other Inquisitions relating to Nottinghamshire, Vol. III: Edward II and Edward III, 1321 to 1350*, Thomas M. Blagg (ed.), *ibid*, VI, 1939; *Documents Relating to the Manor and Soke of Newark-on-Trent*, M. W. Barley (ed.), *ibid*, XVI, 1956; Leicester Museum Wyggeston Hospital Records, 10D/34/138 (159); Rothley Temple Charters 44/28/37, 61, 79 and 112; Shangton Deeds 34DI/56/20; Ferrers Collection, 26D/53/409, 412, 487 and 541; Rev. W. G. D. Fletcher, 'Some Unpublished Documents Relating to Leicestershire', *Leicestershire Architectural and Archaeological Society*, XXIII, Part I, 1895, pp. 213–52; *Regesta Regum Anglo-Normannorum*, II; Doris Mary Stenton, *English Society in the Early Middle Ages (1066–1307)*, The Pelican History of England, 3, 3rd edition, Harmondsworth, 1962; *The Registrum Antiquissimum of the Cathedral Church of Lincoln*, C. W. Foster (ed.), Vol. I, Lincoln Record Society, XXXI, 1931; R. A. Donkin, 'The Cistercian Settlement and the English Royal Forests', *Cîteaux*, XI, 1960, pp. 18–20, 23 and 30; *Calandar of Charter Rolls*, II; *Cartulary of Oseney Abbey*, Vol. V, H. E. Salter(ed.), Oxford Historical Society, XCVIII, 1935; *The Estate Book of Henry de Bray of Harleston, Co. Northants (c. 1289–1340)*, Dorothy Willis (ed.), Camden Third Series, xxvii, 1916; *Carte Nativorum – A Peterborough Cartulary of the Fourteenth Century*, C. N. L. Brooks and M. M. Postan (eds.), Northamptonshire Record Society, 1960; *Luffield Priory Charters*, part I, G. R. Elvey (ed.), *ibid*, XXII, 1968; J. Ambrose Raftis, *The Estates of Ramsey Abbey: A Study in Economic Growth and Organization*, Pontifical Institute of Mediaeval Studies, Studies and Texts, 8, Toronto, 1957; *Regesta Regum Anglo-Normannorum*, H. W. C. Davis (ed.), Oxford, 1913; *The Registrum Antiquissimum of the Cathedral Church of Lincoln*, C. W. Foster (ed.), Vol. II, Lincoln Record Society, XXVIII, 1933; *Cartularium Monasterii de Rameseia*, I, William Henry Hart and Ponsonby A. Lyons (eds.), Rolls Series, 1884; *The Cartulary of Bushmead Priory*, G. Herbert Fowler and Joyce Godber (eds.), Bedfordshire Historical Record Society, XXII, 1945; H. C. Darby, *The Medieval*

Fenland, Cambridge, 1940; *Domesday of St Paul's*, William Hale Hale (ed.), Camden Old Series, LXIX, 1858; *The Registrum Antiquissimum of the Cathedral Church of Lincoln*, C. W. Foster (ed.), Vol. III, Lincoln Record Society XXIX, 1935; *Cartulary of the Abbey of Old Wardon*, G. Herbert Fowler (ed.), Bedfordshire Historical Record Society, XII, 1930; *A Digest of the Charters Preserved in the Cartulary of the Priory of Dunstable*, G. Herbert Fowler (ed.), *ibid*, X, 1926; *The Cartulary of Newnham Priory*, Joyce Godber (ed.), *ibid*, XLIII and XLIV, 1963 and 1964; A. C. Chibnall, *Sherington: Fiefs and Fields of a Buckinghamshire Village*, Cambridge, 1965; *The Thame Cartulary*, H. E. Salter (ed.), Oxfordshire Record Society, XXV and XXVI, 1947 and 1948; *Newington Longeville Charters*, H. E. Salter (ed.), *ibid*, III, 1921; *The Cartulary of Missenden Abbey*, Pt. I, J. G. Jenkins (ed.), Buckinghamshire Record Society, II, 1939; Pt, II, XII, 1962; *A Calendar of the Feet of Fines for the County of Buckingham, 7 Richard I to 44 Henry III*, M. W. Hughes (ed.), *ibid*, IV, 1942; *Chronicon Monasterii de Abingdon*, II, Joseph Stevenson (ed.), Rolls Series, 1858; L. J. Ashford, *The History of the Borough of High Wycombe from its Origins to 1880*, London, 1960; *Luffield Priory Charters*, Part 2, G. R. Elvey (ed.), Northamptonshire Record Society, XXVI, 1975.

2 *Lenton Priory Estate Accounts*, F. B. Stitt (ed.), Thoroton Society, Record Series, XIX, 1959; *Abstracts of the Inquisitiones Post Mortem Relating to Nottinghamshire, Vol. II: Edward I and Edward II, 1279 to 1321*, John Standish (ed.), *ibid*, IV, 1914; *Abstracts of the Inquisitiones Post Mortem and Other Inquisitions Relating to Nottinghamshire, Vol. III: Edward II and Edward III, 1321 to 1350*, Thomas M. Blagg (ed.), *ibid*, VI, 1939; *An Abstract of the Contents of the Burton Chartulary*, Hon. G. Wrottesley (ed.), Staffordshire Record Society, V, pt. 1. 1884; *The Early Rolls of Merton College, Oxford*, J. R. L. Highfield (ed.), Oxford Historical Society, New Series, XVIII, 1964; *The Coucher Book of Selby*, Vol. I, C. C. Hodges (ed.), Yorkshire Archaeological Society, Record Series, XIII, 1893; *Select Documents of the English Lands of the Abbey of Bec*, Marjorie Chibnall (ed.), Camden Third Series, LXXIII, 1957; *Wellingborough Manorial Accounts, A. D. 1258–1323*, Frances M. Page (ed.), Northamptonshire Record Society, VIII, 1936; *The Compotus of the Manor of Kettering for AD 1292*, Charles Wise (ed.), Kettering, 1899; Rev. W. J. B. Kerr, *Higham Ferrers and its Ducal and Royal Castle and Park*, Northampton, 1925; *Cartulary of the Abbey of Old Wardon*, G. Herbert Fowler (ed.), Bedfordshire Historical Record Society, XIII, 1930; J. Ambrose Raftis, *The Estates of Ramsey Abbey: A*

Study in Economic Growth and Organization, Pontifical Institute of Mediaeval Studies and Texts, 3, Toronto, 1957; *The Taxation of 1297*, A. T. Gaydon (ed.), Bedfordshire Historical Record Society, XXXIX, 1959; *Three Records of the Alien Priory of Grove and the Manor of Leighton Buzzard*, Robert Richmond (ed.), *ibid*, VIII, 1924; *Ministers' Accounts of the Earldom of Cornwall*, I; *A Digest of the Charters Preserved in the Cartulary of the Priory of Dunstable*, G. Herbert Fowler (ed.), *ibid*, X, 1926; *Cartulary of Oseney Abbey*, Vol III, H. E. Salter (ed.), Oxford Historical Society, XCI, 1931; G. Herbert Fowler, 'Extents of the Royal Manors of Aylesbury and Brill, circa 1155', *Records of Buckinghamshire*, XI, no. 7, 1926, pp. 401–5; *Pipe Roll of the Bishopric of Winchester*; Frances M. Page, 'A Sketch of the Village of Standon in the Middle Ages', *East Hertfordshire Archaeological Society Transactions*, IX, part III, 1936, pp. 265–70; *Domesday of St Paul's*.

3 *Abstracts of the Inquisitiones Post Mortem relating to Nottinghamshire, Vol. II: Edward I and Edward II, 1279 to 1321*, John Standish (ed.), Thoroton Society, Record Series, IV, 1914; *Abstracts of the Inquisitiones Post Mortem and other Inquisitions Relating to Nottinghamshire, Vol. III: Edward II and Edward III, 1321 to 1350*, Thomas M. Blagg (ed.), *ibid*, VI, 1939; *Cartulary of Oseney Abbey*, H. E. Salter (ed.) IV and V, Oxford Historical Society, XCVII and XCVIII, 1934 and 1935; *A Digest of the Charters Preserved in the Cartulary of the Priory of Dunstable*, G. Herbert Fowler (ed.), Bedfordshire Historical Record Society, X, 1926; Fredk. G. Furney, 'An Agricultural Agreement of the Year 1345 at Mursley and Dunton – with a note upon Walter of "Henley"', *Records of Buckinghamshire*, XIV, Part 5, 1945, pp. 245–64; *Facsimiles of Early Charters from Northamptonshire Collections*, F. M. Stenton (ed.), Northamptonshire Record Society, IV, 1930; *Cartulary of the Abbey of Old Wardon*, G. Herbert Fowler (ed.), Bedfordshire Historical Record Society, XIII, 1930; A. R. H. Baker, 'Howard Levi Gray and English Field Systems: An Evaluation', *Agricultural History*, XXXIX, no. 2; P. D. A. Harvey, *A Medieval Oxfordshire Village: Cuxham 1240 to 1400*, Oxford, 1965; Joan Wake, 'Communitas Villae', *English Historical Review*, XXXVII, 1922, pp. 406–13; *Villeinage in England*; G. C. Homans, *English Villagers of the Thirteenth Century*, Cambridge, Massachusetts, 1941; New York, 1960; *Newington Longeville Charters*, H. E. Salter (ed.), Oxfordshire Record Society, III, 1921.

4 *Abstracts of the Inquisitiones Post Mortem and Other Inquisitions Relating to Nottinghamshire, Vol. III: Edward II and Edward III, 1321 to 1350*,

Thomas M. Blagg (ed.), Thoroton Society, Record Series, VI, 1939; *The Compotus of the Manor of Kettering for AD 1292 (recte 1294/5)*, Charles Wise (ed.), Kettering, 1899; *Calendar of Charter Rolls*, II; *Newstead Priory Cartulary; Estate Book of Henry of Bray; A Digest of the Charters Preserved in the Cartulary of the Priory of Dunstable*, G. Herbert Fowler (ed.), Bedfordshire Historical Record Society, X, 1926.

5 *Abstracts of the Inquisitiones Post Mortem Relating to Nottinghamshire, Vol. II: Edward I and Edward II, 1279 to 1321*, John Standish (ed.), Thoroton Society, Record Series, IV, 1914; *Extents of the Prebends of York, c. 1295, and Extent of Monk Friston, 1320*, T. A. M. Bishop (ed.), Yorkshire Archaeological Society, Record Series, XCIV, 1937; *Domesday of St Paul's*; Rosamond Jane Faith, 'Peasant Families and Inheritance Customs in Medieval England', *Agricultural History Review*, XIV, Part II, 1966, pp. 77–95.

CHAPTER 7

1 This section is based upon the southern England section of *The Agrarian History of England and Wales*, vol. 2, to which the reader may refer for sources.

2 This section is based upon the corresponding section in volume 2, of *The Agrarian History of England and Wales* where the reader may find references to the source material.

3 *Accounts and Surveys of the Wiltshire Lands of Adam de Stratton*, M. W. Farr (ed.), Wiltshire Archaeological and Natural History Society, Records Branch, XIV, 1959; *Liber Henrici de Soliaco; Rentalia et Custumaria Michaelis de Ambresbury, 1235–1252, et Rogeri de Ford, 1252–61*, C. J. Elton, Edmund Hobhouse and T. S. Holmes (eds.), Somerset Record Society, V, 1891; *Abstracts of Wiltshire Inquisitiones Post Mortem Returned into the Court of Chancery in the Reigns of Henry III, Edward I, and Edward II, AD 1242–1326*, E. A. Fry (ed.), British Record Society, Index Library XXXVII, 1908; *Abstracts of Wiltshire Inquisitiones Post Mortem, 1327–1377*, Wiltshire Archaeological and Natural History Society, 1909–14; *The Great Chartulary of Glastonbury*, Aelred Watkin (ed.), Somerset Record Society, LIX, LXIII and LXIV, 1947, 1952, and 1956; Charles D. Drew, 'The Manors of the Iwerne Valley, Dorset: A Study of Early Country Planning', *Proceedings of the*

Dorset Natural History and Archaeological Society, LXIX, 1947, pp. 45–50; *Two Chartularies of the Priory of St Peter at Bath*, William Hunt (ed.), Somerset Record Society, 1893; *Two Cartularies of the Benedictine Abbeys of Muchelney and Athelney in the County of Somerset*, E. H. Bates (ed.), *ibid*, XIV, 1899; *Two Registers Belonging to the Family of Beauchamp of Hatch*, Sir H. C. Maxwell Lyte (ed.), *ibid*, XXXV, 1920; *A Collection of Charters Relating to Goring, Streatley, and the Neighbourhood, 1181–1546* T. R. Gambier-Parry (ed.), Oxfordshire Record Society, XIII and XIV, 1931 and 1932; *Gloucester Cartulary*, III; Rev. W. G. Clark-Maxwell, 'The Customs of Four Manors of the Abbey of Lacock', *Wiltshire Archaeological and Natural History Magazine*, XXXII, 1901–2, pp. 311–46.

4 L. J. Ashford, *The History of the Borough of High Wycombe from its Origins to 1880*, London, 1960; *Rentalia et Custumaria Michaelis de Ambresbury, 1235–1252, et Rogeri de Ford, 1252–1261*, C. J. Elton, Edmund Hobhouse and T. S. Holmes (eds.), Somerset Record Society, V, 1891; *Pipe Roll of the Bishopric of Winchester; Calendar of Charter Rolls, III: Domesday of St Paul's; Calendar of Charter Rolls*, IV; *Liber Henrici de Soliaco*, John Edward Jackson (ed.), The Roxburghe Club, 1882; *Two Cartularies of the Benedictine Abbeys of Muchelney and Athelney in the County of Somerset*, E. H. Bates (ed.), Somerset Record Society, XIV, 1899; *A Cartulary of Buckland Priory in the County of Somerset*, F. W. Weaver (ed.), *ibid*, XXV, 1909; *Select Documents of the English Lands of the Abbey of Bec; Charters and Documents Illustrating the History of the Cathedral City and Diocese of Salisbury*, Rev. E. Rich Jones and Rev. W. Dunn Macray (eds.), Rolls Series, 1891; *The Sandford Cartulary*, Agnes M. Leys (ed.), Oxfordshire Record Society, XIX and XXII, 1938 and 1941.

CHAPTER 8

1 *The Stoneleigh Leger Book*, R. H. Hilton (ed.), Dugdale Society, XXIV, 1960; R. A. Donkin, 'The Cistercian Settlement and the English Royal Forests', *Cîteaux*, XI, 1960, p. 19; *Cartulary of Oseney Abbey*, V. H. E. Salter (ed.), Oxford Historical Society, XCVIII, 1935; *The Staffordshire Chartulary*, Hon. George Wrottesley (ed.), Staffordshire Record Society, III, 1882; *An Abstract of the Contents of the Burton Chartulary*, Hon. G. Wrottesley (ed.), *ibid*, V, Part I, 1884; I. H. Jeayes, *Descriptive Catalogue of the Charters and Muniments belonging to the*

Marquis of Anglesey, *ibid*, Third Series, XXVII, 1937; *The Great Register of Lichfield Cathedral known as Magnum Registrum Album*, H. E. Savage (ed.), *ibid*, Third Series, XIV, 1926; I. H. Jeayes, *Calendar of the Longdon, Lichfield, and Other Staffordshire Charters*, *ibid*, Third Series XXIX, 1940; *The Cartulary of Tutbury Priory*, A. Saltman (ed.), *ibid*, Fourth Series, IV, 1962; *Inquisitiones Post Mortem, Ad Quod Damnum, etc. Staffordshire, Hen. III, Edw. I and Edw. II, 1223–1327*, *ibid*, Third Series, II, 1911; *Inquisitiones Post Mortem, Ad Quod Damnum, Staffordshire, Edw. III*, *ibid*, Third Series, IV, 1913; *Ancient Deeds Preserved at the Wodehouse, Wombourne*, Gerald P. Mander (ed.), *ibid*, Third Series, XVIII, 1930; *A Chartulary of the Priory of St Thomas, The Martyr, near Stafford*, F. Parker (ed.), *ibid*, VIII, pt. I, 1887; *A Chartulary of the Augustine Priory of Trentham*, F. Parker (ed.), *ibid*, XI, 1890; *The Inquests on the Staffordshire Estates of the Audleys of AD 1273, 1276, 1283, 1299, 1308*, *ibid*, New Series, XI, 1908; Jean R. Birrell 'The Forest Economy of the Honour of Tutbury in the Fourteenth and Fifteenth Centuries', *University of Birmingham Historical Journal*, VIII, no. 2, 1962, pp. 114–34; Hon. G. Wrottesley, *A History of the Bagot Family*, *ibid*, New Series XI, 1908; Miss H. L. E. Garbett, *Calendar of Early Charters, etc., In the Possession of Lord Hatherton*, *ibid*, Third Series, XVIII, 1930; Isaac Herbert Jeayes, *The Rydeware Chartulary*, *ibid*, XVI, 1895; *Facsimile of Early Charters from Northamptonshire Collections*, F. M. Stenton (ed.), Northamptonshire Record Society, IV, 1930; *The Shenstone Charters*, George Grazebrook(ed.), Staffordshire Record Society, XVII, 1896; General the Hon. George Wrottesley, 'The Burton Chartulary [Derbyshire Portion]', *Journal of the Derbyshire Archaeological and Natural History Society*, VII, 1895, pp. 97–153; *Derbyshire Charters*, Isaac Herbert Jeayes (ed.), London and Derby, 1906; W. H. Hart, 'A Calendar of the Fines for the County of Derby from their commencement in the Reign of Richard I', *Journal of the Derbyshire Archaeological and Natural History Society*, VII, 1885, pp. 195–217; IX, 1887, pp. 84–93; X, 1888, pp. 151–9; XII, 1890, pp. 24–42; Rev. C. Kerry, 'Darley Abbey Charters Preserved at Belvoir', *ibid*, XVI, 1894, pp. 14–43; *The Chartulary of Darley Abbey*, Reginald R. Darlington (ed.), 2 vols, Kendal, 1945; *The Registrum Antiquissimum of the Cathedral Church of Lincoln*, C. W. Foster (ed.), III, Lincoln Record Society, XXIX, 1935; Rev. J. Charles Cox, 'The Chartulary of the Abbey of Dale', *Journal of the Derbyshire Archaeological and Natural History Society*, XXIV, 1902, pp.82–150; 'Repton Charters', *ibid*, LIII, 1932, pp. 64–89; Reginald R. Darlington, 'The Glapwell Charters', Part I, *ibid*,

LXXVI, 1956, pp. 1–144; Part II, *ibid*, LXXVII, 1957, pp. 145–267; Rev. J. Charles Cox, 'Ancient Documents relating to Tithes in the Peak', *ibid*, V, 1883, pp. 129–64; J. B. Harley, 'Population Trends and Agricultural Developments from the Warwickshire Hundred Rolls in 1279', *Economic History Review*, Second Series, XI, no. 1, August 1958, pp. 15–16; *Gloucestershire Studies*, H. P. R. Finberg (ed.), Leicester, 1957; R. H. Hilton, 'Winchcombe Abbey and the Manor of Sherborne,' *University of Birmingham Historical Journal*, II, no. 1, 1949, pp. 31–52; H. P. R. Finberg, *The Early Charters of the West Midlands*, Leicester, 1961; W. St. Clair Baddeley, 'Early Deeds relating to St Peter's Abbey, Gloucester', *Transactions of the Bristol and Gloucestershire Archaeological Society*, XXXVII, 1914, pp. 221–34 and XXXVIII, 1915, pp. 19–46; *The Great Roll of the Pipe for the First Year of the Reign of King Richard the First, AD 1189–1190*, Joseph Hunter (ed.), London, 1844; *The Red Book of Worcester*, Marjory Hollings (ed.), Worcestershire Historical Society, 1 vol. in 4, 1934–50; John Smith of Nibley, *The Lives of the Berkeleys*, Sir John Maclean (ed.), Gloucester, 1883; H. P. R. Finberg, *Gloucestershire: An Illustrated Essay on the History of the Landscape*, London, 1955; revised edition, London, 1975; *Calendar of Charter Rolls*, II; *The Red Book of Hereford*, A. T. Bannister (ed.), Camden Third Series, XLI, 1929; Rev. C. Ernest Watson, 'The Minchinhampton Custumal and its Place in the Story of the Manor', *Transactions of the Bristol and Gloucestershire Archaeological Society*, LIV, 1932, pp. 203–384; *The Cartulary of Cirencester Abbey*, C. D. Ross (ed.), 2 vols., Oxford, 1964; *Regesta Regum Anglo-Normannorum*, II; *Historia et Cartularium Monasterii Sancti Petri Gloucestriae*, I, William Henry Hart (ed.), Rolls Series, 1883; *Cartulary of Oseney Abbey*, IV, H. E. Salter (ed.), Oxford Historical Society, XCVII, 1934; *The Sandford Cartulary*, Agnes M. Leys (ed.), I and II, Oxfordshire Record Society, XIX and XXII, 1938 and 1941; *The Thame Cartulary*, H. E. Salter (ed.), I and II, Oxfordshire Record Society, XXV and XXVI, 1947 and 1948; *Charters and Documents Illustrating the History of the Cathedral, City and Diocese of Salisbury*, Rev. Rich Jones and Rev. W. Dunn Macray (eds.), 1891.

2 Hon. G. Wrottesley, *An Abstract of the Contents of the Burton Chartulary*, Staffordshire Record Society, V, pt. I, 1884; *A Chartulary of the Priory of St Thomas, The Martyr, Near Stafford*, F. Parker (ed.), *ibid*, VIII, pt. I, 1887; Isaac Herbert Jeayes, *The Rydeware Chartulary*, *ibid*, XVI, 1895; *The Chartulary of Dieulacres Abbey*, Hon. G. Wrottesley (ed.), *ibid*, New

Series, IX, 1906; *The Inquests on the Staffordshire Estates of the Audleys of AD 1273, 1276, 1283, 1299, 1308,* Josiah Wedgwood (ed.), *ibid,* New Series, XI, 1908; *Ancient Deeds Preserved at the Wodehouse, Wombourne,* Gerald P. Mander (ed.), *ibid,* Third Series, XVIII, 1930; *Inquisitiones Post Mortem, Ad Quod Damnum, etc., Staffordshire, Hen. III, Edw. I and Edw. II, 1223–1327, ibid,* Third Series, II, 1911; *Cartulary of Oseney Abbey,* VI, H. E. Salter (ed.), Oxford Historical Society, CI, 1936; General the Hon. George Wrottesley, 'The Burton Chartulary [Derbyshire Portion]', *Journal of the Derbyshire Archaeological and Natural History Society,* VII, 1885, pp. 97–153; *Derbyshire Charters,* Isaac Herbert Jeayes (ed.), London and Derby, 1906; Rev. J. Charles Cox, 'Ancient Documents relating to Tithes in the Peak', *Journal of the Derbyshire Archaeological and Natural History Society,* V, 1883, pp. 129–64; W. M. Hart, 'A Calendar of the Fines for the County of Derby from their Commencement in the Reign of Richard I', *ibid,* VII, 1885, pp. 195–217; X, 1888, pp. 151–9; and XII, 1890, pp. 24–42; Rev. C. Kerry, 'Darley Abbey Charters Preserved at Belvoir', *ibid,* XVI, 1894, pp. 14–43; Rev. J. Charles Cox, 'The Chartulary of the Abbey of Dale', *ibid,* XXIV, pp. 82–150; 'Repton Charters', *ibid,* LIII, 1932, pp. 64–89; Reginald R. Darlington, 'The Glapwell Charters', Part I, *ibid,* LXXVI, 1956; *The Chartulary of Darley Abbey,* R. R. Darlington (ed.), 2 vols, Kendal, 1945; *Select Documents of the English Lands of the Abbey of Bec; Lives of the Berkeleys; Liber Henrici de Soliaco,* Roxburgh Club, 1882; *Gloucester Cartulary,* III; Rev. E. A. Fuller, 'Tenure of Land, by the Customary Tenants, in Cirencester', *Transactions of the Bristol and Gloucestershire Archaeological Society,* II, 1877–8, pp. 285–319; Rev. S. E. Bartlett 'The Manor and Borough of Chipping Campden', *ibid,* IX, 1884–5, pp. 134–95; Rev. C. Ernest Watson, 'The Minchinhampton Custumal and its Place in the Story of the Manor', *ibid,* LIV, 1932, pp. 203–384; *Gloucestershire Studies,* H. P. R. Finberg (ed.), Leicester, 1957; *Ministers' Accounts of the Earldom of Cornwall,* I; P. D. A. Harvey, *A Medieval Oxfordshire Village: Cuxham 1210–1400,* Oxford Historical Series, Oxford, 1965; *Lancashire Inquests, Extents and Feudal Aids,* William Farrer, (ed.), pt. I, AD 1205–AD 1307, Lancashire and Cheshire Record Society, XLVIII, 1903; *A Collection of Charters Relating to Goring, Streatley and the Neighbourhood, 1181–1546,* T. R. Gambier-Perry (ed.), pts 1 and 2, Oxfordshire Record Society, XIII and XIV, 1931 and 1932; *The Thame Cartulary,* H. E. Salter (ed.), I and II, *ibid,* XXV and XXVI, 1947 and 1948; T. H. Lloyd, 'Some Documentary Sidelights and the Deserted Oxfordshire Village of

Brookend', *Oxoniensia*, XXIX and XXX, 1964 and 1965, pp. 116–28; *Pipe Roll of the Bishopric of Wincester*, 1964.

3 *Cartulary of Oseney Abbey*, H. E. Salter (ed.), IV, V, and VI, Oxford Historical Society, XCVII, XCVIII and CI, 1934, 1935 and 1936; *The Sandford Cartulary*, I and II, Agnes M. Leys (ed.), Oxfordshire Record Society, XIX and XXII, 1938 and 1941; *The Thame Cartulary*, I and II, H. E. Salter (ed.), Oxfordshire Record Society, XXV and XXVI, 1947 and 1948; P. D. A. Harvey, *A Medieval Oxfordshire Village: Cuxham 1240 to 1400*, Oxford, 1965; *Liber Henrici de Soliaco*; Rev. C. E. Watson, 'The Spillman Cartulary', *Transactions of the Bristol and Gloucestershire Archaeological Society*, LXI, 1939, pp. 50–94; R. H. Hilton, 'Winchcombe Abbey and the Manor of Sherborne', *University of Birmingham Historical Journal*, II, no. 1, 1949, pp. 31–52; *Gloucestershire Studies*; W. St. Clair Baddeley, 'Early Deeds relating to St Peter's Abbey, Gloucester', *Transactions of the Bristol and Gloucestershire Archaeological Society*, XXXVIII, 1915, pp. 19–46; Finberg, *Gloucestershire; Inquisitiones Post Mortem, Ad Quod Damnum, etc., Staffordshire, Edw. III*, Staffordshire Record Society, Third Series, IV, 1913; W. E. Wightman, 'Open Field Agriculture in the Peak District', *Derbyshire Archaeological Journal*, LXXXI, 1961, pp. 111–25; J. Wilfrid Jackson, 'Terraced Cultivation at Priestcliffe, near Taddington', *ibid*, LXXXII, 1962, pp. 100–2; James C. Jackson, 'Open Field Cultivation in Derbyshire', *ibid*, pp. 54–72; Alan R. H. Baker, 'Open Fields in Derbyshire: Some Reservations about Recent Arguments', *ibid*, LXXXIII, 1963, pp. 77–81; J. P. Carr, 'Open Field Agriculture in Mid-Derbyshire', *ibid*, pp. 66–76; General the Hon. George Wrottesley, 'The Burton Chartulary [Derbyshire Portion]', *Journal of the Derbyshire Archaeological and Natural History Society*, VII, 1885, pp. 97–153; W. R. Holland, 'Alsop and other Charters', *ibid*, VIII, 1886, pp. 98–130; W. H. Hart, 'A Calendar of the Fines for the County of Derby from their Commencement in the reign of Richard I', *ibid*, VII, 1885, pp. 195–217; X, 1883, pp. 151–9; *Cartulary of Darley Abbey*; Rev. J. Charles Cox, 'The Chartulary of the Abbey of Dale', *ibid*, XXXIV, 1902, pp. 82–150: *Ancient Deeds Preserved at the Wodehouse, Wombourne*, Gerald P. Mander (ed.), Staffordshire Record Society, Third Series, XVIII, 1930; *Villeinage in England; A Digest of the Charters Preserved in the Cartulary of the Priory of Dunstable*, G. Herbert Fowler (ed.), Bedfordshire Historical Record Society, X, 1926; *Studies of Field Systems in the British Isles*, Alan R. H. Baker and Robin A. Butlin (eds.), Cambridge, 1973.

4 *Lives of the Berkeleys; Cartulary of Oseney Abbey*, V, H. E. Salter (ed.), Oxford Historical Society, XCVIII, 1935; *A Chartulary of the Augustine Priory of Trentham*, F. Parker (ed.), Staffordshire Record Society, XI, 1890; *The Chartulary of Dieulacres Abbey*, Hon. G. Wrottesley (ed.), *ibid*, New Series, IX, 1906; Hon G. Wrottesley, *A History of the Bagot Family*, *ibid*, New Series, XI, 1908; *Calendar of the Manuscripts in the William Salt Library, Stafford*, M. E. Cornford and E. B. Miller (eds.), *ibid*, Third Series, XI, 1921; *Ancient Deeds Preserved at the Wodehouse, Wombourne*, Gerald P. Mander (ed.), Third Series, XVIII, 1930; I. H. Jeayes, *Calendar of the Longdon, Lichfield and other Staffordshire charters, ibid*, Third Series, XXIX, 1940; *The Place Names of Derbyshire*; W. H. Hart, 'A Calendar of the Fines for the County of Derby from their Commencement in the reign of Richard I', *Journal of the Derbyshire Archaeological and Natural History Society*, VII, 1885, pp. 195–217.

5 *An Abstract of the Contents of the Burton Chartulary*, Hon. G. Wrottesley (ed.), Staffordshire Record Society, V, pt. I, 1884; Hon. George Wrottesley, 'The Burton Chartulary [Derbyshire Portion]', *Journal of the Derbyshire Archaeological and Natural History Society*, VII, 1885, pp. 97–153.

CHAPTER 9

1 W. G. Hoskins and H. P. R. Finberg, *Devonshire Studies*, London, 1952; E. M. Jope and R. I. Threlfall, 'Excavation of a Medieval Settlement at Beere, North Tawton, Devon', *Medieval Archaeology*, II, 1958, pp. 112–40; R. A. Donkin, 'The Cistercian Settlement and the English Royal Forests', *Cîteaux*, XI, 1960; *Pipe Roll Richard I; Devon Feet of Fines*, 2 vols., Devon and Cornwall Record Society, 1912–39; W. G. V. Balchin, *Cornwall: An Illustrated Essay on the History of the Landscape*, London, 1954; F. E. Halliday, *A History of Cornwall*, London, 1959; Charles Henderson, *Essays in Cornish History*, A. C. Rowse and M. I. Henderson (eds.), Oxford, 1935; Rev. S. Baring-Gould, 'Ancient Settlement on Trewortha Marsh', *Journal of the Royal Institution of Cornwall*, XI, part I, April 1892, pp. 57–70 and XI, part II, May 1893, pp. 289–90; John Hatcher, *Rural Economy and Society in the Duchy of Cornwall, 1300–1500*, Cambridge, 1970.

2 H. P. R. Finberg, *Tavistock Abbey: A Study in the Social and Economic History of Devon*, Cambridge Studies in Medieval Life and Thought,

New Series, II, Cambridge, 1951; 2nd edition, Newton Abbot, 1969; K. Ugawa, 'The Economic Development of Some Devon Manors in the Thirteenth Century', *Reports and Transactions of the Devonshire Association*, XCIV, 1962, pp. 630–83; J. Hatcher, 'A Diversified Economy: Later Medieval Cornwall', *Economic History Review*, XXII, no. 2, 1970, pp. 208–27; 'Non-Manorialism in Medieval Cornwall', *Agricultural History Review*, XVIII, pt. 1, 1970, pp. 1–18; *Rural Economy and Society in the Duchy of Cornwall, 1300–1500*, Cambridge, 1970; *English Tin Production and Trade before 1550*, Oxford, 1973; 'Myths, Miners and Agricultural Communities', *Agricultural History Review*, XXII, pt. 1, 1974, pp. 54–61.

3 Robert Dymond, 'The Customs of the Manor of Braunton', *Reports and Transactions of the Devonshire Association*, XX, 1888, pp. 254–303; Sir J. B. Phear, 'Note on "Braunton Great Field"', *ibid*, XXI, 1889, pp. 201–4; Alfred H. Shorter, 'Field Patterns in Brixham Parish, Devon', *ibid*, LXXXII, 1950, pp. 271–80; A. H. Slee, 'The Open Fields of Braunton: Braunton Great Field and Braunton Downs', *ibid*, LXXXIV, 1952, pp. 142–9; Charles Luxton, 'The "Tun" by the Credy: The Earliest Saxon Settlement at Crediton', *ibid*, LXXXVII, 1955, pp. 33–8; W. G. Hoskins and H. P. R. Finberg, *Devonshire Studies*, London, 1957; *Tavistock Abbey*; R. R. Rawson, 'The Open Field in Flintshire, Devonshire and Cornwall', *Economic History Review*, Second Series, VI, no. 1, 1953, pp. 51–4; Alfred H. Shorter, 'Landscore, Stitch and Quillet Fields in Devon', *Devon and Cornwall Notes and Queries*, XXIII, part XII, 1949, pp. 372–80; A. L. Rowse, *Tudor Cornwall*, London, 1941; N. J. G. Pounds, 'Lanhydrock Atlas', *Antiquity*, XIX, 1945, pp. 20–6; N. J. G. Pounds, 'The Lanhydrock Atlas and Cornish Agriculture about 1700', *Annual Report of the Royal Cornwall Polytechnic Society*, New Series, XI, part 3, 1944, pp. 112–45; W. G. V. Balchin, *Cornwall: An Illustrated Essay on the History of the Landscape*, London, 1954; O. G. S. Crawford, 'The Work of Giants', *Antiquity*, X, 1936, p. 162 *et seq.*

4 W. G. Hoskins, *Devon*, London, 1954; Carew, *Calendar of Charter Rolls*, II; Finberg, *Tavistock Abbey*.

CHAPTER 10

1 Roy Millward, *Lancashire: an Illustrated Essay on the History of the Landscape*, London, 1955; R. C. Cunliffe Shaw, *The Royal Forest of*

Lancaster, Preston, 1957; J. H. Lumby. *A Calendar of the Deeds and Papers in the Possession of Sir James de Hoghton, Bart, of Hoghton Tower, Lancashire*, Lancashire and Cheshire Record Society, LXXXVIII, 1936; F. Walker, *Historical Geography of South-West Lancashire before the Industrial Revolution*, Chetham Society, New Series, CIII, 1939; *The Coucher Book or Chartulary of Whalley Abbey*, W. A. Hulton (ed.), Chetham Society, Old Series, X, XI, XVI, and XX, 1847–9; *The Chartulary of Cockersand Abbey of the Premonstratensian Order*, William Farrer (ed.), Chetham Society, New Series, XXXVIII, XXXIX, XL, XLIII, LVI, LVII and LXIV, 1898–1909; *Lancashire Inquests, Extents, and Feudal Aids*, William Farrer (ed.), I, AD 1205–AD 1307, Lancashire and Cheshire Record Society, XLVIII, 1903; II, AD 1310–AD 1333, *ibid*, LIV, 1907; III, AD 1313–AD 1355, *ibid*, LXX, 1915; Thomas Dunham Whitaker, *An History of the Original Parish of Whalley, and Honor of Clitheroe, in the Counties of Lancaster and York*, London, 1818; *Dunkenhalgh Deeds, c. 1200–1600*, G. A. Stocks and James Tait (eds.), Chetham Society, New Series, LXXX, 1921; *The Chartulary of the Cistercian Abbey of St Mary of Sallay, in Craven*, Joseph McNulty (ed.), Yorkshire Archaeological Society, Record Series, LXXXVII and XC, 1933 and 1934; *The Coucher Book of Furness Abbey*, I, J. C. Atkinson (ed.); II, John Brownbill (ed.), Chetham Society, New Series, IX, XI, XIV, LXXIV, LXXVI and LXXVIII, 1886–1919; R. A. Donkin, 'The Cistercian Settlement and the English Royal Forests', *Cîteaux*, XI, 1960; W. N. Thompson, 'Gosforth in the Chartulary of St Bees', *Transactions of the Cumberland and Westmorland Antiquarian and Archaeological Society*, New Series, II, 1902, pp. 307–21; *The Register of the Priory of St Bees*, James Wilson (ed.), Surtees Society CXXVI, 1915; *The Register of the Priory of Wetherhal*, J. E. Prescott (ed.), Cumberland and Westmorland Antiquarian and Archaeological Society, Record or Chartulary Series, I, 1897; *The Register and Records of Holm Cultram*, Francis Grainger and W. G. Collingwood (eds.), *ibid*, VII, 1929; Rev. Frederick W. Ragg, 'Early Barton', *Transactions of the Cumberland and Westmorland Antiquarian and Archaeological Society*, New Series XXIV, 1924, pp. 295–350; *Facsimiles of Early Charters from Northamptonshire Collections*, F. M. Stenton (ed.), Northamptonshire Record Society, 1930; *The Priory of Finchale*, James Raine (ed.), Surtees Society, VI, 1837; *Boldon Buke*, William Greenwell (ed.), Surtees Society, XXV, 1852; G. V. Scammell, 'Seven Charters Relating to the *Familia* of Bishop Hugh du Puiset', *Archaeologia Aeliana*, Fourth Series, XXXIV, 1956, pp. 77–90; *The Chartulary of Brinkburn Priory*, William Page (ed.),

Surtees Society, XC, 1893; *Pipe Roll I Richard I; Calendar of Charter Rolls*, I; *Chartularium Abbathiae de Novo Monasterio*, J. T. Fowler (ed.), Surtees Society, LXVI, 1878; *The Priory of Hexham*, James Raine (ed.), Surtees Society, XLIV and XLVI, 1864 and 1865; T. A. M. Bishop, 'Assarting and the Growth of the Open Field', *Economic History Review*, VI, 1935, pp. 18–25; *Ministers' Accounts of the Earldom of Cornwall 1296–1297*, L. Margaret Midgley (ed.), Camden Third Series, LXVI and LXVIII, 1942 and 1945; *West Yorkshire Deeds*, Wilfrid Robertshaw (ed.), Bradford Historical and Antiquarian Society, Local Record Series, II, 1931–6; *Early Yorkshire Charters*, III, 1916; *Early Yorkshire Charters*, VII, 1947; *The Coucher Book of the Cistercian Abbey of Kirkstall*, W. T. Lancaster and W. Paley Baildon (eds.), Thoresby Society, VIII, 1904; *The Chartulary of the Augustinian Priory of St John the Evangelist of the Park of Healaugh*, J. S. Purvis (ed.), Yorkshire Archaeological Society, Record Series, XCII, 1936; *Yorkshire Deeds*, VII, Charles Travis Clay (ed.), *ibid*, LXXXIII, 1932; *Yorkshire Deeds*, X, Mrs M. J. Stanley-Price (ed.), *ibid*, CXX, 1955; *Early Yorkshire Charters*, VI, 1939; VIII, 1949; X, 1955; XI 1963; G. C. Homans, *English Villagers of the Thirteenth Century*, Cambridge, Massachusetts, 1941; New York, 1960; *Extents of the Prebends of York, c. 1295, and Extent of Monk Friston, 1320*, T. A. M. Bishop (ed.), Yorkshire Archaeological Society, Record Series, XCIV, 1937; Bryan Waites, 'The Monastic Settlement of North-East Yorkshire', *Yorkshire Archaeological Journal*, XL, 1961, pp. 478–95; 'The Monastic Grange as a Factor in the Settlement of North-East Yorkshire', *ibid*, XL, 1962, pp. 627–56; *Early Yorkshire Charters*, I, 1914; IX, 1952; *Cartularium Abbathiae de Rievalle*, J. C. Atkinson (ed.), Surtees Society, LXXXIII, 1889; *Cartularium Abbathiae de Whitby*, J. C. Atkinson (ed.), *ibid*, LXIX and LXXII, 1879–1881; *Early Yorkshire Charters*, IV, 1935 and V, 1936; *Yorkshire Deeds*, VIII, Charles Travis Clay (ed.), Yorkshire Archaeological Society, Record Series, CII, 1940; *The Coucher Book of Selby*, J. T. Fowler (ed.), *ibid*, X and XIII, 1891 and 1893; *Early Yorkshire Charters*, XII, 1965.

2 *Mamecestre*, John Harland (ed.), Chetham Society, Old Series, LIII and LVI, 1861; *A Calendar of the Deeds and Papers in the Possession of Sir James de Hoghton, Bart, of Hoghton Tower, Lancashire*, J. H. Lumby (ed.), Lancashire and Cheshire Record Society, LXXXVIII, 1936; *Lancashire Deeds, I, Shuttleworth Deeds, pt. I*, John Parker (ed.), Chetham Society, New Series, XCI, 1934; *The Coucher Book or Chartulary of Whalley Abbey*, W. A. Hulton (ed.), Chetham Society, Old Series, X, XI, XVI,

and XX, 1847–9; *The Chartulary of Cockersand Abbey of the Premonstratensian Order*, William Farrer (ed.), Chetham Society, New Series, XXXVIII, XXXIX, XL, XLIII, LVI, LVII, and LXIV, 1898–1909; *The Chartulary of the Cistercian Abbey of St Mary of Sallay in Craven*, Joseph McNulty (ed.), Yorkshire Archaeological Society, Record Series, LXXXVII and XC, 1933 and 1934; G. H. Tupling, *The Economic History of Rossendale*, Chetham Society, New Series, LXXXVI, 1927; *Lancashire Inquests, Extents and Feudal Aids*, William Farrer (ed.), Lancashire and Cheshire Record Office, XLVIII, LIV and LXX, 1903, 1907 and 1915; *Two Compoti of the Lancashire and Cheshire Manors of Henry de Lacy, Earl of Lincoln, 24 and 33 Edward I*, P. A. Lyons (ed.), Chetham Society, Old Series, CXII, 1884; *The Coucher Book of Furness Abbey*, I, J. C. Atkinson (ed.); II, John Brownbill (ed.), Chetham Society, New Series, IX, XI, XIV, LXXIV, LXXVI, and LXXVIII, 1886–1919; Rev. W. Ragg, 'Shap and Rosgill and Some of the Early Owners', *Transactions of the Cumberland and Westmorland Antiquarian and Archaeological Society*, New Series, XIV, 1914, pp. 1–62; *The Register of the Priory of Wetherhal*, J. E. Prescott (ed.), Cumberland Westmorland Antiquarian and Archaeological Society, Record or Chartulary Series, I, 1897; Rev. Frederick W. Ragg, 'Five Documents concerning Sizergh, Strickland and Barton', *Transactions of the Cumberland and Westmorland Antiquarian and Archaeological Society*, New Series, XVIII, 1918, pp. 131–60; W. N. Thompson, 'Gosforth in the Chartulary of St Bees', *ibid*, II, 1902, pp. 307–21; *The Register and Records of Holm Cultram*, Francis Grainger (ed.), Cumberland and Westmorland Antiquarian and Archaeological Society, Record or Chartulary Series, VII, 1929; *The Register of the Priory of St Bees*, James Wilson (ed.), Surtees Society, CXXVI, 1915; J. L. Kirkby, 'Some Early Records of Cumberland Lay Subsidies', *Transactions of the Cumberland and Westmorland Antiquarian and Archaeological Society*, New Series, LIII, 1954, pp. 63–8; J. Crawford Hodgson, 'Temple Thornton Farm Accounts, 1308', *Archaeologia Aeliana*, XVII, 1895, pp. 40–52; *Chartularium Abbathiae de Novo Monasterio*, J. T. Fowler (ed.), Surtees Society, LXVI, 1878; *The Priory of Hexham*, James Raine (ed.), *ibid*, XLIV and XLVI, 1864–5; *The Chartulary of Brinkburn Priory*, William Page (ed.), *ibid*, XC, 1893; *Boldon Buke*, William Greenwell (ed.), *ibid*, XXV, 1852; *Bishop Hatfield's Survey*, William Greenwell (ed.), *ibid*, XXXII, 1857; *The Inventories and Account Rolls of the Benedictine Houses or Cells of Jarrow and Monk-Wearmouth*, James Raine (ed.), *ibid*, XXIX, 1854; *The Priory of Finchale*, James Raine (ed.), *ibid*, VI, 1837; *Yorkshire*

Inquisitions of the Reigns of Henry III and Edward I, William Brown (ed.), Yorkshire Archaeological Society, Record Series, XII, XXIII, XXXI and XXXVII, 1892–1906; *Early Yorkshire Charters*, II, 1916; *Yorkshire Deeds*, X, Mrs M. J. Stanley-Price (ed.), *ibid*, CXX, 1955; T. W. Hanson, 'Cattle Ranches of Sowerbyshire', *Transactions of the Halifax Antiquarian Society*, 1949, pp. 49–59; *Ministers' Accounts of the Earldom of Cornwall*, II; 'Compoti of the Yorkshire Estates of Henry de Lacy, Earl of Lincoln (Part II)', *Yorkshire Archaeological Journal*, XIII, 1895, pp. 405–15; *West Yorkshire Deeds*, Wilfrid Robertshaw (ed.), Bradford Historical and Antiquarian Society, Local Record Series, II, 1931–6; *Cartularium Abbathiae de Rievalle*, J. C. Atkinson (ed.), Surtees Society, LXXXIII, 1889; *Pedes Finium Ebor, Regnante Johanne, AD MCXCIX–AD MCCXIV*, W. Brown (ed.), *ibid*, XCIV, 1897; *Charters Relating to Possessions of Kirkstall Abbey in Allerton*, F. R. Kitson (ed.), Thoresby Society, IV, 1895; *The Calverley Charters Presented to the British Museum by Sir Walter Calverley Trevelyan, Baronet*, William Paley Baildon and Samuel Margerison (eds.), *ibid*, VI, 1904; *The Coucher Book of the Cistercian Abbey of Kirkstall*, W. T. Lancaster and W. Paley Baildon (eds.), *ibid*, VIII, 1904; *Documents Relating to the Manor and Borough of Leeds, 1066–1400*, John Le Patourel (ed.), *ibid*, XLV, 1956; *Early Yorkshire Charters*, I, 1914; VI, 1939; VII, 1947; VIII, 1949; and XI, 1963; *Yorkshire Deeds*, IX, M. E. Hebditch (ed.), Yorkshire Archaeological Society, Record Series, CXI, 1948; *Yorkshire Deeds*, III, William Brown (ed.), *ibid*, LXIII, 1922; *Yorkshire Deeds*, IV, V, VI and VII, Charles Travis Clay (ed.), *ibid*, LXV, LXIX, LXXVI and LXXXIII, 1924–32; *The Chartulary of the Augustinian Priory of St John the Evangelist of the Park of Healaugh*, J. S. Purvis (ed.), *ibid*, XCII, 1936; *Yorkshire Deeds*, I and II, William Brown (ed.), *ibid*, XXXIX and L, 1909–14; *The Chartulary of St John of Pontefract*, Richard Holmes (ed.), *ibid*, XXV and XXX, 1899–1902; *Extents of the Prebends of York, c. 1295 and Extent of Monk Friston, 1320*, T. A. M. Bishop (ed.), ibid, XCIV, 1937; *Feet of Fines for the County of York from 1218 to 1231*, John Parker (ed.), *ibid*, LXII, 1921; *Abstracts of the Chartularies of the Priory of Monkbretton*, J. W. Walker (ed.), *ibid*, LXVI, 1924; *Yorkshire Lay Subsidy*, William Brown (ed.), *ibid*, XVI, 1894; *The Coucher Book of Selby*, J. T. Fowler (ed.), *ibid*, X and XIII, 1891–3; *Early Yorkshire Charters*, IV, 1935; X, 1955 and XII, 1965; Sir George Duckett, 'Charters of the Priory of Swine in Holderness', *Yorkshire Archaeological Journal*, VI, 1881, pp. 113–24; Kaoru Ugawa, *Lay Estates in Medieval England*, Tokyo, 1966 (in Japanese); *Calendar of Charter Rolls*, I; *Durham Episcopal*

Charters, H. S. Offler (ed.), Surtees Society, CLXXIX, 1968; A. S. Ellis, 'Yorkshire Deeds', *Yorkshire Archaeological Journal*, XII, 1893. pp. 92–115; *Early Yorkshire Charters*, III, 1916, V, 1936 and IX, 1952; *Cartularium Prioratus de Gyseburne*, W. Brown (ed.), Surtees Society, LXXXVI and LXXXIX, 1889–94.

3 Howard Levi Gray, *English Field Systems*, Cambridge, Massachusetts, 1915; R. A. Butlin, 'Northumbrian Field Systems', *Agricultural History Review*, XII, 1964, pp. 99–120; J. Z. Titow, 'Medieval England and the Open-field System', *Past and Present*, XXXII, pp. 97–8; *A Calendar of the Deeds and Papers in the Possession of Sir James de Hoghton, Bart, of Hoghton Tower, Lancashire*, J. H. Lumby (ed.), Lancashire and Cheshire Record Society, LXXXVIII, 1936; *Lancashire Inquests*, II, ibid, LIV, 1907; *A Calendar of that Part of the Collection of Deeds and Papers of the Moore Family, of Bankhall, Co. Lanc., Now in the Liverpool Public Library*, ibid, LXVII, 1913; G. Youd, 'The Common Fields of Lancashire', *Transactions of the Historic Society of Lancashire and Cheshire*, CXIII, 1961, pp. 1–41; R. Cunliffe Shaw, 'The Townfields of Lancashire', *ibid*, CXIV, 1962, pp. 23–36; Frank Tyrer, 'The Common Fields of Little Crosby', *ibid*, pp. 37–48; F. J. Singleton, 'The Influence of Geographical Factors on the Development of the Common Fields of Lancashire', *ibid*, CXV, 1964, pp. 31–40; T. Hesketh Hodgson, 'The Village Community in Cumberland, as instanced at Halltown, near Rocliff', *Transactions of the Cumberland and Westmorland Antiquarian and Archaeological Society*, Old Series, XII, 1893, pp. 133–40; T. H. B. Graham, 'The Common Fields of Hayton', *ibid*, New Series, VIII, 1908, pp. 340–51; Francis Grainger, 'Agriculture in Cumberland in Ancient Times', *ibid*, IX, 1909, pp. 120–46; T. H. B. Graham, 'The Townfields of Cumberland', *ibid*, X, 1910, pp. 118–34; XIII, 1913, pp. 1–13; Gertrude M. Simpson, 'Townfields of Threlkeld, Mardale, Wet Sleddale and Langdale', *ibid*, XXIX, 1929, pp. 266–72; R. E. Porter, 'The Townfields of Coniston', *ibid*, pp. 273–7; Wilson Butler, 'Townfields of Broughton and Subberthwaite in Furness', *ibid*, pp. 293–302; G. Elliott, 'The System of Cultivation and Evidence of Enclosure in the Cumberland Open Fields in the Sixteenth Century', *ibid*, LIX, 1960, pp. 85–104; M. W. Beresford, 'Glebe Terriers and Open Field Yorkshire', *Yorkshire Archaeological Journal*, XXXVII, 1936, pp. 86–97; John Lister, 'Local Illustrations of Seebohm's "English Village Community"', *Bradford Antiquary*, I, 1888, pp. 254–66; *The Chartulary of St John of Pontefract*, I, Richard Holmes (ed.), Yorkshire

Archaeological Society, Record Series, XXV, 1899; *Yorkshire Deeds*, VI, IX and X; *ibid*, LXXVI, CXI, and CXX, 1930, 1948, and 1955; *The Coucher Book of Selby*, J. T. Fowler (ed.), *ibid*, X and XIII, 1891 and 1893; A. S. Ellis, 'Yorkshire Deeds', *Yorkshire Archaeological Journal*, XII, 1893, pp. 92–115; T. A. M. Bishop, 'An Extent of Barton in Richmondshire, 1309', *ibid*, XXXII, 1936, pp. 86–97; T. A. M. Bishop, 'Assarting and the Growth of the Open Fields', *Economic History Review*, VI, 1935–6; Robert A. Dodgshon, 'Infield-Outfield and the Territorial Expansion of the English Township', *Journal of Historical Geography*, I, 4, 1975, pp. 327–45; 'Scandinavian "Solskifte" and the Division of Land in Eastern Scotland', *Scottish Studies*, XIX, 1975, pp. 1–14; 'The Landholding Foundations of the Open-field System', *Past and Present*, LXVII, 1975, pp. 3–29; 'Towards an Understanding and Definition of Runrig: The Evidence for Roxburghshire and Berwickshire', *Transactions of the Institute of British Geographers*, LXIV, 1975, pp. 15–33.

4 *Ministers' Accounts of the Earldom of Cornwall, II: Yorkshire Deeds*, V and VII, Yorkshire Archaeological Society, Record Series, LXIX and LXXXIII, 1926 and 1932; *The Coucher Book or Chartulary of Whalley Abbey*, I, W. A. Hulton (ed.), Chetham Society Old Series, X, 1847; *Bishop Hatfield's Survey*, William Greenwell (ed.), Surtees Society, XXXII, 1857; *Chartularium Abbathiae de Novo Monasterio*, J. T. Fowler (ed.), *ibid*, LXVI, 1878; G. Elliot, 'The System of Cultivation and Evidence of Enclosure in the Cumberland Open Fields in the Sixteenth Century', *Transactions of the Cumberland and Westmorland Antiquarian and Archaeological Society*, LXIX, 1966, pp. 85–104; *The Register and Records of Holm Cultram*, Francis Grainger and W. G. Collingwood (eds), Cumberland and Westmorland Antiquarian and Archaeological Society, Record or Chartulary Series, VII, 1929; *The Register of the Priory of Wetherhal*, J. E. Prescott (ed.), *ibid*, I, 1897.

5 *Lancashire Inquests*, II and III, Lancashire and Cheshire Record Society, LIV and LXX, 1907 and 1915, *Yorkshire Inquisitions*, I, Yorkshire Archaeological Society, Record Series, XII, 1892.

CHAPTER 11

1 H. J. Hewitt, *Mediaeval Cheshire: An Economic and Social History of Cheshire in the Reigns of the Three Edwards*, Chetham Society, New Series, LXXXVIII, 1929: *The Chartulary or Register of the Abbey of St Werburgh, Chester*, James Tait (ed.), *ibid*, LXXIX and LXXXII, 1920 and 1923; *The Coucher Book or Chartulary of Whalley Abbey*, I, W. A. Hulton (ed.), *ibid*, Old Series, X, 1847; *Transactions of the Historic Society of Lancashire and Cheshire*, New Series, IX, 1893, pp. 219–20; Dorothy Sylvester, 'A Note on Medieval Three-course Arable Systems in Cheshire', *ibid*, New Series, CX, 1958, pp. 183–6; *The Ledger Book of Vale Royal Abbey*, John Brownbill (ed.), Lancashire and Cheshire Record Society, LXVIII, 1914; *The Chartulary of Dieulacres Abbey*, Hon. G. Wrottesley (ed.), Staffordshire Record Society, New Series, IX, 1906; R. A. Donkin, 'The Cistercian Settlement and the English Royal Forests', *Cîteaux*, XI, 1960; *Historia et Cartularium Monasterii Sancti Petri Gloucestriae*, I, William Henry Hart (ed.), Rolls Series, 1863; *Red Book of Hereford: The Great Register of Lichfield Cathedral Known as Magnum Registrum Album*, H. E. Savage, Staffordshire Record Society, Third Series, XIV, 1926; *Ancient Deeds Preserved at the Wodehouse, Wombourne*, Gerald P. Mander (ed.), *ibid*, XVIII, 1930; W. K. Boyd, 'Extent of the Manor of Ellesmere, 28 October, 1280', *Transactions of the Shropshire Archaeological and Natural History Society*, Second Series, XI, 1899, pp. 252–9; W. K. Boyd, 'Shropshire Feet of Fines, AD 1196–1211', *ibid*, Second Series, X, 1898, pp. 307–30; A. J. Roderick, 'Open-field Agriculture in Herefordshire in the Later Middle Ages', *Transactions of the Woolhope Naturalists' Field Club*, XXXIII, 1949, 1950 and 1951, pp. 55–67; *The Domesday Geography of Midland England*, H. C. Darby and I. B. Terrett (eds.), Cambridge, 1954; *Cartularium Prioratus S. Johannis Evang. de Brecon*, R. W. Banks (ed.), Archaeologia Cambrensis, Fourth Series, XIII and XIV, 1882 and 1883, pp. 275–308 and 18–311; *Calendar of Charter Rolls*, I; *Survey of the Honour of Denbigh*, Paul Vinogradoff and Frank Morgan (eds.), Records of the Social and Economic History of England and Wales, I, London, 1914; *Regesta Regum Anglo-Normannorum*, II; William Rees, *South Wales and the March, 1284–1415, A Social and Agrarian Study*, Oxford, 1924; reprinted 1974.

2 Giraldus Cambrensis, *The Itinerary Through Wales: Description of Wales*, London, 1908; *Ministers' Accounts for the Lordships of Abergavenny, Skenfrith, and White Castle*, A. J. Roderick and William Rees (eds.), South Wales and Monmouthshire Record Society, II and III, 1950 and 1954; William Rees, 'The Temple Manor of Llanmadoc', *Bulletin of the Board of Celtic Studies*, XIII, part III, 1949; *The Black Book of St David's*, J. W. Willis Bund (ed.), Cymmrodorion Record Series, V, 1902; John Griffiths, 'Two Early Ministerial Accounts for North Wales', *Bulletin of the Board of Celtic Studies*, IX, part I, 1937, pp. 50–70; John Griffiths, 'Early Accounts relating to North Wales, temp. Edward I', *ibid*, XV, Part II, 1953, pp. 145–51; William Rees, *South Wales and the March, 1284–1415, A Social and Agrarian Study*, Oxford, 1924; reprinted, 1974; T. Jones Pierce, 'A Lleyn Lay Subsidy Account', *Bulletin of the Board of Celtic Studies*, V, part I, 1929, pp. 54–71; T. Jones Pierce, 'Two Early Caernarvonshire Accounts, I, Lay Subsidy Account 242/50B (AD 1293)', *ibid*, V, Part II, 1930, pp. 142–8; Frederic Seebohm, *The Tribal System in Wales*, London, 1904; W. K. Boyd, 'Shropshire Feet of Fines, AD 1196–1211', *Transactions of the Shropshire Archaeological and Natural History Society*, 1898, pp. 307–30; A. J. Roderick, 'Open-field Agriculture in Herefordshire in the later Middle Ages', *Transactions of the Woolhope Naturalists' Field Club*, XXXIII, 1949, 1950, and 1951, pp. 55–67; H. J. Hewitt, *Mediaeval Cheshire: An Economic and Social History of Cheshire in the Reigns of the Three Edwards*, Chetham Society, New Series, LXXXVIII, 1929; *Cheshire in the Pipe Rolls, 1158–1301*, R. Stewart-Brown (ed.), Lancashire and Cheshire Record Society, XCII, 1938; *The Chartulary or Register of the Abbey of St Werburgh, Chester*, James Tait (ed.), Chetham Society, New Series, LXXIX and LXXXII, 1920 and 1923.

3 *Ancient Laws and Institutes of Wales*, I. I am supposing that all quotations really are the work of Hywel Dda, not of some interpolator. If the quotations date from the second half of the twelfth century the arguments still hold good, and fit better with what we know about new settlement in Wales and elsewhere, particularly northern England, during this century. J. G. Edwards, 'The Historical Study of the Welsh Lawbooks', *Transactions of the Royal Historical Society*, Fifth Series, XII, 1962, pp. 141–55; 'The Welsh Laws', *Welsh History Review*, 1963. The co-tillage clauses are a late-twelfth-century addition. *The Latin Texts of the Welsh Laws*, Hywel David Emanuel (ed.), Cardiff, University of Wales History and Law Series, XXII, 1967; T. P. Ellis, *Welsh Tribal*

Law and Custom in the Middle Ages, 2 vols, Oxford, 1926; Margaret Davies, 'Rhosili Open Field and Related South Wales Field Patterns', *Agricultural History Review*, IV, part II, 1956, pp. 80–96; Dorothy Sylvester, 'The Common Fields of the Coastlands of Gwent', *ibid*, VI, part I, 1958, pp. 9–26; R. R. Rawson, 'The Open Field in Flintshire, Devonshire, and Cornwall', *Economic History Review*, Second Series, VI, no. 1, 1953, pp. 51–2; *Black Book of St David's*; *Survey of the Honour of Denbigh*; G. R. J. Jones, 'The Llanynys Quillets: A Measure of Landscape Transformation in North Wales', *Transactions of the Denbighshire Historical Society*, XIII, 1964, pp. 135–58; Dorothy Sylvester, 'Settlement Patterns in Rural Flintshire (excluding Maelor Saesneg)', *Proceedings of the Flintshire Historical Society*, XV, 1954–5, pp. 6–42; Dorothy Sylvester, 'Rural Settlement in Cheshire: Some Problems of Origin and Classification', *Transactions of the Historic Society of Lancashire and Cheshire*, CI, 1949–50, pp. 1–38; Dorothy Sylvester, 'The Open Fields of Cheshire', *ibid*, CVIII, 1956, pp. 1–33; Vera Chapman, 'Open Fields in West Cheshire', *ibid*, CIV, 1952, pp. 35–59; Dorothy Sylvester, 'The Rural Landscape of Eastern Montgomeryshire', *Montgomeryshire Collections*, 1955; Dorothy Sylvester, 'A Note on Medieval Three-course Arable Systems in Cheshire', *Transactions of the Historic Society of Lancashire and Cheshire*, CX, 1958, pp. 183–6; A. J. Roderick, 'Open-field Agriculture in Herefordshire in the Later Middle Ages', *Transactions of the Woolhope Naturalists' Field Club*, XXXIII, 1949, 1950 and 1951, pp. 55–67; G. R. J. Jones, 'Some Medieval Rural Settlements in North Wales', *Institute of British Geographers, Publications No. 19, Transactions and Papers 1953*, pp. 51–72; G. R. J. Jones, 'Medieval Open Fields and Associated Settlement Patterns in North-West Wales', *Geographie et Histoire Agraires*, Actes du colloque international organisé par la Faculté des Lettres de l'Université de Nancy (Nancy 2–7 septembre 1957), Nancy, 1959; G. R. J. Jones, 'Wales', *The Advancement of Science*, XV, no. 60, 1959, pp. 338–42.

4 H. J. Hewitt, *Mediaeval Cheshire: An Economic and Social History of Cheshire in the Reigns of the Three Edwards*, Chetham Society, New Series, 88, 1929; *The Ledger Book of Vale Royal Abbey*, John Brownbill (ed.), Lancashire and Cheshire Record Society, LXVIII, 1914; *The Chartulary or Register of the Abbey of St Werburgh, Chester*, James Tait (ed.), Chetham Society, New Series, LXXIX and LXXXII, 1920 and 1923; *Ministers' Accounts of the Lordship of Abergavenny*; George

Owen, *The Description of Pembrokeshire*, Henry Owen (ed.), Cymmrodorion Record Series, II, 2 vols in 4, 1892–1936.

5 *The Ledger Book of Vale Royal Abbey*, John Brownbill (ed.), Lancashire and Cheshire Record Society, LXVIII, 1914; W. K. Boyd, 'Extent of the Manor of Ellesmere, 28 October, 1280', *Transactions of the Shropshire Archaeological and Natural History Society*, Second Series, XI, 1899, pp. 252–9; *Red Book of Hereford*; A. W. Wade-Evans, *Welsh Medieval Law*, Oxford, 1909; Charles I. Elton, *Origins of English History*, London, 1890; *Ancient Laws and Institutes of Wales*, I; T. Jones-Pierce, 'Some Tendencies in the Agrarian History of Caernarvonshire During the Later Middle Ages', *Caernarvonshire Historical Society, Transactions*, I, 1938–9, pp. 13–36; 'Medieval Settlement in Anglesey', *Anglesey Antiquarian and Field Club: Transactions*, 1951, pp. 1–33; 'Agrarian Aspects of the Tribal System in Medieval Wales', *Géographie et Histoire Agraires*, pp. 329–37; *Vadstena Symposium*, pp. 182–9; G. R. J. Jones, 'The Tribal System in Wales: A Reassessment in the Light of Settlement Studies', *Welsh History Review*, I, no. 2, 1961, pp. 111–32; G. R. J. Jones, 'Post-Roman Wales', *The Agrarian History of England and Wales*, H. P. R. Finberg (ed.), Cambridge, 1972, pp. 281–382.

CHAPTER 12

1 The essential works are still Sir Frederick Pollock and Frederick William Maitland, *The History of English Law before the Time of Edward I*, 2nd edition, S. F. C. Milsom (ed.), Cambridge, 1968, II, Chapter VII, Family Law, pp. 364–447, especially Section I, 'Marriage', pp. 364–99; H. S. Bennett, *Life on the English Manor: A Study of Peasant Conditions, 1150–1400*, Paperback Edition, Cambridge, 1960, pp. 240–8; and George Caspar Homans, *English Villagers of the Thirteenth Century*, reissued New York, 1960, Book II, Families, pp. 109–219. See *The Agrarian History of England and Wales*, vol. 2, for the source material on the *anilepimen*. The Norwich Cathedral Priory Account Rolls refer to payments to *anilepimen* on the priory's Norfolk estates, and Ada Elizabeth Levett discussed them in her posthumous paper 'Merchet and Marriage Custom' in *Studies in Manorial History*, Oxford, 1938; reprinted, London, 1963, pp. 235–47; Ramsey Cartulary, I; BM Cotton Claudius C. XI; BM Cotton Claudius D XIII; BM Harley 3977; Oldfield Register of Crowland Abbey, BM Harley 5845, ff. 25d–26d,

printed with reasonable accuracy in Richard Gough, 'History and Antiquities of Croyland Abbey', *Bibliotheca Topographica Brittanica*, London, 1783, XI, Appendix I, pp. 55–7; BM Additional 35296 and Harley 742; Myntling Register, Spalding Gentlemen's Society; and *Court Roll of Chalgrave Manor, 1278–1313*, Marian K. Dale (ed.), Bedfordshire Historical Record Society, XXVIII, 1950.

INDEX